The Change of
a Lifetime

The Change of
a Lifetime

EMPLOYMENT PATTERNS AMONG

JAPAN'S MANAGERIAL ELITE

John C. Beck   *Martha N. Beck*

UNIVERSITY OF HAWAII PRESS / HONOLULU

94 95 96 97 98 99   5 4 3 2 1

Library of Congress Cataloging-in-Publication Data
Beck, John C., 1959–
The change of a lifetime : employment patterns among Japan's
managerial elite / John C. Beck, Martha N. Beck.
p.   cm.
Includes bibliographical references and index.
ISBN 0–8248–1503–3 (cloth). — ISBN 0–8248–1529–7 (paper)
1. Executives—Japan. 2. Job security—Japan. 3. Occupational
mobility—Japan. 4. Elite (Social Sciences)—Japan. I. Beck,
Martha Nibley, 1962– . II. Title.
HD38.25.J3B43   1993
331.7'616584'00952—dc20   93–41946
CIP

University of Hawaii Press books are printed on acid-free
paper and meet the guidelines for permanence and durability
of the Council of Library Resources

Design by Ken Miyamoto

CONTENTS

ABBREVIATIONS

AS	*Asahi Shinbun*
BT	*Business Tokyo*
FEER	*Far Eastern Economic Review*
JEJ	*Japan Economic Journal*
JEN	Japan Economic Newswire
KN	*Kyodo News*
LAT	*Los Angeles Times*
MS	*Mainichi Shinbun*
NKS	*Nihon Keizai Shinbun*
NSS	*Nikkei Sangyō Shinbun*
ST	*Straits Times* (Singapore)
WSJ	*Wall Street Journal*
YS	*Yomiuri Shinbun*

CHAPTER ONE

Introduction

THE SUMMER OF 1979 found Ken'ichi Takahashi thoroughly unhappy with his job. There seemed to be no justifiable reason for Takahashi's discontent. He was doing as well as anyone with his background could be expected to do. In fact, having graduated from a university generally acknowledged to be somewhat less than topnotch, Takahashi had been lucky to move into a job with a well-known and respected steel-producing firm. His classmates, most of whom had ended up in somewhat less prestigious organizations, had looked upon Takahashi with mild envy. For the rest of their lives, as each of them diligently climbed the corporate ladder, Takahashi would be a little ahead of most of his schoolmates.

At the time, this had been more than enough to make Takahashi excited with his job, pleased that he had thrown in his lot with a firm that could support him in every way throughout the remainder of his career. He had worked hard, those first years, spending day after day in the tedious tasks given to "beginners" at the firm and night after night drinking beer and sake with his co-workers. Like most of them, Takahashi had spent the first two decades in the company moving slowly and predictably from one promotional level to the next, changing the title that preceded the name on his business cards with appropriate pride and pleasure. At thirty he had married one of the company secretaries, and the marriage had been welcomed in the firm with a generous bonus and great congratulations. Takahashi was a company man.

In 1976 Takahashi had been transferred from the Tokyo office to a branch of their firm in Kumamoto. He and his wife considered it providential that the transfer had come just as their oldest child and only son was ready to move from elementary school into junior high school. Of

1

course, they would have followed company orders whenever they had come, but as it happened their son could make the move without creating much discontinuity in his education. As Takahashi knew, such discontinuity could have repercussions for the rest of the boy's life. Their little girl had had to move from her Tokyo school to another elementary school in Kumamoto, which was unfortunate, but of course not so tragic for a girl as it would have been for a boy. Takahashi and his wife were deeply grateful for the consideration of the company in timing the Kumamoto transfer.

Still, it was about the time he had been moved that Takahashi had begun to feel something was wrong. The Kumamoto office didn't seem to have as much connection to Tokyo as he had hoped, and he noticed with a slight chill how few of the Kumamoto people ever seemed to move back to the main office and the chance at a directorship. The real shock came in the summer of 1978, when Takahashi was passed over for a promotion he had almost been taking for granted. Takahashi began to notice things he didn't like about his job. He had to admit that he often found the work tedious, his immediate superior often made decisions with which Takahashi disagreed, and the president of the Kumamoto branch office was a bitter old man who had been ousted from the Tokyo office by some obscure political infighting and who had sat at his Kumamoto desk nursing his grudges ever since. It was not lost on Takahashi, watching the president's defeated expression and hearing the slight grumbling that wafted from his desk after a phone conversation with Tokyo, that he himself could end up in the old man's position not so many years down the road.

The 1979 promotions rolled around, and Takahashi was passed over again. This was the last straw. For weeks he found going to work almost unbearable. He tried to find solace in the fact that at least his family seemed happy in Kumamoto. However, Takahashi knew chances were that the next set of transfers would involve a move back to Tokyo or to some other "outpost" of the company in a position much like the one he had now. A transfer to a new city would take his wife away from her friends in their neighborhood and his son out of a junior high school where he had just been elected student body president. Unless, of course, Takahashi went to live at the new post alone—*tanshin funin*. He couldn't bear that thought. As it was now, when he accompanied his fellow workers to the bars after hours, he could think of nothing to say to them. While they laughed and complained and consulted and conversed, Takahashi stared sullenly into his beer and wondered if this would be the reward for his years of devotion to the firm. What would it be like if he were alone? On one of these nights, after enough beer to make him stagger a bit walking to his home and his family, Takahashi decided to quit.

Of course, he told no one. The decision to resign was unthinkable. It was preposterous. The company had supported him, had been his mother, father, sisters, and brothers since he was practically an adolescent. Company friends had told him whom to marry, where to live, how to behave. The tiny company pin on his lapel and the title on his business card had been his identity, had told him how he should react to others and others how they should react to him. Without the company, he and his family would be nothing. His wife would be scorned by former friends, his children mocked at school. And yet the job was intolerable. Takahashi had racked his brains night and day for months, trying to figure out how he could stand it. There was no way. He had to leave.

Takahashi began secretly hunting for work at another firm, one that could give his family some of the stability and identity he planned to relinquish with his job. But his attempts were halfhearted, based on a feeble hope for the impossible. In his heart Takahashi knew that if he quit his present position, no other company in Japan would be interested in hiring him. He would be damaged goods, a traitor, with no loyalty or decency. And yet the more he berated himself for these loathsome attributes, the more set Takahashi became on leaving his firm. There was a strange sort of exhilaration in doing something so base, so antisocial, so manifestly wicked, as quitting his job. It gave him a heady sense of freedom, as though he were a turncoat samurai out of his wife's favorite TV drama, planning to murder his master and travel free, a masterless *rōnin,* over the countryside. It was dreadful, but it had style.

Takahashi's wife did not agree with this conclusion. Nor did her parents or his. Takahashi's children were opposed to the change, knowing implicitly that their peers would find out and belittle them in a thousand excruciating ways. His two sisters were appalled, pleading the cause of Takahashi's innocent wife and children to him in strident tones over the telephone. The news of Takahashi's insane plans had spread through the family like wildfire almost before he had finished whispering them to his wife one night after a fortifying fifth of whiskey. Before he even left for work the next morning the phone had begun to ring, and since then it had been ringing almost nonstop. Surely he wasn't serious, the telephone shouted to Takahashi in one familiar voice after another. Surely he couldn't do this to his family, his children, his feeble, aging parents who had sacrificed so much on his behalf. Takahashi's uncle called to read him a newspaper article about an executive who had quit and shortly thereafter committed suicide. His brother-in-law Yukio called to remind him that Takahashi's quitting could have negative repercussions on his own career if Yukio's firm found out they were related. His mother called, again and again, to discuss the long and difficult labor she had experienced at his birth and how tenderly she had raised him from a scrawny, sickly infant. But the more phone calls Takahashi received, the harder it was for him to go to work every morning and the more disengaged he felt from his company. He tried to close his mind and let his family's criticisms bounce off him. His performance at work suffered. No one there seemed to like him much anymore. Takahashi was just waiting for the slightest sign of something to jump to, and then he would jump.

"Something to jump to" occurred to Takahashi one day as he sat in his favorite little sushi bar eating lunch. There it was! Freedom to work one's own hours, be one's own boss. No one to snub him for being a traitor. Takahashi excitedly telephoned an old elementary school friend who had inherited his father's sushi business. Sushi became his secret avocation. He worked far into the night setting up a concern, finding out about the business, whom he should hire, how to find a location. Takahashi's wife, listening to his side of the conversations, pursed her lips and said nothing. She could see he was set on the thing. Her life of happiness and ease as a company wife was over. There was nothing she could do but hang on to the battered fragments of what she had married. She kept her tears to herself and concentrated on ensuring that her son would do as well as possible in school, considering the circumstances. He was her last hope.

At last the sushi bar was ready to go, and Takahashi announced his decision to his superiors at work. The scandal was staggering, even worse than he had expected. The telephone calls from his family, which had been tapering off into disgusted silence, were more than replaced by calls from co-workers, the company directors, prestigious acquaintances whom Takahashi remembered only dimly from college days, and even some of his old professors. It was the same story all over again. This wasn't like him, surely he didn't mean it, they could understand his problems but those problems could be worked out, the company was willing to forgive him and let him start out fresh, as though none of this had ever happened. Takahashi closed his mind and responded with endless numbing apologies, but he would not change his mind. It was impossible to do so at this point anyway. No matter what they said, Takahashi knew perfectly well that the company personnel would never forget nor be able to wholly forgive what he had done. His life as a salaryman was over, and there was no use in looking back.

In 1980, when the new promotions were assigned, a group of celebrating executives from Takahashi's old company burst through the door of his struggling sushi shop. It was an awkward moment, to say the least, as Takahashi in his white apron and hat stood dumbly behind the bar looking at the blue-suited images of what he had been. The moment of strained silence was quickly covered up by orders of sushi all around; the men ate quickly and left immediately. The whole occasion had left Takahashi rather sad and thoughtful. The sushi business was harder than he had expected, and he was always aware of a nagging financial insecurity he had never felt as a salaryman. He missed the camaraderie, the predictability, the assurance that had come with being a company man. But looking back, Takahashi could not regret having left his company. Hard as life was now for him and his family, he could not have borne an endless struggle to go nowhere in his old firm. On balance, Takahashi decided with a sigh, he was better off selling sushi. He only wished, with his whole heart, that there had been an easier way.

Takeshi Abe spoke reasonably good German. Abe knew that this, as much as or more than his managerial skills, had been the reason for the mess he'd found himself in during the winter of 1986. Much later, Abe considered the whole affair something of an embarrassment and hoped everyone would forget about it. But at the time, it had been really quite exciting.

In 1986 Abe had been working for a staid and steady Japanese pharmaceuticals firm, an old company with a good name and reputation. Abe had graduated from a top university and been able to take his pick of companies, so his joining the firm had honestly been a personal choice. Abe was a cautious person, and he liked the odds on a career in pharmaceuticals. He reasoned that people would do without oil, steel, or even bank accounts in an emergency, but there was always a demand for medicines. Once on board at the top pharmaceuticals firm in Japan, he knew his job was safe.

Abe's typically conservative approach to life was another reason that the 1986 fiasco was so strange. There seemed to have been little to precipitate it. Abe had done well in the company's sales department, and by that year he had been promoted to a fairly prestigious level. He knew he would never make president or director—that was for people who risked losing it all by taking political sides in the firm—but he was comfortable where he was. Secure. The company took care of all his needs and those of his wife and sons. There was no need for Abe even to consider doing anything so drastic as he had actually done.

The call from that headhunter had started it all. Abe's careful nature was accompanied by a sort of awe toward people who risked, who gambled, who took things into their own hands. He'd seen a television documentary on headhunters not a week before the man had called him, and the whole concept of executive search firms made his pulse quicken with forbidden allure. Abe could scarcely imagine a whole enterprise devoted to convincing people to leave their jobs for other companies. There was something frightening and exotic about it. Abe's wife, who had watched the program with him, said she was sure it was somehow involved with organized crime, but Abe didn't think so. As the commentator on the documentary had said, times were changing. That headhunters were to be found in Japan gave evidence of those changes.

Then, that same week, Abe had picked up the telephone on his desk to hear the voice of a man introducing himself as an official of an executive search firm. Abe wondered retrospectively why he hadn't simply hung up on the man—the documentary was to blame, no doubt. Instead of hanging up, Abe had frozen in his chair, holding the receiver with rigid hands and pretended nonchalance. The headhunter laid out his position. He was working for a German pharmaceutical firm—was he correct in understanding that Abe spoke German? Abe darted a glance around the crowded office and croaked "Yes" into the receiver. The German firm was trying to enter the Japanese market and had already set up a successful branch in the Tohoku region. Was it true that Abe had been born and raised in Tohoku? "Yes," Abe whispered hoarsely. Good, said the headhunter, then this position would give him a chance to return to his home town—if he decided to consider it. The position for which Abe was being considered, incidentally, was vice-president in charge of sales, the highest position open in Japan. Did Abe find this interesting? Abe's lips twitched. He knew very well that he could never hope to attain such a prestigious level in his present firm. The headhunter went on. The salary being offered for the vice-president's position was—he quoted a figure that made Abe's head spin. Was Abe at all interested in talking to him further? the headhunter inquired innocently. Abe peered furtively at the people around him, with whom he had spent every day and most of the night for more than twenty years. He was astonished to hear his own voice, strained and unnatural, saying "Yes" into the telephone. The headhunter had quickly mentioned where and when they might meet for lunch, and Abe was relieved. The man was suggesting a crowded hotel lobby some distance from Abe's firm as the rendezvous point. It was unlikely that they would be spotted or recognized there. Abe said "Yes" a few more times into the receiver and hung up in a daze.

For the rest of that day Abe had forced himself to act as though nothing unusual had happened. He felt a pang of guilt whenever he spoke to his friend Nagai, who had been with the company two years longer than Abe and who had recently been appointed head of personnel. He remembered how, years earlier, Nagai had presented himself to the president when Abe had bungled a sale, taking full responsibility and not even mentioning Abe's name. That evening, looking across the karaoke bar at the smiling, reddened faces of his co-workers, Abe had felt so moved by his own rendition of "You Needed Me" that he had been forced to stop singing and wipe his eyes. Nevertheless, he couldn't stop the ringing in his ears of the headhunter's voice saying "vice-president in charge of sales" and quoting that fabulous salary over and over again. Abe knew that he should call the man back and cancel their meeting, but he didn't even have a telephone number. These headhunters knew their business.

Abe could scarcely believe it when, on the appointed day at the appointed hour, he found himself wandering through the hotel lobby casting nervous glances at anyone who looked particularly ruthless or risque. But the headhunter who met him near the paging phones seemed surprisingly normal. Abe had been soothed into relaxation by the man's courteous manner and honest face. This letting down his guard, he later realized, had been a mistake. Somehow the headhunter had gotten Abe to display more interest than he had intended to, and before Abe knew what was happening they had scheduled another meeting, this time with a German official present. At that meeting, later in the week, Abe had become so flustered attempting to speak decent German that he had found himself agreeing to let the company fly him to Europe to meet with the directors. It was all moving too fast for Abe, and yet he knew he must really be interested. He'd let it go this far.

Abe's superior had frowned when Abe told him that he was taking some of his vacation time. It wasn't that he didn't have plenty of vacation time saved up; in twenty-three years Abe had never taken more than two days of vacation per year. He knew it seemed odd for him to be going now, especially in the midst of a developing sale. When he told his boss he had to take care of family problems, the man's frown became a sympathetic smile. Abe hardly even felt guilty, since he hadn't been stretching the truth. He was having family problems. When he had told his wife about the headhunter, the German company, and the upcoming trip to Europe, a chill had settled over their relationship with a suddenness that made Abe feel as though he had walked into a meat freezer. Abe felt his resolve to consider the job change growing as he argued all night with his wife in favor of the trip. Eventually he had simply put his foot down— although not before repeating the salary mentioned by the headhunter several dozen times—and the conflict at home had died down to icy silence.

The European trip had been thrilling. As soon as the plane had taken off from Tokyo, Abe had felt a growing sense of adventure and freedom that had increased throughout his stay in Germany. He had felt bold and unrestrained as he had greeted the company president in his newly practiced German. The company was pleased with him, he could sense it. Abe was pleased with them as well. He could see unlimited potential for them in Japan, he told them. He knew that if he were in charge of sales, he could carry the German company to successes they had never dreamed of. Abe felt quite giddy. After several meetings, the German firm had made him an offer. The salary, which Abe had assumed the headhunter was exaggerating, proved to be even more than he had been told. Abe felt quite dizzy at the thought of it. He shook hands with the Germans again. Everyone agreed that Abe should take six months to make an amicable departure from his firm. On the plane home to Japan, Abe celebrated his future with a hearty glass of dark German beer.

The "amicable departure" presented some difficulties. For a week after his return from Germany, Abe said nothing to anyone at the company. The guilt at what he had done, and was intending to do, hung around him like a cloud. Finally, he invited Nagai out for drinks at a rather private bar. As he gradually unfolded the plan to Nagai, the other man's face changed from surprise to wonder to anger to deep sadness. Abe was smitten with remorse. Still, Nagai was kindly as always. He did not understand young people, he said (although Abe was only five years younger), and he had thought Abe was a different sort of person than he seemed to be. But that was simply his own mistake. Abe should do whatever was best for him. Abe's heart had swelled with friendship. Everything was going to be fine.

It was about this time that unexpected things started to happen around the company. Abe began to hear comments from co-workers about his rosy future with the firm and the inadvisability of any Japanese leaving his employer. Abe would nod, looking at them closely. Certainly they shouldn't know anything about his plans, and there was nothing to make him suspect that they did. Still, it was odd that so many people, so suddenly, had begun to mention to Abe the virtues of loyalty and the privilege of working for a firm that was more like a family. Maybe they had always talked this way, and Abe's guilt just made him notice it more than usual. The guilt was tremendous, he had to admit it. Every comment on the Japanese salaryman's fidelity to the firm tore at Abe's heart, and every soulful glance from Nagai made him feel more and more like a traitor.

One day the president had called him in. Abe's heart raced, and he felt the blood drain from his face as he answered the summons. They'd found out, he was sure of it. What would they do to him? Whatever it was, he probably deserved worse. Abe steeled himself for retribution. Although the room was cool, sweat trickled down his back as he bowed to the president and awaited his punishment. "Congratulations, Mr. Abe," said the president. "In recognition of your fine performance over the past quarter, we have decided to promote you to general manager in Tokyo." Abe had nearly fainted. He bowed again, his mind racing. General manager of the biggest operation in the company? What had he done recently to merit this promotion? He'd been trying to do his job, but certainly he'd done no better than before—worse, if anything, because of the German thing. It was absurd. It wasn't even time for promotions; they were always made in the summer. And the president had been so kind, so paternal. Abe's guilt and shame at his treacherous behavior almost overwhelmed him as he walked back to his desk.

The next day, after a sleepless night, Abe had telephoned the headhunter with trembling fingers. This whole thing had been a terrible mistake. He'd let himself be carried away in some newfangled modern trend. He might as well have spiked his hair and gone to dance with the teenagers in Harajuku. When the headhunter answered the phone, Abe said miserably that he was very sorry, terribly, terribly sorry, but he simply could not accept the job with the German pharmaceutical firm. The headhunter's voice grew heated. Abe had already shaken on the deal; the Germans were expecting him. Yes, Abe said, he knew, he was terribly sorry, so sorry, there were family problems (this was absolutely true, thought Abe, thinking of his wife's increasingly steely demeanor), he simply could not accept the job. After fifteen minutes the headhunter appeared to be defeated. He was sorry, too, he told Abe. And the Germans would be very, *very* sorry. Abe had broken a deal, he said, and they had been relying on him; but if Abe could not take the job, there was nothing more to be said. They hung up.

Abe felt as though a huge weight had been lifted from his shoulders. He thought happily how pleased his wife would be, how Nagai's face would light up, how he could show his loyalty and gratitude to the president for his unheard-of promotion. There was a nagging unease in Abe's mind when he thought about the German company. They had spent a lot of time and money on him, flown him to Europe, wined him and dined him, and seemed to trust him. It was troubling. Still, they would understand. They were used to people quitting abruptly and breaking their promises. After all, Abe reasoned, they were not Japanese.

Hiroshi Yamada was almost thirty-eight, and he knew if he was going to make a move it had better be soon. He had always been a man of action, proud of his intelligence, his ambition, and his youth. The first two he would always have; the third was fading. Yamada had been born in the ruins at the beginning of the Reconstruction and had grown up with Japan itself into a successful practitioner of business. He had worked desperately hard in school for the sake of his parents, who had lost everything—including, in his father's case, an arm—during the war. For his parents and his nation, Yamada had tested at the top of every class, been accepted at Tokyo University, and joined one of Japan's most successful banks shortly after graduation. He was a soldier like his father, he often thought, he was just fighting a different battle.

Yamada loved his job with the bank. At first he had gotten by mainly on ambition. The tasks at the bottom of the ladder in his firm were not particularly exciting. He had done them, and done them well, because he knew they were the foundations of future success, for him as well as his company. He had never really expected to get much fulfillment out of the work itself. That had changed when Yamada moved into investment banking. Not long after receiving this new assignment, Yamada had suddenly realized that going to work was more exciting than he had ever dreamed it could be. He loved the tension, the long hours of controlled desperation preparing a deal, and the powerful burst of adrenaline when the time finally came to act. Investment banking was like a drug for Yamada. He worked hard, tossed down beer with his co-workers long into the night, and slept too little. It was thrilling.

Yamada's obvious enjoyment of his work had gotten him a spot on the newest team organized by the bank. He was second in command of a special branch of the firm that dealt in mergers and acquisitions. Now Yamada looked at his old colleagues the way a fighter pilot looks at the ground crew. Mergers and acquisitions was even more intoxicating than other aspects of investment banking, packed with powerful secrets and secret power. Yamada worked even longer hours than he had before. His wife and daughter figured in his mind only as sleeping faces half hidden by the quilted futons he tiptoed past on his return from evenings spent talking business in the bars. He was exhausted, he was exhilarated, and he was completely content.

But Yamada had not gotten where he was through contentment. It began to bother him that the company seemed to take his brilliance and diligence for granted. He had worked long and hard to become a *kachō*, but once he had achieved the position it seemed somewhat less than enough to reward his spectacular performance. There was no real reason for Yamada to feel constrained, no hint that his climb up the ladder had stopped, but he felt impatient. The positions above him in the bank were all filled with middle-aged executives who would have to age into retirement before any spots would open for Yamada's generation. The bank was top-heavy, clogged with these older men who were content to inch upward according to their birthdays and not their accomplishments. To Yamada, who knew he was working harder than any four of his superiors, the long wait for promotion seemed absurd.

There was little hope that Yamada's firm would defy tradition by promoting him past his seniors. He had heard that some firms had begun to do such things, but he knew it would be a long time before his bank joined those ranks. Part of the reason for the enormous success that had made the bank desirable to Yamada in the first place was its conservative, thoroughly Japanese approach. The bank followed tried and true methods on a grand scale. It would never take risks or make preposterous leaps like hiring science graduates or even women (as Yamada had read some firms were doing) or challenging the seniority system. It was frustrating. Yamada knew that much of his energy came from his youth. By the time he had reached a level where he could have some real influence in the bank, he would be too old to care about making changes.

Despite these problems, the daily pleasure of making big deals and taking big risks was enough to make Yamada more than happy in his job. Uncharacteristically, he had almost forgotten that transfers were coming up until a superior had whispered to him that the word around the company was that Yamada was likely to be moved off the mergers and acquisitions team within the month. Yamada had bristled at the thought. Where, he asked his boss, were they going to send him? The answer was appalling: corporate planning, or perhaps personnel. Yamada was furious. He felt he would suffocate if he were forced into the mild, tedious drudgery of—he hated to even think the word—personnel. Or even worse, *corporate planning*. It was simply too much to tolerate.

The rumors about his impending transfer made Yamada feel that his thirty-eighth birthday was terribly important. He was still young enough —barely, he thought—to come on board at another bank as an expert in mergers and acquisitions. Yamada wasn't blind; he'd read the magazines. He was backed up on the mergers and acquisitions team by a squadron of young subordinates who admired and trusted him. He had heard them talk about job hoppers, about high fliers who could simply leave a firm and join another as experts in their fields. This was 1990, and the traditional ways were fast becoming obsolete. It was not like Yamada to stay with the old-fashioned when the new beckoned to him on the horizon.

The day before his birthday, Yamada got a call from a headhunter. He was not surprised—after all, he had received at least three such calls in the past—but this time was different. A Japanese bank was looking for a well-qualified executive to head up a new division in mergers and acquisitions. Was there any chance Yamada might be interested in the position? Yamada immediately set up an appointment with the headhunter, replaced the phone on the hook, and sat for a moment drumming his fingers on his desk. As a new top graduate from Todai, Yamada had briefly considered the very bank that was now trying to recruit him. Back then, he had passed them off as second tier, a step down, not worth his while. But he understood from his younger colleagues that now this bank was highly regarded as an innovator. It had been on the list of top twenty companies for new graduates this year. What was more, this bank had instituted several new tactics (that was obvious from the fact that Yamada was being recruited) that Yamada felt would help Japan keep up with the future. He could do worse. Yamada rapped the top of his desk with his knuckles. Corporate planning indeed!

He confided in a few subordinates, young men who were themselves often wooed by scouts and who knew the scuttlebutt about comparative wages, benefits, and promotion opportunities. The whole thing was very tempting. Yamada mentioned the issue briefly to his wife, who seemed to think that the increase in salary would be worth it—especially since he seemed so happy doing mergers and acquisitions. Their daughter Etsuko was still young; his move would not hurt her future. Yamada's wife knew two other women whose husbands had changed jobs, and they could afford to fly home and visit their own parents several times a year. Yamada's wife had always been dazzled by his success, and she assured him that she would back him up no matter what he decided. His parents seemed confused by talk of a job change—wasn't he happy where he was?—but they were sure Yamada would do his best to make them proud of him. He always had. His wife's parents were somewhat less enthusiastic about the job change. In fact, they called him a treacherous son-in-law and swore they would never have allowed him to marry their daughter if they had known he would disgrace her in this fashion. Yamada shrugged off their anger, knowing it would ease if his salary and his title both improved.

The meetings with the headhunter went well, as did further meetings with the bank's administrators. The salary was tempting, the work enticing, and there would be a rather large proportion of job-changers in Yamada's new division. He would be working with the best and the brightest from across Japan. Promotion opportunities seemed virtually unlimited, tied as they were to performance rather than seniority. It took Yamada only a few hours to decide that he couldn't refuse the bank's offer. He told his superiors at the old bank that he was regrettably forced to leave for family reasons—his aging parents, trouble with his father's health . . . The directors were most unhappy, but there was nothing they could do. Yamada said his good-byes with many deep bows and sincere apologies. He regretted having to leave the bank, but after all there were many who could fill his position. He had not been allowed to work to his full potential anyway. Yamada took his gang of subordinates out to a hostess bar, where they toasted him again and again. One of them whispered to Yamada that he was considering leaving the firm for an American investment bank. Yamada ordered another drink for him and promised that they would talk.

On his first day with the new bank, Yamada took a few minutes to call his parents in Hokkaido. Yes, he told them, it looked like a great job. He had more freedom in his work than he had ever had with the old firm, and he expected to enjoy working with a group of enthusiastic and progressive people. He would call them and tell them more once he'd had a little time to adjust. Yamada's parents seemed happy. He had done well for them all his life, and he was still doing well. As Yamada reminded his parents, neither he nor his country had reached the top by refusing to move into the future.

The stories of Mssrs. Takahashi, Abe, and Yamada are derived from personal histories of real Japanese executives. They are meant to illustrate what we believe to be a widespread alteration in the sanctions and expectations surrounding one of Japanese management's most famous elements: the lifetime employment system. *Shūshin koyō seido,* as the Japanese know their tradition of "permanent" employment, has been acknowledged by scholars from both Eastern and Western cultures as one of the essential pillars upon which the Japanese built their postwar economic miracle. Simplistically described, this system is a tradition of corporate paternalism, in which the executive is socially and psychologically bound to his company in a process that seems to many Westerners to be closer to adoption than merely hiring. The largely implicit understanding between the Japanese "company man" and his firm is that each party owes the other a lifetime bond of loyalty that is not only financial, but highly social.

The most casual glance at the Japanese corporate world reveals the differences in corporate loyalty between most Japanese salarymen and their Western counterparts. Any Western executive who has spent a week doing business in Japan soon notices that the businessmen in that country identify themselves and each other in terms of the corporate pins they wear on their lapels and the titles that appear on their business cards. Japanese executives work long hours and almost never use their full allotment of vacation time. They usually spend their evenings, even after work, in the company of other employees from their own firms rather than at home with their families. Their closest associations and sources of personal advice tend to be found at the office. In short, Japanese salarymen are apparently more socially bound to their places of work than are Western businessmen. To the casual observer, the phrase "one big, happy family" seems to ring less hollow in a Japanese firm than it might in many Western ones.

Behind the impressive devotion of the Japanese salaryman to his firm lies a long history of social structures and cultural norms. Perhaps the clearest modern manifestation of these phenomena is the lifetime employment system. When a Japanese college graduate is hired by a company, both the firm and the new employee know that they can reasonably expect their relationship to last throughout the executive's career. On one hand, the company doing the hiring is making an unstated but understood pledge that it will assure the newly hired member secure and lasting employment, generous benefits, and the intangibles of social support and identity. On the other hand, the employee is generally expected to stay with the firm for the rest of his working life. Although it is not illegal for an executive to quit his job or move to another firm, the impropriety of such an action in the context of Japanese culture has made job hopping much more rare in that country than in Western nations.

Some Western scholars, analyzing the management strategies that have propelled Japan to its economic prosperity, have recommended that something more like the Japanese employment system should be imitated by Western companies (Dore 1973; Lincoln and Kalleberg 1990). Other analysts, while admitting that the lifetime employment system has been crucial to Japan's success, claim that the system is so dependent on culture and socialization that it will always be subject to a kind of Japanese monopoly. A middle road between the first two extremes, however, suggests that that country's lifetime employment system is neither the solution to the managerial woes of other nations nor an indestructible bastion of Japanese cultural heritage (Aoki 1988). As Japan comes to resemble other nations in terms of its involvement in the world market and the internationalization of its operations, the permanency of the "permanent employment" system seems to be growing less certain. This book will document changes in some Japanese structures, behaviors, and attitudes that indicate a change in the character and the extent of the lifetime employment system.

The Corporate Elite and the Lifetime Employment System

In order to discuss any change, it is first necessary to have a clear picture of exactly what the lifetime employment system is. Given its notoriety and the influence it has clearly had on Japanese economic practice, many Westerners are surprised to find that the lifetime employment system has never been pervasive over all classes of workers. It has in fact been limited to a small but prestigious and powerful group of highly educated employees. It has been estimated that fewer than 20 percent of the workers in Japan are involved in the lifetime employment system (Taira 1962, 167; Cole 1979, 61). The three case histories recounted at the beginning of this chapter are taken from the top stratum of Japanese business society—a group that might be called the "corporate elite."[1] This book will focus on this small group of workers, not to imply that their experiences are representative of the experiences all Japanese workers experience, but to illustrate and use the fact that elite workers are the most effective sample in which to examine changes in the lifetime employment system.

The overwhelming majority of the corporate elite in Japan are males who fulfill two main qualifications: they have university degrees, and they work in large Japanese enterprises. Women are almost automatically excluded from the lifetime employment system. Recently a few companies have broken with the tradition of relegating women to "O.L." ("office lady") positions and have considered some female employees for lifetime employment. In general, however, the feminist movement has made few inroads into Japanese corporate life. Most "elite" female employees, even those with degrees from the best universities, are expected to quit work as soon as they find an eligible marriage partner. Yoshino writes that

> a university education constitutes, with few exceptions, the single most important prerequisite to qualifying for managerial rank. Not only is a university education required but a very strong preference traditionally has been shown for graduates of a limited number of leading universities. (Yoshino 1967, 227–228)

The alumni of these prestigious institutions are more likely than any other group of Japanese workers to move into the lifetime employment system. The association between highly selective educational institutions and large firms in Japan represents a strong bond between the various organs of social status in that country. As Rohlen put it: "The association of permanent employment with high status is one of the most prominent characteristics of the Japanese company scene, and it colors the entire statistical spectrum" (Rohlen 1974, 92). The comparison between the status ranking and paternalism of premodern Japanese society and the present corporate-education hierarchy is intriguing even to the newest Japan enthusiast, and we will discuss it briefly below. Chapter 2 of this work will offer a simple description of how the relationship between high status and permanent employment evolved through Japanese history. For the present purposes, however, it is more important to realize that the system, as it exists, seems to create or reinforce a remarkable consistency in the behaviors and attitudes of some of the most prestigious members of Japanese society.

> With the managerial revolution, most of the Japanese elite have now been incorporated into large organizations, and their pattern of life has become essentially that of high-level salary men. . . . They follow the same pattern of regular hours, regular pay, regular vacation. Although they have higher standards of consumption and participate more actively in political and community life than the average salary man, they do not have the independence in action that the independent entrepreneur had. Their activities, like those of lower-level salary men, are subject to their groups' consensus about the interest of the firm. (Vogel 1963, 266)

Not only is the lifestyle of the permanent employee limited largely to high-status workers, but high-status workers tend to limit their job choices to positions offering lifetime employment. Unlike lower-level salarymen (white-collar workers who have only high school degrees or who have college degrees but work in small firms), almost all of elite Japanese salarymen (college graduates who work in large firms) are involved in the permanent employment system. Many large manufacturing firms offer lifetime jobs to all male employees of the firm, from directors to forklift drivers; but while smaller firms are willing to give their managers

the promise of permanent employment, the rank and file are often subject to the buffetings of the external labor market. The corporate elite are
thus one group almost universally involved in the lifetime employment
system. Furthermore, their conspicuous position at the top of an over-
arching national hierarchy ensures that this group is not only unusually
uniform, but also easy to distinguish.

Our final reason for focusing our analysis on corporate elites is a theoretical one. While the thoroughness of the Japanese elites' involvement in
lifetime employment makes this group particularly sensitive to the impact
of changes in the employment system, the high status of elites makes
them more likely to transmit alterations from individuals back into
organizations and the broader environment. Both Weber's analysis of
forms of authority and the social psychological literature on leadership
acknowledge that social status plays a role in an individual's power to
change the attitudes and behaviors of larger groups of people.

Certainly, status is one of the most important determinants of social
influence in Japan. The imperative of allegiance to one's social superiors
has been seen as the Japanese alternative to the Western norm of adherence to absolute philosophical standards as behavioral guides. Standard
acceptable behavior patterns in Japan apparently never have been absolute. Vogel noted that the men and women of Mamachi (the Tokyo
neighborhood he observed)

> do not have an articulated system of thought which embodies their fun-
> damental beliefs. . . . [They] prefer to think that they have no particu-
> lar values and explain their behavior not as resulting from convictions
> or values, but from situations or customs, as if they had not internalized
> the customs. Many eagerly discuss various philosophies of life as if the
> philosophies had nothing to do with their own convictions. (Vogel
> 1963, 142)

Proper behavior for Vogel's Mamachi residents was determined by the
group with which the individual most identified. Members of the group
were almost necessarily deferential to those with the highest status. In
Japan, then, "societal norms" do not appear to emanate from numinous
ethical strictures, but from the most prestigious group in the society at
any given time. Yoshino points out that harmony is an important value in
Japan because of the "great importance ascribed to collectivity" (Yoshino
1967, 11). If it is to consistently preserve harmony, a value or value system must be considered reasonable. If it is perceived as unreasonable,
whatever is best for the group at any given time takes its place as the most
preferable attitude or behavior. However, any Westerner who assumes
that the harmony of a group-generated value system is democratic should

recall the hierarchical nature of Japan's "vertical society." In Japan, the opinions of one who is older, better educated, has a better "title," or comes from a more elite family tend to carry the most weight in a "group" decision. Hiyoshi Nakamura, a social psychologist, found that in modern Japan the higher the individual's status, the more room he will be given to deviate from group and social norms (Nakamura 1978, 638–641). Status, then, has a tremendous impact on the ability an individual might have to affect group, organizational, economic, or culture structures and standards.

Theory and logic both support the notion that higher-status employees, who command more power and resources than lower-status workers, will as individuals create the most obvious possible impact on the employment system.[2] It is for this reason, as well as those discussed above, that this work will concentrate on the elite business manager.

Methods

A variety of methodological approaches contributes to the scientific validity of any social analysis, and this becomes more and more true the broader the phenomenon under study. For this reason we employed as many different approaches to obtaining information on Japan's corporate elite as time and resources would permit. Some of these are tried and true methods used by almost every social analyst. Others involved more unusual tactics. Together, we believe they provided many different internal validity checks and yielded a more accurate representation of the Japanese lifetime employment system than any one of them might have in isolation. Nevertheless, a few caveats are in order. In trying to confine our study to corporate elites—male college graduates from "elite" colleges in managerial-track positions in "elite" firms (see n. 1)—we were somewhat hampered by the limited availability of large-scale data sources. Most published surveys of college graduates and elite-firm employees categorize the data along only one of these criteria, and we have been forced to make do with drawing on one category or another for large-scale significance.[3] Only in our interviews were we able to focus narrowly on individuals who we were positive fit the full range of requirements for membership in the "corporate elite." However, the close correlations between the information obtained by interviewing and the less exactly defined statistical samples convinced us that the latter type of evidence was a valid representation of trends among Japan's corporate elite. We are confident that the use of a broad range of analytical tools in studying this segment of Japanese society has allowed us to "triangulate" on something approaching truth.

DOCUMENTARY EVIDENCE

Perhaps the most accessible source for information on Japan's lifetime employment system is documentary evidence. Besides consulting academic articles and journals, we reviewed the literature addressing lifetime employment in the Japanese mass media over the past five years. Most of these reports came from newspaper and popular literature accounts that sensationalize the degree to which the lifetime employment system is breaking down. With this caution, it is still significant that the mass media are talking about a profound change taking place in Japan. For one thing, even sensationalized accounts are often based on some factual evidence. For another, information disseminated through popular media can have a significant effect on the individual's attitudes toward job changing. The mere fact that a corporate executive who might be considering changing jobs can read in the morning newspaper about other Japanese business elites who changed jobs (and have been successful and happy because of it) might make that executive more likely to move to another company. We wish to emphasize again that our reliance on the media is due to our conviction that a thorough examination of public perception on this issue is crucial for understanding the changing attitudes and values toward job hopping in Japan.

INTERVIEWS

This conclusion was supported by personal accounts we obtained through interviews. To obtain a reasonably varied interview sample, we conducted our interviews with three different groups of Japanese elites. These groups, which we will later describe in more detail, consisted of business managers, university seniors from colleges in and around Tokyo, and finally, salarymen who were in the process of changing jobs.

Our purpose in interviewing business managers was to understand as thoroughly as possible the way Japanese organizations respond both to individual behavior and environmental shifts. The managers we interviewed held a variety of positions at various levels in their respective organizations. The largest percentage of those interviewed were *torishimariyaku* (directors) and *buchō* (general managers)—most of whom were in charge of personnel or personnel planning. We also made a point of interviewing branch managers and *kachō* to see how they viewed job changing in their ranks and what they were doing to stop or encourage it. (Not surprisingly, we found that those in personnel planning had the strongest and most clearly formed opinions about the future course of the organization and the probable effect of variations in the employment system. But almost everyone had an opinion about the past, and all the interviews proved useful in evaluating the relationships among individ-

ual, organization, and environment in terms of lifetime employment.)
Interviewees in this first group worked in Japanese companies and in foreign firms operating in Japan.

We also interviewed at least twenty college seniors from different universities in the Tokyo area. We asked the students about their upcoming job decision, their careers, families, attitudes toward work, and visions of the future of Japan. We found very few differences in attitudes across schools. The considerable variety that did exist in the students' ideas about the future seemed to stem largely from differences in their backgrounds before college. On an informal level, one of the most interesting aspects of these interviews was the contrast between the answers we received in 1987–1988 and those one of the authors had been given by Japanese college students five years earlier. While the author had not conducted formal interviews with the students at that time, the attitudes of today's college graduates seemed to differ significantly.

Finally, we were lucky enough to interview a number of job changers —those rare business elites who had recently decided to make the move into a new company. Despite the well-publicized scarcity of such people in Japan's lifetime employment system, we were able to interview well over a hundred who had changed jobs since this project began. We asked each subject about his background, work experiences prior to changing jobs, and feelings about the move after having completed it. The career histories of these individuals were varied: some were moving from one Japanese firm to another, while many others had moved from Japanese to foreign firms; some had changed companies only once, while some were contemplating a second or third organizational switch. All were quite open about the way a job change had affected their careers, families, and friends.

PARTICIPANT OBSERVATION

The unusually free access we had to job changers, as well as those contemplating a change, was due in part to an "intervention" methodology we were able to employ for more than four months. During this time one of the authors was employed as a senior consultant at a major foreign-capitalized executive search firm in Tokyo. As a headhunter, he was able to work on roughly ten projects devoted to locating replacements for senior management positions in various industries. Four of the searches involved the investment banking industry; two were in pharmaceuticals; two were in insurance; and two were for business management positions in high-tech firms. Over the course of the four months, we would estimate that he spoke with more than 250 people about the possibility of making job changes.

Through his work he was exposed not only to the searches in which he was directly involved, but to all the searches in the office. (More than fifty searches were under way while he was employed in this firm.) The usefulness of this methodology for understanding the elite employment system in Japan came not only from the job itself, but also from the authors' being identified as an executive recruiter and his wife in more casual social situations. This identification meant that almost all conversations during that period of employment centered on the questions at the heart of this study. The attitudes and behaviors expressed toward the topic of job changing in some ways seem more trustworthy than those gleaned from more formal interviews and questionnaires.

QUESTIONNAIRES

While interviews provided many of the in-depth qualitative data we felt to be helpful in understanding Japan's employment system, they lacked the potential for generalization inherent in quantitative information. The interview subjects were necessarily preselected, and their responses to questions did not have the uniformity necessary for comparison. For these reasons, another important part of the research methodology we employed to understand the changes taking place in the lifetime employment system was survey questionnaires. Through the kindness of Recruit Research Company, we were able to carefully analyze surveys on jobs and job changing issues that Recruit had conducted over the past ten years. We were limited to using the company's published cross-tabular data for past surveys but were given the original data for the most recent surveys 1986 to 1987 and were able to perform statistical analysis on those data ourselves.

Even more important than these surveys, however, was the opportunity we had to use the company's Recruit Realtime Research (RRR) system to survey six hundred randomly selected salarymen in the Tokyo area, with questions we designed ourselves. Three hundred subjects responded to this survey. More than half of the respondents were college graduates, and of those, most were in large companies. Since we were interested in college graduates even if they had changed jobs to a smaller company, company size was not a factor in reducing the size of this sample. The survey was conducted in August 1988, making these data the most recent and the most directly related to the topic of the lifetime employment system among elites.

We believed that a survey centered in Tokyo would give us the best chance of assessing the current climate of corporate elites—a climate that is influential in other parts of Japan as well. Because mass media and educational decisions are centralized in Tokyo, Tokyo culture and belief systems have been spread throughout the country. Tokyo's influence is particularly pervasive in the realm of business. More than 70 percent of corporate headquarters of large companies in the country are in Tokyo. Even if a business manager has never lived in Tokyo (a rather unlikely possibility for a middle-aged businessman), he is likely to have visited often enough to know which combination of ten subway lines would take him from one point to another in the city. The homogeneity of Japan's corporate employment system, even as compared to the general homogeneity of the national culture, make the Japanese business world a uniquely suitable context in which to study social change. Alterations in the institution are rarer and more immediately obvious to the observer than they might be in many other naturally occurring social systems.

The combination of literature review, interviewing various samples, participant observation, and analysis of survey data yielded what we believe is a valid description of Japan's employment system as far as the corporate elite are concerned. The condition of this high-status group, in turn, provides a clue to larger-scale phenomena in Japanese business and its environment. By identifying one element in this homogeneous environment that is highly sensitive to change and by using as many means as possible to describe that element accurately, we attempted to approximate the chemist's experiment in the massive and complex laboratory of the social world.

Overview and Conclusion

This book describes what we believe to be significant changes in Japan's lifetime employment system for the managerial elite over the past few years. Chapter 2 sets the stage for this discussion by examining some of the historical underpinnings of the system. Chapter 3 describes the lifetime employment system in the postwar period. Chapter 4 considers some of the reasons for the impregnability of "permanent" employment as well as the evidence of a pronounced alteration during the late 1980s: behaviors and attitudes alike of Japanese elite employees and organizations show increasing tolerance toward the heretofore unheard-of act of changing jobs. Some of the more important reasons for the increases in motive and opportunity for job changing are addressed in chapter 5. Most of these reasons can be found in broad-scale environmental changes, such as Japan's current demographic situation, the slowing of growth in the Japanese economy, the related need for Japan's corporations to diversify, and the country's increasing involvement in the world market. We are convinced that at the level they are being experienced in today's Japan, these changes are both unprecedented and impossible for the present Japanese employment system to accommodate without changing the system itself. The next two chapters discuss the changes that have been taking place in the system since the late 1980s. Chapter 6 considers the increased opportunities for job mobility being provided by organizations, and chapter 7 addresses the increased motivations for individual elites to job hop. For this reason, as chapter 8 points out, we disagree with some scholars' dismissal of recent trends away from traditional lifetime employment as a mere temporary anomaly. Instead, we expect to see some significant transformations in Japan's permanent employment system as the nation adapts to a changing internal and global environment. The implications of these changes for Japanese competitiveness are discussed at the end of this final chapter.

The phenomenal success of Japanese enterprise in the postwar era and the unique and impressive characteristics of its managerial practice have been a source of curiosity and even envy to Western managers for the past few decades. The lifetime employment system is one of the most dramatic examples of the "Japaneseness" of Japanese management. Unquestionably, this system has contributed to the rapid rise of the nation's economic prosperity. Whether the aim is to imitate, discard, or compete with the lifetime employment system, it is first necessary to understand it.

But *shūshin koyō seido* is not a monolithic, immutable structure, as many casual Western observers believe. We have emphasized "casual" here because our experience in talking to a variety of people about the subject of Japanese lifetime employment convinces us that there exists in most Westerners' minds a "common view" of the monolithic Japanese employment system. Many academics have stated their arguments with a great deal of care (usually involving the extensive use of caveats and footnotes), but they still leave the reader with the impression that some static form of "traditional" employment system exists in Japan.[4] In some cases we have restated arguments more strongly and with fewer qualifications than any particular scholar would likely do because we are trying to get at the impression left for the Western reading public. We do not attack any particular author, but we do dispute the popular ideas that still exist about an immutable employment system in Japan.

We maintain that the system is changing as the society that engendered it changes and that the present alterations in the nature of Japan's lifetime employment comprise a fundamental aspect of the system itself. In this book we attempt to describe Japanese "permanent employment" as a fluid phenomenon that changes and adapts over time and differing economic situations. In the process, we hope to provide an understanding of the system that is itself more adaptable, more congruent with actual circumstances, and hence more theoretically and practically useful than some other Western analyses.

CHAPTER TWO

The History of Elite Employment Decisions in Japan

THE JAPANESE corporate elite have been identified with lifetime employment since the system first came into being. Permanent employment has always been more associated with the managerial class than with lower-level employees. Gordon's extensive study of labor relations in Japan noted that only following World War II did lifetime employment become a pervasive system among blue-collar workers in Japan (Gordon 1985). For the elite university graduates, however, the system fell into place well before the war (Taira 1962, 150–168). In this chapter we examine the structures, standards, and sanctions that have influenced the employment decisions of Japan's managerial elites from the "traditional" Japan of the Tokugawa period to the present. The image that emerges from this historical perspective is one of constant interplay between ideological standards (particularly the standard of loyalty), the concrete demands of structural economic factors, and social sanctions that constrain behavior for Japanese individuals.

Historically, the norms and institutions that controled the Japanese elites' social behaviors were the same that eventually came to be accepted structures and social standards for the general populace. But at any given time, the structures, standards, and sanctions surrounding the decisions about employment made by those in the managerial classes differed slightly from those of the broader society.[1] By limiting this analysis to one class—one very important class—we reduce the variation in elements impinging on the employment decision. Taking this very specific focus is especially informative because, despite the historical centrality of the managerial work force to Japan's employment system, the history of this

country's white-collar workers remains largely unstudied. Kinmonth
maintains that

> white-collar workers, their lifestyle, employment, and compensation,
> have been given only journalistic coverage and standard histories of the
> labor and social movements virtually ignore their existence, as do major
> statistical studies. (Kinmonth 1981, 7)

It is important to keep in mind the breadth of factors that influence a
managerial-class employee's decision to join or leave a company. These
factors include aspects of Japanese national ideology, personal loyalties,
and communal obligations as well as contractual employment arrangements. We have therefore examined the history of employment decision
making by considering elements of the social, political, economic, and
commercial climates that might have helped determine the actions of
individual businessmen. This investigation shows that the employment
decision in Japan, while based on a variety of political and economic factors, is influenced most fundamentally by the network of social norms
and sanctions that characterize Japanese society. It also shows that the
employment system in Japan has always been able to conform itself to
the economic and societal environment in which it exists.

Japanese Loyalty

One of the most popular works ever written for the Japanese theater is
Chūshingura (The Treasury of Loyal Retainers). This puppet play, first
produced in 1748, is one of the most explicit exemplifications of the
famous Japanese ethic of loyalty—an ethic often cited as one of the key
ingredients in modern Japan's lifetime employment system. Chūshingura
is the story of forty-seven samurai whose master is betrayed and forced to
commit suicide. The forty-seven, having pledged lifelong devotion to
their leader, refuse to rescind that commitment until he is avenged. They
execute the culprit, commit ritual suicide in recompense, and achieve
immortality for their rectitude, their courage, and above all for their
loyalty.[2]

Loyalty—in a guise that appears to Westerners as the most extreme
form of that virtue—is one of the ideological values most identified with
Japan. Neither Western nor Japanese observers have failed to notice the
perpetuation of this value in modern Japan, and nowhere is the comparison between the forty-seven samurai of Chūshingura easier to draw than
in the institution of permanent employment. The loyalty ethic that
underlies permanent employment has been described proudly by the Japanese and covetously by Westerners as one of the keys to Japan's phenomenal economic success. Certainly it is one of the standards that gov-

erns the employment decisions of the nation's executive elites. Permanent employment is more an attitude of managers than of employees. The position that enterprise loyalty is important to employees, "although it has a very real basis, must be understood as the dominant *management* ideology that has pervaded much of Japanese industrialization in the twentieth century" (Cole and Tominaga 1976, 88).

Of these three factors, economic changes are perhaps most obvious and most amenable to quantitative measurement. Sanctions, although their influence is apparent on a societal scale, usually exert that influence at the individual level. The historical evidence for such sanctions therefore tends to be anecdotal. Such evidence, although perhaps not as "hard" as economic data, is nonetheless verifiable and reasonably robust. The effect of ideological standards is more elusive. This is not because standards are not explicit—in Japan, as we will point out, they are often extremely explicit—but because they are particularly susceptible to misinterpretation. To understand the actions of individual Japanese in the face of given economic circumstances, however, an accurate comprehension of such basic values is essential. Many Western observers of Japan have employed a kind of Weberian *Verstehen* to Japanese values, attempting, as Weber himself recommended, to

> accept these values as given data, then . . . try to understand the action motivated by them on the basis of whatever opportunities for approximate emotional and intellectual interpretation seem to be available at different points in its course. (Weber 1978, 6)

While such an approach yields more explanatory power than a culture-biased Western analysis of Japan, it contains its own set of pitfalls. The cultural observer who sympathizes with "foreign" values risks believing that he or she in fact empathizes with them and may proceed to present an approximate picture of human behavior as an absolutely accurate one. Popular literature and opinion concerning Japan, and particularly Japanese employment practices, tend to fall into this trap. For this reason the Japanese ethic exemplified by the forty-seven samurai of *Chūshingura* is often assumed by Western commentators to be simply an exaggerated form of Occidental loyalty. To look at the history of the Japanese employment system from this perspective is to encounter baffling inconsistencies. As this chapter points out, Japan's employment history seems at some times to adhere closely to a public, nationwide standard of employee loyalty and at others to respond to a highly rational economic calculus on the part of those same employees. Such transitions would be contradictory under a Western loyalty ethic, which rests on an emotional commitment to the object of fealty regardless of, or even in spite of, economic advantage.

Another contribution Max Weber gave social science was the notion that

> not ideas, but material and ideal interests, directly govern man's con-
> duct. Yet very frequently the "world images" that have been created
> by ideas have, like switchmen, determined the tracks along which
> action has been pushed by the dynamic of interest. (Gerth and Mills
> 1946, 280)

A careful examination of the loyalty ethic, one of the "switchmen" that has most influenced Japanese employment patterns, clarifies the course the nation's elite workers have taken as the "dynamic of interest" has changed from the time of the forty-seven *rōnin* to the age of the *sara-riiman*. A digression to this topic is intended to create a frame of refer-ence for the historical data that comprise the bulk of this chapter.

In the great division Western philosophy created between reason and passion, rationality and emotion, "loyalty" falls on the side of the roman-tic. The romantics of the European Enlightenment condemned rational-ity as the evil that had banished genuine human affections from social conduct and relationships. When such simple virtues were replaced by rational calculation, action was tainted by a coldness that obliterated compassion and replaced it with coercion. Western culture today echoes the romantic assumption that steadfastness in relationships is based on a moral stance in which rationally calculated personal advantage has no place. Thus, even such acute observers as Ruth Benedict see in the strik-ing loyalty of much Japanese conduct a highly emotional commitment to the object of that fealty—one that, following the Occidental sanctions of loyalty, would persist despite any change in the circumstances of the indi-vidual. This perspective is apparent, for example, in Benedict's discus-sion of Japanese prisoners of war who apparently switched loyalty from Japan to the Allied forces once they had been captured (Benedict 1967). The explanations for this conduct offered by Benedict are set firmly in a Western concept of loyalty. They are first, that the Japanese did not expect their soldiers to be taken alive and had therefore failed to indoctri-nate them in proper prisoner-of-war behavior; and second, that the cap-tured Japanese considered themselves "dead" to their own country and resigned themselves to cooperation out of combined despair and precon-ditioned obedience.

Both aspects of this explanation bear a good deal of credence. But it is remarkable that Benedict fails to consider one obvious aspect of the Japa-nese prisoners' switch of loyalties: that once in the hands of the enemy, it is to any prisoner's advantage to cooperate. The possibility that this obvi-ous fact may have contributed to the Japanese prisoners' behavior does not occur to Benedict, we believe, because the author knew the Japanese to be intensely *loyal*—and that to change allegiances for reasons of personal advantage flies in the face of the Western definition of loyalty. This omission of the factor of personal gain from the ethic of loyalty is a recurrent theme in Western assessments of Japanese behavior, not least in the literature on permanent employment. The remarkable devotion of an executive to his firm, and of the company to him, is seen by many Westerners as an almost incomprehensibly thorough adherence to the ideal of fealty. This loyalty, it is assumed, is instilled in the Japanese to the degree that it overrides an American-style response to the opportunity to maximize one's own economic success.

As this chapter shows, the actual behavior of Japanese employees over time responds much more closely to a personal rational calculus than one might expect, given this image of the Japanese as the epitome of Western-style loyalty. Simplistically put, the data show that the Japanese elites have historically clung most rigidly to the practice of lifetime employment when economic conditions made it advantageous to do so. In periods when opportunities within companies seemed less promising and when other opportunities knocked from outside firms, job changing and entrepreneurialism rose drastically despite the continued reification of loyalty as a primary Japanese value. In this fact lies an apparent contradiction that often impedes Westerners' understanding of Japan. Is the Japanese employee really as devoted to the company as he seems, or is he merely playing the role of the idealist, using it as a facade to hide a cool assessment of his own advantage?

The answer to this question that emerges from the historical evidence on employment standards, structures, and sanctions in Japan is, yes. And, of course, no. The answer is Janus-faced because the question assumes a dichotomy that is Western, not Japanese, in its origins. In fact, Japanese employment decisions appear to be based on criteria that are both rational and emotional, both economic and ideological. The patterns of Japanese employment seem consistent and logical only if one dispenses with the notion that these two elements of human nature necessarily oppose each other—for in Japan they are often inextricably interconnected.

One can imagine situations in which an American executive might affix absolute loyalty to his or her organization. Most of these involve personal relationships that might equally well exist outside the scope of the company—for example, the person might work for a family firm or might have started the company. In such cases, the American employee might offer absolute allegiance to the job, but for the primary reason that such allegiance would constitute personal loyalty to family or to self. Even in the case of the most thoroughgoing "organization man" in the United States, the relationship of executive to employer is seen primarily as contractual and value-rational, centering on the exchange of labor for material wealth. Such a relationship is expected to be separate and qualitatively different from the executive's relationship, for example, to spouse and children. These "personal" connections are seen as primarily nonrational, emotional, and associated with a depth of mutual loyalty not expected in corporate association.

The separation of these two realms of human activity—the economic and the emotional—seems right and proper to the American. In fact the combination of the two sides is often viewed as troublesome and inappropriate, especially in the workplace. The Japanese, by contrast, tend to see rational and emotional considerations as interdependent and interconnected. Their version of society operates more smoothly the more the two elements are locked together. Thus, for example, American firms have explicit rules and unwritten social sanctions to discourage the development of romantic relationships between office personnel, while the Japanese condone discreet matchmaking between employees of the same company. The Westerner tries to disaggregate rational and passionate issues, while the Japanese sees such disaggregation as a disturbance in the proper order of things.

To understand the history of employment in Japan, then, it is essential to allow an analytical framework wherein an executive's career is not merely an economic arrangement nor an emotional commitment, but an agreement that involves the offering of almost every aspect of the employee's life—economic productivity inextricably intermingled with emotional fealty—to the company. In exchange for this unrestricted contribution of self, however, the employer is fully expected to return to the employee the equivalent of what he or she has contributed; in other words, the worker's whole economic and emotional life. Corporate loyalty is thus emotionally complete but rationally conditional. This combination of rational and nonrational commitment in the Japanese concept of loyalty—or rather the failure of the Japanese world view to dichotomize the two—helps clarify aspects of that loyalty that can be a source of amazement to casual Western observers. The unconditional totality with which the Japanese can devote themselves to an organization, and the paradoxical suddenness with which that devotion might shift its locus, is as evident in the history of lifetime employment as it is in Benedict's example of prisoner-of-war behavior. The latter met with disbelief and astonishment when observed by American soldiers; the former is equally incomprehensible from a purely Western businessperson's world view.

The standard of loyalty, with this uniquely Japanese meaning, has made an important contribution to the nation's employment system from the late premodern era to the present. We have devoted considerable attention to this standard because it is a conceptually consistent theme in the history of Japan's lifetime employment system. The remainder of this chapter discusses the ways in which the ideal of employee loyalty interacted with structures and sanctions throughout the tumultuous changes that brought Japan from an isolated feudal empire to an international economic giant. The conclusion summarizes what we believe to be the patterns of Japanese employment behavior that emerge from an analysis of the historical data and suggests ways in which these patterns can be interpreted to elucidate the condition of Japan's present employment system.

Tokugawa Period

The Tokugawa period, which stretched from the late sixteenth century until the fall of the shogunate in 1868, was the final era of "traditional" Japanese history: its conclusion ushered in what is known as the "modern" era. If the modern institutions of Japan have their roots in the country's traditional past, as many of them seem to, one would expect to unearth evidence of those roots in the Tokugawa period. And in fact, many elements of modern Japan's employment system do appear to be prefigured in the hierarchically structured class system of Tokugawa. The most obvious of these are the period's heavy-handed ideological emphasis on harmonious relationships and loyalty and the methods and mechanisms by which social norms were maintained.

Structurally, Tokugawa society was the formal concretization of what Chie Nakane calls modern Japan's "vertical society." There was little if any of what Westerners would call "individualism" in the Japan of the Tokugawa period (Dore 1958, 376). Each person in Tokugawa society was defined almost completely by the station held by his or her family. This status identification placed significant limits on what one could be or do within the Japanese social, cultural, and economic context. Samurai were on the top of the social heap in Tokugawa Japan, with farmers, artisans, and merchants ranking below them (in that order). To actively participate in the activities of a lower class was unthinkable.[3]

Strict boundaries between samurai and merchant classes were formalized in the first half of the eighteenth century. During the Genroku period (1688–1704), the merchant class developed a luxurious and flamboyant lifestyle, characterized by the kabuki theater and *ukiyo-e* paintings of that period. Eventually the more well-to-do samurai also began to indulge in these luxuries and the sumptuary display of wealth that went with them (Fairbank, Reischauer, and Craig 1978, 424). Shogun Yoshimune (1716–1745), appalled by this turn of events, issued the *shinki hatto* edict, which prohibited the start of new businesses and restricted

the show of material goods (Hirschmeier and Yui 1981, 19). This supposedly allowed the samurai to return their attention to the business of
public welfare with an eye singly to the good of the nation (Yoshino
1967, 54).

Under the samurai ethic of the Tokugawa period, it was understood
that economic activities were important primarily as contributions to
political objectives (Yoshino 1967, 14). Nevertheless, a large portion of
late-Tokugawa villagers were involved in some kind of "business." Farmers who had large holdings often hired farm hands for rice cultivation
and then employed them during the winter season in a cottage industry
such as weaving, trading, or financial operations (Hirschmeier 1970,
27). During the late Tokugawa period artisans who could not bear working under a single *oyakata* (foreman) for most of their lives bought their
master's *kabu* (guild privileges) and went into business for themselves
(Hazama 1976, 24). Even some samurai went into business, but they
kept their samurai background a secret to avoid the stigma associated
with mercantile activity (Hirschmeier and Yui 1981, 57).[4] The number
and heterogeneity of those entering the merchant class catalyzed a change
in popular attitude toward commercial activity. The derogatory apho-
rism that "warrior means willpower, peasant means taxpaying, artisan
means work, merchant means *smiling*" (Hirschmeier 1970, 16) was
increasingly displaced by the belief that merchants could be as important
to the good of Japan as the samurai.

The benefits of mercantile activity could not be ignored in view of
Japan's tremendous economic growth during the late Tokugawa (Hirschmeier and Yui 1981, 15). The samurai class—even the high samurai—
realized that the power in society was shifting toward the merchant class
(Yoshino 1967, 17). Their response was to form fief-sponsored semi-
monopolies in many of the industries where merchants were gaining an
upper hand (Yoshino 1967, 15). With this move, the stigma that had
been attached to business and mercantile activities since the *shinki hatto*
began to fade away. There are even accounts of lower-class samurai selling their samurai titles to buy businesses (Yamamura 1967, 144).[5] The
end of Tokugawa saw a loosening of the rigid structures that had characterized Japanese society since the period began.

The structural limitations Tokugawa society placed on individualism
went hand in hand with the ideological centrality of harmonious human
relationships during this time. Long before the Tokugawa began, in the
seventh century A.D., the great Prince Shotoku had canonized harmony
and obedience as the highest ideals of Japanese society (Nakamura 1964,
712). Philosophical tenets imported from China further strengthened the
importance of the "human nexus" (Nakamura 1964, 414) in Japan: loyalty to specific individuals featured prominently in Buddhist teachings

(Nakamura 1964, 51), and Confucian ethics centered on the "five important relationships" *(wulun)* among family members, subjects, rulers, and friends.[6] Tokugawa Japan brought to its apex this definition of morality, a morality founded on a relativistic, socially determined ideal whose ultimate standard was to preserve the harmony of relationships. Loyalty to one's social superiors was a key element in this harmony. The "highest virtue was considered to be sacrifice of the self for the sake of the sovereign, the family (especially the parents) or the community" (Reischauer 1970, 142).

The idealization of loyalty and the importance of the human nexus were, to a large degree, standards of the samurai class, but they were gradually transmitted to the rest of Japanese society. As Hirschmeier and Yui put it:

> The samurai class, which was presented as a model for society, was being emulated by the other classes so that the Confucian value system came to permeate the whole of Tokugawa society, shaping it into a homogeneous people with rigidly defined behavior patterns. (Hirschmeier and Yui 1981, 13)

These standards for samurai stressed both "absolute loyalty to one's lord and unswerving filial piety" and "learning and scholarship" (Yoshino 1967, 5). In the late eighteenth century Ekken Kaibara, a well-known ideologue (who wrote "on behalf of his lord") (Kinmonth 1981, 57), urged the populace to be diligent "above and beyond official duties," to pay attention to human relations, to give in to group opinion, and to "avoid displays of intelligence" (Kinmonth 1981, 327). This ethic was admirably suited to the interests of the Tokugawa ruling class, whose position made them vulnerable to betrayal by their lower-ranking retainers. The ideal of absolute loyalty was the upper class's most effective protection, and Tokugawa rulers pushed it to its limit.

The application of popular ideology to the practice of business in Tokugawa Japan can be seen in the example of the Mitsui family code, originally a will written by Mitsui family head Hachirobei in 1694. It was slightly rewritten and institutionalized as the house code by Hachirobei's son in 1722. The most striking feature of the Mitsui canon is its similarity to official and unofficial codes of conduct in modern Japanese businesses. Mitsui's three-hundred-year-old standards persisted almost unchanged from the Tokugawa period to the present.

If the class-based and ideologically governed activities of the Tokugawa Japanese provide the structural and moral base for modern employment decision making, the mechanisms by which social norms were enforced during Tokugawa prefigures the system of sanctions that characterize the paternalistic atmosphere of the modern company. The family and the community were the primary agents of social control in the Tokugawa period. Because family membership involved taking the name of the family, it was obvious who was an insider and who was an outsider to each family group (Vogel 1967, 111). The head of the household was responsible for disciplining those who behaved improperly. The most extreme forms of punishment involved ostracism and expulsion, measures that served not only to discipline the offending individual but also to vindicate his family in the eyes of the community (Hirschmeier and Yui 1981, 15). Informal sanctions by the members of the Tokugawa community were in fact the primary means by which "contracts" were enforced within the villages. Neither the sanctions nor the contracts were of a type that was common in the West. Contracts were either verbal agreements between parties or tacit understanding of how a good villager should act.[7] Enforcement was frequently a matter of "psychological and communal pressure" (Yoshino 1967, 7).

Such pressures were not the only social controls brought to bear on deviant individuals in Tokugawa Japan. In the merchant and artisan classes, sanctions for improper behavior were usually internalized in the commercial house or trade guild. In the houses, where power was held centrally by the owners, excessive internal competition could be punished by expulsion. In the guilds, where power was less centralized, traditions guarded against unproductive competition. One example is in the *jinrikisha* guild, where it was taboo for one rickshaw runner to overtake another (Hearn 1923, 403). In the case of a break with understood rules of propriety (as in the example of one guild member luring away another's customer), the member's guild privileges were revoked and, consequently, his right to practice his craft rescinded (Hirschmeier and Yui 1981, 37).

EMPLOYMENT PATTERNS FOR ELITES DURING TOKUGAWA

Since familial relationships were responsible for enforcement of norms and obligations in Tokugawa society, the most obvious and effective method of organizational control was to create similar ties within the company (whether real blood relationships existed or not). The replication of a kinship model in a setting without blood ties was most strikingly demonstrated by the artisans. A young apprentice artisan went to live in the home of his overseer or *oyakata* (literally, "parent person"). The apprentice formed "quasi-parent-child relationships" *(oyabun-kobun)* with his master and "quasi-sibling relationships" *(kyōdai-bun)* with the other workers (Hazama 1976, 24–25).

Most businesses in the Tokugawa period were started by individual entrepreneurs and had become "family" enterprises. Many of the employees were blood relatives, but even those who were not came to depend heavily on their employers for both physical and emotional needs that would normally be supplied by parents. This aspect of early Japanese paternalism "establishes a consistent dependent relationship between employer and employee which emotionally may work itself out in the form of a need to be wanted or loved on the part of the employee" (Bennett and Ishino 1963, 226). It was not only the employee who received emotional sustenance from the employer. The employee and employer were each expected to feel *ninjō* for the other. Yoshino defines *ninjō* as "an understanding response to another's *hidden* feelings of deprivation and despair" (Yoshino 1967, 7).

Because of the closeness of these relationships and the weight of the obligations they entailed, hiring a new employee into a Tokugawa business was a very serious proposition. In the Noda *shōyu* (soy sauce) manufacture, the family-member owners (not the nonfamily managers) did this recruiting and "relied heavily on connections with kinsmen and members of the local community for recommendations" (Fruin 1983, 46). The familial and communal ties gave the owners some punitive recourse if the hire did not work out. In the Mitsui house, extra precautions were taken to ensure that none would bring shame to the name of Mitsui or the young apprentices' families. The boys were hired at the age of puberty (twelve or thirteen years old) and "lived with the manager rather like household servants. Their lives both on and off duty were regulated in the minutest detail" (Crawcour 1978, 227). These new hires were called *detchi* (apprentice). They usually served without pay, except for food, lodging, and clothing, until they became *tedai* (clerks) at the age of seventeen or eighteen (Hirschmeier and Yui 1981, 59). This period without pay may conceivably have been instigated to prevent apprentices from accumulating money and moving on to a more lucrative position, but it seems likely that the intense family and community pressures would have sufficed to prevent such a breach of ethics. The most important function of the *detchi* period was rather the opportunity for young employees to prove uncompromising loyalty to the house. It was by no means a matter of course that all apprentices would display that kind of loyalty: Crawcour's study of Minaguchiya, a Nagoya draper, shows that almost all of the *detchi* "left within a few years after they were hired" (Crawcour 1978, 276–282).

The decision to join a commercial house in Tokugawa Japan was rarely an individual one. The twelve- or thirteen-year-old did not set off on a series of job interviews in various houses. Rather, the members of his family arranged employment with a house in much the same way that the family would arrange his marriage. Usually it was second or third sons, who would not take over the family farm, who were hired out to become apprentices in the merchant houses.

Once an apprentice became a clerk, the family members observed
him closely to see if he had the "right stuff" to become a *bantō* (manager). What mattered here was not economic background, seniority, or
blood ties, but ability (Yamamura 1967, 44).[8] Owners were looking for
skilled managers to keep the house economically viable through the
next generation.[9] Unfortunately there were not many *bantō* positions
available in late Tokugawa Japan. Most houses hired only one *bantō*,
who eventually became responsible for running the entire company
(Hirschmeier and Yui 1981, 38–39).[10] More often than not, this *bantō*
was adopted into the family (Fruin 1983, 45). It is little wonder, then,
that there were not enough positions for all apprentices or clerks to
become *bantō*, and most had to return to their family farms (Taichi
1981, 24). This was accomplished with the least possible loss of face.
At the age of thirty, when *tedai* were eligible to become *bantō*, they
were sent home for a short leave. If the *tedai* were not called back to the
company from this leave, they knew they had not been promoted
(Hirschmeier and Yui 1981, 39).

Appointment to the position of *bantō* was not the final rung in the
climb to the top of the merchant community in Tokugawa Japan; owners
always held out incentives to their managers to elicit more faithful service. The loyal *bantō* could be given his own firm to run as a branch
(bekke) of the main family firm (Yoshino 1967, 40). This would not be a
completely autonomous position. The right of *bekke* could be revoked if
the "proper" respect were not paid to the owners of the main family business *(honke)* (Hirschmeier and Yui 1981, 40).

Class structure and samurai standards formed a backdrop to the pervasive social control of employment decision making in Tokugawa
Japan. The family controlled a youth's entry into the business world, but
exit from the path toward *bantō* status was often an individual decision.
Once an individual left the house, he took himself out of the running for
promotion in any house business and was left to lower-status farming or
labor employment.

Meiji Period

STRUCTURE

The Meiji period, which began in 1868, was prefaced by an increased
need and respect for commercial activity in Japanese society. After the
psychological blow the Japanese received from the arrival of Admiral
Perry and his black ships in 1853, Japan's leaders adopted the ideal of
fukoku kyōhei (rich country, strong army). They reasoned that the only
way to build an army strong enough to gain the respect of Western powers was to first build a rich country. Japan would be nothing in Westerners' eyes until the country could compete technologically and economi-

cally with the other "imperial" powers. Thus, for the first time since the
Genroku period, the government acknowledged the need for a strong
economy and emphasized commercial productivity.

Kozo Yamamura argues that the first Japanese citizens to take advantage of this new emphasis on business were pure opportunists. He cites as
an example the self-centered attitude of Yataro Iwasaki, founder of Mitsubishi, who sold his samurai title to start a lumber business and
appeared willing to go to any ends to make sure his business thrived
(Yamamura 1967, 155).[11] The early Meiji period was known as *udemae
shakai*—"a society in which only ability counted as a self-made younger
brother could laugh at the petty authority of his poverty-stricken elder
brother" (Dore 1967, 129). During this period the concept of *risshin,* or
getting ahead in life, became very important in Japan. The bonds that
had held social mobility to a minimum in feudal Japan were loosened,
and people from all classes struggled to move up in the world.

The first wave of entrepreneurs came from all classes and backgrounds. Mannari points out that three-fourths of Meiji businessmen
came from commoner backgrounds (Mannari 1965, 57).[12] Many of
these "commoners" were merchants or landlords who had the capital—
and at last, the freedom—to set up businesses (Hirschmeier and Yui
1981, 111). It was the ports (trade and shipbuilding) that gave these
entrepreneurs their start. The Yasudas, Okuras, Asanos, Otanis, and
Morimuras of the Japanese business world all forsook their "humble"
origins and built their personal business success into trading empires
(Hirschmeier and Yui 1981, 95). Even some samurai got involved in the
early commercial activity in Meiji Japan, but they were usually samurai
of lower rank, many of whom had fallen "into dire poverty in the second
half of the Tokugawa period" (Hirschmeier and Yui 1981, 14).

As we will see, Meiji business acquired many of its standards from the
samurai class. But it was the merchant, artisan, and farm traditions that
gave modern Japanese business its earliest structure. The merchant class,
perhaps, had the greatest influence on modern business structure in
Japan. Merchant houses were the only commercial infrastructure in place
when Japan began to modernize. Thus it was natural that these houses
formed the basis for the most powerful businesses (especially the quasi-
governmental businesses such as shipyards, arsenals, and mints) in Meiji
Japan—the *zaibatsu*. Since merchant houses were developed in a period
of economic stability and class immobility, however, they did not provide
a pattern to deal with a mobile work force in Meiji's opportunistic business climate. During the early years of Meiji, the *zaibatsu* found that
many young managers who were pessimistic about their opportunities
for advancement in their original firms might switch jobs until they
found a company in which they could climb a bit higher in the corporate
hierarchy.

It was the artisan class that helped form early business mobility patterns. Seeking to gain as much skill as possible, artisans in the early Meiji undertook a series of short job stints in a variety of firms. (Gordon 1985, 19).[13] Blue-collar workers and their employers adopted an artisan-based system, which stipulated that a worker's beginning and subsequent wage was based on the individual's skill level at the time of entry. Therefore, a worker who had entered a company as an apprentice would make much less than one who entered the firm as a highly skilled worker, even if their present skill levels were equal. Thus it was to the advantage of most blue-collar workers to change jobs often, increasing their base-level pay as they moved from company to company (Gordon 1985, 45). Meiji white-collar workers (particularly those with technical educations) may have had a similar attitude about the acquisition of skills in a variety of companies. Hiroshi Hazama (1976, 27) reports that "educated factory workers in Japan tended to be discontented with their jobs; they didn't like doing the same thing for a long time and liked to do a variety of jobs on the side." (Hazama 1976, 27)

Thomas Smith argues that the work patterns of the artisan class were not stable enough to become the norm for business management (Smith 1960). That standard was established by the sons of influential and well-to-do landlords who went to the cities to build their fortunes in Meiji's newly founded businesses. These boys combined the values of hard work and parsimony with values of Confucian diligence. They rose quickly in the corporations of Meiji Japan. Smith's statistics show that by the turn of the century, 45 percent of the business elite were sons of landlords (Smith 1960, 100). Whether because of the attitudes of these men or simply the lack of promotion opportunities in late Meiji, the high turnover rates of the 1870s and 1880s had practically disappeared by 1900.

At the turn of the century, a policy of hiring only recent graduates became prominent in some of the larger Japanese firms. At Mitsui, the practice of hiring college graduates more than five years after their graduation came to an end. Crawcour asserts that at this time there was "agreement in principle to recruit only school leavers and internalize training" (Crawcour 1978, 238). Highly skilled workers, such as those with university educations, could have used the threat of desertion to "hold modern industry to ransom, as it were, in the absence of some such agreed strategy by employers" (Crawcour 1978, 238).

Whether or not employers were collaborating against their employees, there was much less opportunity for either horizontal or vertical mobility in late Meiji Japan than in the early years of the period. Yonekawa points out that graduates who had entered companies before the 1890s were "assigned to such important posts as directors and general managers of departments or of overseas branches in their early forties and they generally tended to retain these positions until the early 1920s" (Yonekawa

1984, 208). The stability of these managers' career paths meant that by the end of the century there were few high-ranking positions for new college graduates. Kinmonth notes that a private university degree—which in the 1870s practically assured the graduate of a job as a secretary in the government or as a manager in commerce—might lead to a ¥10-a-month job on the bottom rungs of a low-status bureaucracy in the 1890s (Kinmonth 1981, 133). An 1891 article in a magazine for Japanese youth claimed that half of the graduates of private college who had studied politics and economics were unemployed after leaving school.[14]

STANDARDS

While early Meiji Japan was full of new opportunities and innovative structures (when compared with the feudal period), most of the stated policies and practices governing individual behavior persisted unchanged. The basic unit of social control in Meiji Japan was still the family; loyalty and the human nexus still dominated Japanese values. Introductions were still very important to finding a job. Dore points out that "employers who were willing to take all comers, unintroduced and unguaranteed, were rare" (Dore 1967, 127). In almost all economic activities of this time, even "unrelated persons" were arranged to "function together in an artificial or simulated kinship group" (Yoshino 1967, 67). Even within areas of such "personal" interest as *risshin*, the stated motivating factor was less personal ambition than family pride.[15] Thus Tokugawa virtues such as loyalty were still valued, but the focus of that loyalty had switched in response to structural changes.

The Mitsui family code, perhaps more than any other written document, is indicative of the continuity in business standards that existed between Tokugawa and Meiji Japan. In 1900, after two centuries, Lord Hachirobei's will was still so pertinent to the conduct of Japanese business that Mitsui instituted a policy of requiring all new recruits into the company to swear an allegiance to the code. Byron Marshall points out that, in general, the substance of the ideology surrounding business had changed little from feudal times to the Meiji period (Marshall 1967, 3).

EDUCATION

Along with the ever-present focus on loyalty, one of the most important Tokugawa traditions to carry over into Meiji Japan was the emphasis on education. Many scholars have argued that this emphasis on academic discipline was a major reason for Japan's rapid rise as an industrial power. The place of education in Meiji society became even more exalted in conjunction with the spirit of opportunism and the demise of strictly "ascriptive criteria of status." Thomas Smith argues that education took the place of ascriptive status to some extent, making a diploma "both a certification of knowledge and a 'pedigree' " (Smith 1960, 100).

The use of such "pedigrees" in Tokugawa Japan had been limited mainly to determining which high-ranking samurai could enter public service. Thus in the earliest years of the Meiji period, education (college education in particular) was considered the path to becoming a government bureaucrat. It required considerable effort to shift the emphasis on education from the public to the private sector. Yukichi Fukuzawa was as important as any other single person in making education important to the business world. He was the founder of Keio Gijuku University and author of hundreds of pamphlets and books that expounded the philosophy of *fukoku kyōhei*. In the early years of Meiji Japan the government paid large salaries to Westerners who came to teach workers and managers how to function in government-sponsored industries such as shipbuilding, iron works, and so on. Ideologues like Fukuzawa saw their role as instilling self-sufficiency in the Japanese people—and how else could the people become self-sufficient but by education? Dore argues that the message in Fukuzawa's *Gakumon no Susume* "was a culmination of and not a break with the Tokugawa tradition" (Dore 1965, 312). Even so, Fukuzawa's message was a strong one: "It is merely by employing himself in learning, knowing many things well, that a man becomes respected, that he becomes a rich man. The man without learning becomes a poor man, an inferior man."[16]

Although this emphasis on education had germinated in the samurai tradition of the Tokugawa, Fukuzawa had to fight against some of the other ideologies of this same warrior class to extend the ideal of education to economic and business leaders. In the early days of Meiji Japan, graduates of the elite Tokyo Imperial University (today's Tokyo University) "were so imbued with their importance to the nation that most refused any position in private enterprise—no matter how well paid" (Hirschmeier and Yui 1981, 78). Instead they entered government service because the Tokugawa samurai tradition taught that it was "inhuman to bow down to money" (Marshall 1967, 42). With three out of four 1878 Tokyo University graduates coming from samurai origins (Kinmonth 1981, 61), Fukuzawa was fighting against stiff odds. Moreover, what had been chiefly samurai culture in the Tokugawa had become popular culture in Meiji Japan. Sydney Crawcour reports that "the distinction between samurai and popular culture was tending to become a little blurred in some areas even before the Restoration" (Crawcour 1978, 120). Fukuzawa tried to separate "self-respect" from the samurai's social prestige and instead equate it with education and "business success."[17]

The big merchant houses (precursors to the *zaibatsu*) were the first private businesses to listen to Fukuzawa's ideas and recognize the importance of recruiting college graduates. The university graduate's importance lay both in skills and in status. Yataro Iwasaki (founder of Mitsubishi) boasted as he began recruiting Keio and Hitotsubashi university graduates that "in the whole of the Japanese Empire there shall be no other enterprise surpassing us in managerial ability" (Wray 1984, 25). In all of Meiji society, these college graduates were "regarded with awe" (Hirschmeier and Yui 1981, 77). Some of the prestigious aura that surrounded the university graduate also adhered to the company that could lure him away from a government position.

Even when samurai-class Japanese began to accept the importance of commerce and the social role of businessmen, an impediment to the successful integration of social status and commercial endeavor remained in the fact that Meiji merchants had as much disrespect for the educated as the educated had for merchants. Samurai-class college graduates were seen as too self-important to respect the primacy of the customer in business dealings. In the early 1880s, when Mitsui Trading began recruiting college graduates, the managing director was careful to instruct the graduates "to be as well-dressed as other clerks, so that customers might not recognize their status; once customers gave them credit on their performance, then their educational background could be revealed" (Yonekawa 1984, 206).

Meiji merchants placed high importance on such elements of business as proper dress and perfect manners. The surplus of "aspirants over opportunities" is one of the three reasons Kinmonth gives for the importance of "proper decorum" in the Japanese business world of the early twentieth century, along with the fact that there were no clear hallmarks of achievement and that the work situation involved relations of people with varying status and power (Kinmonth 1981, 74). The company became an almost courtly setting, where favors and advancement were based largely on conformity to exacting rules of etiquette. The businessman's primary concerns became his relations with various people in the firm, and white-collar workers realized that promotion and salary increases were "received in exchange for conformity to group life *(dantai seikatsu)* of the bureaucratic, governmental, business and academic organizations that employed them" (Kinmonth 1981, 326).

Social Sanctions

Modern Western business has no set of social sanctions comparable to those that created and reinforced the centrality of decorum to the Japanese managerial system. Crawcour comments that

> while the [modern system of recruiting only graduates fresh out of college and promoting on the basis of human relations] itself is a creative reaction to changing circumstances, and as such is innovative rather than traditional, what gives the system its characteristic flavor is the web of non-material sanctions by which employees and society as a

whole have been conditioned to accept the system as both morally good and individually satisfying. (Crawcour 1978, 239)

If policies and practices that companies had adopted toward their managerial class employees in the Meiji period were to function effectively (indeed, if they were to function at all), an accompanying ideology had to be successfully propounded. The ideology that emerged still marched under the banner of traditional Japanese loyalty. However, in contrast to the entrepreneurial nationalism that had been preached throughout the early years this period, late Meiji standards reemphasized the notions of loyalty to one's employer.

The philosophy of Sontoku Ninomiya, a nineteenth-century philosopher, epitomizes the virtues of loyalty and hard work promulgated during the later years of Meiji Japan. Ninomiya taught that the most important duty of a man is "to repay [his] obligation to society in general and to [his] employer in particular." To reinforce this doctrine in the minds of future Meiji businessmen, Ninomiya's statue was erected in most elementary school yards at the turn of the century (Crawcour 1978, 240). Eiichi Shibusawa, a prominent Meiji bureaucrat, further bolstered Ninomiya's ideas. He stated that "in order to get along in society and serve the State, we must by all means abandon this idea of independence and self-reliance, and reject egoism completely" (Kinmonth 1981, 339). One concrete example of the enforcement of this philosophy could be found in Mitsubishi, where even though managers "were given far-reaching decision power, they were never permitted to forget that they were nothing but retainers of the House of Iwasaki" (Hirschmeier 1970, 25). In this way, the self-serving entrepreneur, who was given some measure of status and respect in early Meiji Japan,

> never had much scope to gain power, nor with the continuance of the Tokugawa preference for advancement by learning and dependent service rather than self-seeking money-making, has he had much chance to gain prestige as the admired type, the representative of the ethos of the society. (Dore 1958, 391)

One interesting irony about the ideologies that held managers "in place" in Meiji Japan is that these same managers were involved in the creation of the norms (Crawcour 1978, 241).[18] In fact, the onus of adhering to standard practices rested most heavily on the elite members of Japanese society. Hirschmeier and Yui point out that the higher a businessman rose in Meiji Japan, the more he had to comply with the "pressure of public opinion and expectation . . . at least outwardly" (Hirschmeier and Yui 1981, 96). Lafcadio Hearn, an acute observer of Japan at the turn of the century, enumerated the sanctions that held the high-status Meiji businessman in his place. Hearn describes social pressure coming from above (from superiors), from "his fellows and equals," and from below "represented by the general sentiment of his inferiors. And this last sort of coercion is not the least formidable" (Hearn 1923, 373). These pressures intensified, rather than lessened, as a Meiji business elite climbed the corporate ladder. Hearn maintained that once in a leadership position,

> less than ever before, does he belong to himself. He belongs to a family, to a party, to a government: privately he is bound by custom, publicly he must act according to order only, and never dream of yielding to any impulses at variance with order, however generous or sensible such impulses may be. A word might ruin him: he has learnt to use no words unnecessarily. By silent submission and tireless observation of duty he may rise and rise quickly. (Hearn 1923, 402)

The well-placed Meiji businessman, therefore, cared deeply about right and wrong (as defined by his peer group) and was held tightly in the web of social norms and sanctions that controlled his every action in the employment system.

EMPLOYMENT PATTERNS OF ELITES DURING MEIJI

The decision of a managerial-track employee to join a company in Meiji was a much more mature, informed decision than that made by the Tokugawa business elite. The Meiji managerial-track candidates generally were college graduates; thus, they were older than their Tokugawa counterparts when they entered their first company. They were also less tied to traditional structures such as the family and the community. In fact, the college years in which the student moved away from home to attend school

> were the one time in the life-cycle of an educated Japanese when he was not directly under parental pressure or cramming for examinations and the one time when he was not worried about finding or keeping a job. Higher school [college] was the one moment in his existence when he could indulge his ego without worrying about what it would do for his chances for *risshin* (personal advancement). (Kinmonth 1981, 340)

Thus the Meiji college graduate, unlike the Tokugawa merchant house employee, made an individual decision to work in a particular company. This decision was informed by relationships with family and friends, but for the most part, economic opportunities drove the original decision-making process.

When the early Meiji college graduate considered the economics of *shūshoku* (entering a company), there was certainly plenty of reason to consider private business. The university students were doted on by private businessmen "who were willing to support them during their university years. After graduation these youngsters moved immediately into top positions, receiving about ten times the salary of a local bank manager" (Kinmonth 1981, 77–78). The young graduates were assured of a short path to the top of the company, even if more senior managers were already employed. In Mitsubishi, even though a number of employees followed Iwasaki from Tosa to manage the privatized company, it was the graduates of Keio or Tokyo Kaisei Gakko (Tokyo University) who rose quickly because they were "better educated" (Wray 1984, 27).

Although conditions were extremely favorable for college graduates in their firms, companies like Mitsui and Mitsubishi had a problem recruiting the top students. Instead, college graduates sought to involve themselves in the national industrial scene by becoming "high-prestige" bureaucrats for the Ministry of Industry, which had been formed in 1870 to "establish government pilot enterprises, and promote industrial enterprise" (Hirschmeier and Yui 1981, 86). For the most part, however, the Japanese were following the industrialization model of the West, which called for their industrial and commercial ventures to be in the hands of private citizens. One particularly talented and influential man who rose to the task of privatization was Eiichi Shibusawa.

Shibusawa had already made a name for himself in the Finance Ministry before resigning to become the president of Japan's First National Bank. He and an English adviser, Alexander Allan Shand, wrote the regulations and rules that were to govern modern Japanese banking (Hirschmeier and Yui 1981, 101). More important, Shibusawa was a role model for other educated elite in Meiji Japan (Yoshino 1967, 62). His philosophy—a restatement of Fukuzawa's theme that one could engage in business and still serve the country—appealed to college graduates, who had samurai educations even when their family background was not samurai. In fact, Shibusawa is credited with developing a new word for "businessman," *jitsugyōka,* which did not have the pejorative connotations of the terms that described merchants in Tokugawa Japan. Along with a new name, he bestowed a new definition on the Meiji businessman: "someone who works with honesty for the establishment of industry" (Hirschmeier 1970, 172). Shibusawa's philosophy led even the most opportunistic businessmen of the time to—at least publicly—espouse an ethic of loyalty that emphasized the enrichment of Japan. Ichizaemon Morimura, a trader who was later made a baron, expressed these patriotic motivations succinctly:

> Even supposing one tries, and no profit is gained, or one suffers a loss; if it is to the good of the State, then one should continue to try. I state positively that the secret to success in business is the determination to work for the sake of society and of mankind as well as for the future of the

nation, even if it mean sacrificing oneself. (Wakamiya 1929; trans. Marshall 1967, 35–36)

With Shibusawa's example firmly in mind, college graduates began to be more willing to join private business. By 1900 the percentage of college students entering business after graduation from Tokyo University, Keio, Tokyo Higher Commercial (later Hitotsubashi), and Tokyo Technical (later Tokyo Institute of Technology) was 16.9 percent, 35.3 percent, 73.5 percent, and 49.5 percent respectively (Yonekawa 1984, 194).

It was not only Shibusawa's example that sent many college graduates looking for commercial employment around the turn of the century. By the mid-1880s, the government was eagerly divesting itself of the pilot industries in which it had been involved from 1870 onward. This divestiture provided two reasons for graduates to consider private business. The most important reason was that students who had wanted a job in industry could no longer obtain hands-on industrial jobs in the Ministry of Industry. (In fact, by the 1890s it was becoming hard to find any government position after graduation [Dore 1973].) The second reason more and more graduates entered private business was that alumni of their prestigious colleges were often the managers of the privatized companies the Ministry of Industry had established. The proposition of joining a company in which college education was valued was much more appealing than going to work for a merchant family.

By the turn of the century, even the merchant families and successful opportunists were placing much greater emphasis on hiring college graduates. Skill and learning were not the only qualities that Iwasaki of Mitsubishi was after when he began hiring graduates of Keio and Tokyo universities (Wray 1984, 25). He was also looking for connections. To keep channels of communication open with these all-important bureaucrats, companies redoubled their efforts to recruit graduates from the universities that were supplying the government ministries. Like Mitsubishi, Mitsui Trading hired students from Keio and Tokyo universities; but when the de facto managing director, Takashi Masuda, was made a member of the School Council, Mitsui cemented ties with Hitotsubashi University. From the 1880s onward, Masuda's position gave Mitsui an inside track to recruiting college graduates (Yonekawa 1984, 203). Sumitomo was a dyed-in-the-wool merchant *family* until the family elders realized that to be successful in the twentieth-century business environment they needed the services of college graduates. Sumitomo began regular recruiting at Tokyo University in 1896 (Hirschmeier and Yui 1981, 167).

The Mitsui, Mitsubishi, and Sumitomo *zaibatsu* all offered something to college graduates that smaller private firms could not—security. By the turn of the century *zaibatsu* were almost as popular with graduates as government employment, since a job there had become as safe as employment within a government ministry (Yonekawa 1984, 204). In fact, Yasuzo Horie argues that some of the samurai-educated graduates preferred working for the *zaibatsu* to a career in government "precisely because the lifelong employment in the service of one family appealed to their traditional values of loyalty (Horie 1967, quoted in Hirschmeier 1970, 25)." It is worth noting that this loyalty was seen not as running only from employee to a firm, but entailed the ability of the corporation to offer a lifetime's security for a lifetime's labor.

Although this kind of job security was one attractive feature of the *zaibatsu* in Meiji Japan, it appears that there was still a great deal of interfirm mobility at this time. Especially in the early years after the Restoration, companies looked for experienced managers to staff their growing economic concerns. Some of these high-level employees came from government, like Taijiro Yoshikawa, "the most important executive" during the first decade of business at N.Y.K., Mitsubishi's shipping line. Yoshikawa had been an educator and administrator at the Ministry of Education until entering Mitsubishi in 1878 "through the recommendation of a former Keio classmate" (Wray 1984, 231).

Yoshikawa's case typified the movement from the public to the private sector that was common at the beginning of the Meiji period. Movement across private firms was also fairly widespread in these early years. Tsunehiko Yui has written a biographical article about Hikojiro Nakamigawa, who became the managing director of Mitsui Bank after a checkered career in a variety of occupations. Nakamigawa served as the editor of *Jiji Shinpō*, Fukuzawa's paper, until he was thirty-three years old and decided to get out and start his own trading firm. His efforts at entrepreneurship failed within a year, but through connections he had formed while editor, he was asked to become president of Sanyo Railway Company. He had been with Sanyo for about ten years when he accepted Mitsui Bank's offer of a directorship (Yui 1970, 43).

These examples of midcareer job changes do not appear to have been isolated events. Of the fifty college graduates who were assigned to manage Mitsubishi's Takashima mines in 1881, only half remained in the company after two years. This mobility appears to have been a product of employee dissatisfaction rather than demand. The dreary work and the fact that many of these new graduates were not yet "accustomed to regular and group work" are two reasons cited for the high turnover rate (Yonekawa 1984, 205). Yonekawa's study of Hitotsubashi graduates in Mitsui Trading shows that between 1885 and 1896, the quitting rate in the first five years ranged from 20 percent to 45 percent (Yonekawa 1984, 207). By the turn of the century, there was still "no clear evidence of the existence of a life-time employment system" in the largest Japanese companies (Yonekawa 1984, 206).

Around the turn of the century, economic, ideological, and social sanctions began to discourage midcareer job changes among university graduates in the large *zaibatsu* (Yonekawa 1984, 207). In contrast to the early Meiji period, late Meiji Japan saw emerging a new pattern that

> still exists in some form today. There is free competition, free entry, the principle of personal achievement dominates—until the entry into a group and then the group takes over under the principle of human harmony, with more unwritten than written rules, which nevertheless are silently and strictly observed. (Hirschmeier and Yui 1981, 122)

Taisho and Early Showa

STRUCTURES

The professionalization of management in Japan became firmly established in the early 1900s as more and more companies began to limit their management hiring exclusively to college graduates. The increasing popularity of graduates was not limited to the echelons of upper management. Some Japanese were convinced that all employees destined for higher ranks should be required to hold college degrees. Seisha Iwashita, president of Kitahama Bank in 1904, stated that

> unless someone has higher education one cannot place reliance on him as an up-to-date banker or company employee—I have paid considerable attention to this problem from the beginning, have studied it and made tests. The results of my findings are that someone who rose from the position of apprentice can in no way compare with someone who graduated from college.[19]

During the early 1900s, the number of colleges and college students rose precipitously in Japan (Eisuke 1986, 158).[20] The effect that increasing college attendance had on the structure of management can be seen in figures Aonuma has estimated from a careful analysis of various company records. He estimates that in 1900 less than 5 percent of the business leaders in Japan were "graduates of universities or higher technical institutes." By 1928, two-thirds of these leaders were college graduates. (By 1962, one-fourth of the nation's executive elite would be hired from Tokyo University, 60 percent from Todai, Kyoto, Hitotsubashi, Tokyo Technical, Keio, and Waseda combined [Aonuma 1965, 117].)

The big trading houses, which had for years cultivated and helped perpetuate the apprentice system, moved toward hiring college graduates during the late years of Meiji. But while the trading houses took their share of college graduates during the early part of the century, there were plenty of degree holders left over for the smaller private firms. As Japan industrialized, these firms hired university graduates to implement the process of modernization and afforded the graduates every opportunity to rise easily and rapidly through the corporate ranks; it was thus only natural that many degree holders would seek positions in private companies. But the same opportunities that meant easy success for graduates at the beginning of this period drew young Japanese onto the university fast track in unprecedented numbers. With the absolute increase in the number of colleges and graduates in Japan during this time and the simultaneous increase in graduate hires, Kinmonth estimates that "the soul of the early Showa graduates was worth 50 percent less than the middle-Meiji graduate" (Kinmonth 1981, 314–315).

STANDARDS

The glut of talented, well-educated Japanese managers in firms in the early twentieth century was intimately linked to the standards that came to dominate Japanese business conduct during this period. The everpresent loyalty ethic, which had emphasized nation building through individual effort in the early years of Meiji, shifted its focus as the period matured. The increasing prosperity of the Japanese economy was accompanied by a reemphasis on loyalty to one's organization and superiors. Kinmonth notes similarities between the standards espoused by salarymen of this period and the samurai in late Tokugawa.

> At 5 or 6 percent of the population, there had been more samurai than the Tokugawa order needed to staff its offices. Those who would maintain their position or even rise a bit did so by competing in rule-following diligence and bribery. Once graduated, the educated youth [of the early twentieth century] was in a similar position to the samurai who had been differentiated from the masses by birth. His education performed the same function, but unfortunately there were more of his kind than the Meiji order (carried over into the Taisho-Showa years) needed. (Kinmonth 1981, 328)

The ideological pendulum, which had swung so far to the side of individualism and entrepreneurship during Meiji, thus returned to a more organizational orientation by the early 1900s. As we have seen, in early Meiji it was the strong individualist or even the charismatic eccentric who was able to rise to the top of newly formed organizations. During these early years, the acquisition of a college degree had been an anomaly that contributed to the graduate's aura of unorthodoxy. The mere fact that a new employee had a college degree had singled him out as one in a handful of nontraditionalists in Japan and had made him a likely candidate for quick success.

By the early Showa era (1920s), however, Japanese companies were awash in a sea of the same college degrees that had gained their original desirability by virtue of their rarity. Under these circumstances, corporate success for degree holders became dependent on excelling within a brimming pool of graduate talent, rather than bobbing effortlessly to the top of a largely uneducated work force. The "formalization of the criteria for entry and promotion" in the bureaucracies ensured that the individual manager's rise would be neither quick nor particularly easy (Dore 1967, 133). The only way to achieve it, amid so many bright young men with similar backgrounds and similar skills, was to conform absolutely to a set of rules at least as strict as those in place in Japanese samurai society. During the early Showa "any deviance from social, corporate or agency norms required a choice between individualism and unemployment" (Kinmonth 1981, 339).

The corporate recruiters of the early Showa no longer filled management openings by simply skimming off the best and brightest graduates of the universities. Instead, hiring decisions were carefully weighed on the basis of a "personality first" policy (Kinmonth 1981, 310–311). In fact, if a job candidate proved "too" talented, his inability to blend in with corporate norms might create more of an internal problem for the firm than if he were not talented enough. The overabundance of college graduates eager to join companies also narrowed the criteria by which potential employees could be compared. Recruiters became ever more alert to and aware of minute details about students' lives. Turn-of-the-century university magazines warned students whose siblings had died not to reveal the fact, lest the recruiter read into this some genetic weakness running through the family (Kinmonth 1981, 322).

The students who survived the minute scrutiny of recruiters and were hired by a company entered the days of *daigakude no yōchien* (literally, "kindergarten for college graduates"). For the first few years of employment, the newly hired executive was allowed to perform only the most menial tasks. These were supposedly meant to train the him in basics of the business, but actually the newcomer usually got little more out of the experience than the ability to bow "so that his muscles moved without any conscious thought on his part" (Kinmonth 1981, 314).

From the company's point of view, however, these first years of training were useful in evaluating a new recruit. The new graduate's obedience and loyalty could be tested in the context of his menial tasks without seriously affecting the operation of the firm. That these virtues—obedience and loyalty—were assigned paramount importance was evidenced by the fact that the new recruit was given no opportunity to exercise or display his other talents even if he had them. On the contrary, the last thing anyone wanted in a firm was a "high-flyer" who was "lacking in stability, given to argumentation, and prone to boredom in the company environment" (Kinmonth 1981, 311).

With the new emphasis on loyalty in companies, the education system began to eliminate stories about individual successes from primary school readers. Instead, school children were regaled with "anecdotes of loyal retainers devoted to the service of the Imperial Throne" (Dore 1967, 137). The idea of changing jobs was obviously antithetical to such a standard. In theory, then, the new graduates entering a corporation in the early 1900s had no intention of ever leaving their firms for more promising or satisfying jobs. According to Kinmonth, the ambitious young executive of this era

> should not be cynical or calculating in his display of diligence. It had to come from the heart, and he should resolve that he would not move to another firm. The aspirant should work as though he expected his efforts would lead to his being called away by another firm, but because of his extra display, he would usually find himself recognized by his own employer. (Kinmonth 1981, 318)

In return for this devotion, companies ostensibly offered recruits the assurance of a virtually unassailable career, with lifelong security, if not spectacular success, ensured by the paternalistic firm. The reality of employment practice during the early part of the twentieth century, how-ever, fell conspicuously short of this ideal. The cohort of university grad-uates entering business during this period had been educated in the early Meiji, when loyalty was understood to be feudalistic. The brightest and most ambitious had competed to excel, not because they wished to devote a lifetime's service to a single company, but because they expected to be rewarded for their unusual talents. Thus despite the strong social sanctions supporting lifetime employment during this period, "those rewarded least according to ability, the better-educated employees, particularly the university graduates, left in large numbers" (Fruin 1983, 230).

That Japanese companies were well aware of the problems they faced in retaining highly skilled and gifted employees is evidenced by the fact that they provided material incentives to highly valued managers. Such employees were often offered high bonuses as part of the company's "life-time loyalty" to them. Thus Toyoji Wada, senior executive director of Fuji Spinning Company, was "to receive in one year the unheard-of sum of 300,000 yen because the firm had made an extraordinary profit of 3 million yen. The directors were each to receive 150,000 yen" (Hirsch-meier and Yui 1981, 201). Top professional managers received as much as 10 percent of net profit—and also received status shares of company stocks (Yoshino 1967, 116). The expectation was that such material rewards along with the all-embracing social network of the firm would comprise a fair trade for these skilled employees' unstinting devotion. And in fact, the promise of such high incentives served to cement the norm of lifetime employment for the elite managers of the early Showa era. The experience of Jisuke Shinshima, an employee of the Kashiwa family enterprise born in 1891, shows the combination of economic and emotional factors that contributed to "permanent employment." "I was afraid I would be left behind by the competitors," wrote Jisuke; "from time to time I even thought of quitting and starting out on my own, but I continued, in spite of my complaints." When Shinshima was twenty-seven, the president of the Kashiwa firm rewarded the young man's loyalty by presenting him with a bride (chosen from among the local girls) and a house—gifts that understandably cemented Jisuke's feelings of obligation and devotion to the company (Fruin 1983, 146).

Not only were managers evaluated and rewarded for their own loyalty to the company, their skill as managers was largely judged by their ability to instill the same values and behavior in the workers under their jurisdiction. No other managerial skill was more positively sanctioned than the ability to avoid disturbances among company personnel. Marshall, in his study of business elite ideology during the prewar period, found that "the ability to handle men and avoid discord was the characteristic most highly praised in discussions of talented business executives" (Marshall 1967, 101). No matter what the condition of the firm in regard to production and profits, and no matter how poorly fitted a given manager might be for correcting such defects, the fact that quitting the firm would reflect badly both on the employee himself (who would be openly exposing his inability to "fit in") and on his boss (who would have obviously failed to make him fit) usually served to keep an executive from changing jobs. When the exacting reciprocal rewards of the lifetime employment "contract" were not met by either employer or employee, however, Showa managers often switched firms.

Hirschmeier and Yui note that during the prewar period "as the non-zaibatsu companies lacked the loyalty concepts which were by tradition built into the *zaibatsu* system, [executives] felt free to change companies and did so sometimes in order to move to the top" (Hirschmeier and Yui 1981, 171). Breaches of the implicit loyalty contract were broken by the companies as well as individuals, and "companies would also hire their prospective managers away from each other" (Hirschmeier and Yui 1981, 171).

This activity was not limited to the hiring of managers in midcareer. Companies also fired employees, in violation of the reigning paternalistic standards. When the depression of 1920 made retaining employees more costly than losing their loyalty, many large firms cut hundreds of workers from their white-collar payrolls.[21] Large firms like Mitsui and N.Y.K. occasionally employed both layoffs and reduced recruiting to cope with difficult economic conditions (Wray 1984, 467–468; Yonekawa 1984, 208). Those fired often included older college graduates, who would be replaced by newly graduated recruits at a much lower wage (Kinmonth 1981, 284). A widely circulated periodical designed to facilitate its readers' efforts to secure good jobs reflected the tension still extant in a corporate system that preached lifetime employment but practiced a much more pragmatic approach to hiring and firing:

> Although large firms may have been moving in the direction of the so-called lifetime employment that is so conspicuous in Post World War II Japan, works such as the *Guide* assumed that firing was possible and a likely fate unless one strove above and beyond official duties and properly fitted into corporate life. Similarly, it was not assumed that the *sarariiman* would spend his whole life at one firm even if he was not fired. (Kinmonth 1981, 319)

By the mid-1930s, even though lifetime employment was becoming almost universally recognized as the Japanese executive ideal, a group of Osaka salarymen still cited "being fired" as their single greatest fear (Hoshino 1937, 101).[22]

Thus, although hiring, firing, and job changing were often based on present economic structural realities ("if anything, the prime limitation on changing employees would appear to have been the absolute scarcity of jobs in this period, not any institutional or ideological barriers" [Kinmonth 1981, 319]), the cumulative course of these decisions over the whole society in the course of the prewar period led to an employment system that relied heavily on traditional ideological standards and sanctions. The overall trend, of industrial growth, provided a climate more suited to the organizational man of the modern era than to the entrepreneur of Meiji Japan. Yonekawa concludes that "it was largely due to the companies' long-term expansion that, despite some adjustment in the number of employees in certain years of the 1920s there emerged a tendency toward a *de facto* lifetime employment in the years prior to the second world war" (Yonekawa 1984, 214).

KIKKOMAN: A CASE STUDY

Perhaps the best in-depth examination of one Japanese company during the prewar period is Mark Fruin's comprehensive description of Kikkoman, the soy sauce producer. Kikkoman's employment practices provide a more specific illustration of the broad national trends we have discussed so far. The company was typically devoted to lifetime employment. Whenever possible, new recruits were drawn from the ranks of local boys, whose personal lives were thought to be more consonant with the combination of personal and economic attachment to Kikkoman and who were furthermore caught up in a web of social structures and sanctions well within reach of company influence. It was not unusual during this period for well-educated employees to leave Kikkoman in search of greener pastures (Fruin 1983, 277).

Fruin's cursory examination of "persistency" patterns for managers hired from Kikkoman's incorporation in 1914 up to 1976 shows that the longevity of a white-collar worker's job tended to vary with the economic condition of the company. Fruin divides the company's history into three periods, basing this division on the most dramatic changes in the economic well-being of the firm. During the first period, from 1918 until 1930, Kikkoman (then named Noda Shoyu) enjoyed the rapid growth that was to make it a corporate giant. Fruin's figures on employment persistency as well as the number of experienced managers hired during this time show close adherence to a policy of lifetime hiring. During the second period, from 1932 to 1948, Kikkoman experienced notably less growth than it had until that time. This period of economic decline shows a decrease in the job persistency of the firm's employees and a correspondingly high propensity for the company to hire experienced managers. In the final period Fruin investigates, from 1949 to 1976, Kikkoman reasserted itself as an economic power, regained momentum for growth, and returned to the patterns of high job persistency and hiring of less experienced workers that had characterized the early years of the twentieth century. In short, "employees who entered [Kikkoman] in periods of economic upswing tended to . . . stay with the firm longest" (Fruin 1978, 267–300).[23]

Kikkoman echoed on an organizational scale the tendencies of the Japanese business world as a whole. The explicit assumption was for lifetime employment, but the ability to realize the ideal seemed contingent on economic conditions. The parallel between national trends and Kikkoman's corporate practices was not coincidental. The Japanese government, which was becoming increasingly involved in the economy throughout the first half of the century, took an active role in promoting "permanent employment" structures, standards, and sanctions within this firm as in many others. Especially after 1930,

> as the emerging military government in Japan began to control credit, to limit access to and prices of raw materials, and to interfere in labor markets through civil and military conscription, companies like Noda Shoyu (Kikkoman) were encouraged to move increasingly toward

practices like life-time employment and seniority-based compensation, whenever practical, as a way of minimizing variable costs in an uncertain and unpredictable economic environment. (Fruin 1983, 230–231).

This increasing focus on the economic need for a national loyalty ethic —loyalty defined as an executive's duty to his organization—would once again shift abruptly as the economic push of the prewar period turned into the war itself.

The World War II Period

With the beginning of World War II, Japan moved into the international arena on a scale, and with a suddenness, unprecedented in the nation's history. This sudden "internationalization" would shape much of the country's economic history from its inception onward. But as Japan's role in the worldwide conflict took shape, it was the condition of war itself, rather than Japan's entry into the world arena, that had the most profound immediate influence on the standards, sanctions, and structures of employment.

Until the war, Japan had had relatively little experience with other nations but a great deal with the complexities of combat. Until internationalization during the Meiji Restoration, the hierarchical structure of Japanese society had been capped by an upper class dedicated to the sword and the military conduct it symbolized. The ideological response to the war was a renewed emphasis on a code of military honor. Sanctions on behavior also closely approximated the traditional samurai code. The corporate executive, no less than the military man, was caught up in the passionate nationalism and devotion to the emperor demanded of every Japanese citizen. The focus of loyalty had once again shifted away from fealty toward economic organizations except as that fealty might serve Japan. Business success, and the trappings of such success, were redefined by national circumstance.

> During the war it became a matter of honour to have a simple life-style. To be rich was almost something of a disgrace. Luxury was made a national enemy. . . . Presidents and executive directors of large businesses were for all these reasons keen on stressing their selfless work and dedication for production and for the war. (Hirschmeier and Yui 1981, 246)

For those who had not succeeded in climbing to the top of the corporate ladder, sacrificing personal goals to the good of an embattled Japan provided a paradoxically personal incentive.

Hirschmeier and Yui found that "fervent nationalism took an easier grip on the nation in that it provided vicarious alternative satisfaction to

those who had been disappointed in the struggle for success" (Hirschmeier and Yui 1981, 246). Thus executives, like virtually every other sector of wartime Japan's society, had every reason to promptly and proudly
embrace the twentieth-century version of a traditional militaristic standard. "Permanent employment" was now a military virtue.

During the war, as during earlier periods of economic stability, rates of
executive persistency were relatively high. The demand created by the
war not only led to tremendous expansion in many Japanese industries, it
also united these industries as a team working against a common enemy.
The relative lack of competitiveness between firms and the economic stability meant that neither companies nor employees had much structural
incentive to flout lifetime employment standards. An additional structural support for permanent employment was provided by the wartime
bureaucracy. Under the military Control Boards, the nation's executive
talent was drawn into a limited number of very large firms. To accommodate Japan's best businessmen within a more centralized industrial system, the ranks of middle and lower management in key firms were hugely
expanded. Thus between 1923 and 1941 Tokyo Maritime Insurance
increased its white-collar work force from one hundred to one thousand
employees. Toshiba, then known as Shibaura, expanded its management
from 2,000 to 20,000 between 1939 and 1944 (Hirschmeier and Yui
1981, 252–255). There was little need for executives to feel hemmed in
by their jobs or to seek better opportunities in a different firm. Few structural barriers stood between the salaryman and his fulfillment of a samu-
rai-like devotion to his company and, through his role in the company,
his nation.

The explicit as well as the more subtle sanctions on the executive's
behavior in World War II Japan were also reminiscent of the samurai era.
For the loyal retainer in a wartime Japanese company, as for the vassal of
a Tokugawa *daimyō,* decorum, fidelity, and displays of loyalty were
more likely to be rewarded than brilliance or initiative. Under conditions
of war even more than in peacetime, privileges were most likely to be
gained by unswerving fidelity to social norms and social contacts. The
most noticeable thing about executives who succeeded during the war,
according to Kinmonth, was that "they had cultivated proper contacts
. . . made sure that their relations with superiors were most cordial and
ingratiating . . . and had committed no infraction of the rules and permitted themselves no deviations that could be used against them by competitors" (Kinmonth 1981, 341–343).

Japan's disastrous defeat in 1945, as much as any event in the nation's
history, brought out what to Western eyes is one of the culture's most
enigmatic qualities. Ronald Dore coined the phrase "flexible rigidity" to
describe this quality in Japan's business practices; the same oxymoronic

description could be applied to Japan's artistic, philosophical, technological, and social responses to periods of foreign intrusion. The combination of powerful traditional norms and eclectic acceptance of alien ideas has historically made Japan unusually able to adapt, rather than succumb, to outside influences.

Never was this capacity more severely tested than in the aftermath of World War II. The extremely rigid social structures, standards, and sanctions Japan had maintained during the war were shaken from top to bottom by its defeat. The material devastation that shattered the lives of Japan's lowliest peasant reverberated to the highest and most idealized pinnacle of the national hierarchy as Japan acknowledged its military inferiority and the emperor denied his own divinity. Physically and spiritually, Japan was in ruins. In addition, the Western conquerors brought with them an egalitarian ideology, with its accompanying social and political structures, that was antithetical to Japan's traditional emphasis on hierarchy.

One of the most immediate consequences of this upheaval was the abrupt rearrangement of certain social patterns in existence at the end of the war. For Japan's white-collar work force, this meant the purging of 3,600 key executives from Japan's leading corporations, including 56 members of *zaibatsu* families, and their replacement by less ideologically dangerous upper-middle-level managers (Yoshino 1967, 2). Masaru Ibuka, president of Sony, found a historical parallel for the immediate postwar years in the Warring States period which had preceded the Tokugawa era. In contrast to the corporate system of the pre–World War II years, when *junjo* (the proper order of things) had established clear lines of authority from the emperor through the government to the *zaibatsu* and on down to the humblest of enterprises, Ibuka noted that "the formerly crucial connections with *zaibatsu* banks and imperial university classmates have become less significant than the capacity of individuals to combine the factors of production in a better way;" in addition to its similarity to the disorganization of the Warring States period, the immediate aftermath of World War II paralleled the Meiji era's enthusiastic absorption of Western technologies and the entrepreneurialism that accompanied it. As the venerable *zaibatsu* underwent their forced reorganization, entrepreneurial ventures such as Honda and Sony sprang up in the chaos following Japan's defeat like blades of grass in a plowed field.

The restructuring of social and corporate networks, and the increased leeway for individual initiative it created, fit in well with the egalitarianism of Japan's conquerors. As the United States set out to rebuild Japan in something approximating its own image, the concept of democracy as a social ideal diffused rapidly through the remnants of the imperial order.

Japan's traditional identification of physical and military strength with spiritual strength helped create an immediate—and to Western eyes para-doxical—willingness for the Japanese to study and accept the alien ideals of their conquerors. Nationwide standardization of mass media, such as newspapers, allowed new ideologies to be spread evenly and effectively throughout the country. NHK, Japan's dominant broadcasting firm, became "perhaps the chief educator of propriety and ethics, notably of the families, with its wholesome and morally high standard programs" (Hirschmeier and Yui 1981, 275). All over the country, from almost uni-form sources, the Japanese were exposed to moral standards heavily influenced by the nation's military defeat and the implied ideological superiority of the victors. This infusion of foreign ideas seemed at first to constitute a dramatic philosophical break from Japan's tradition—so much so that Yoshino saw a more radical ideological change between the pre- and postwar periods than between Tokugawa and Meiji (Yoshino 1967, 37).

Both the physical destruction incurred by the war and the egalitarian ideology of the victorious West led to an upsurge in individualistic stan-dards. Dore found that achievement was more emphasized relative to ascription in postwar Japan than it had been earlier in the nation's his-tory (Dore 1967, 7). The characteristic Japanese emphasis on loyalty remained, but its focus had once again changed from devotion to a hierarchical superior and responsibility to inferiors, to the loyalty one Japanese owed another as an equal (Yoshino 1967, 43). Paradoxically, the respect for the United States as a superior nation enhanced the acceptance of egalitarianism in Japan. Bennett noted two dramatic changes in social standards after the war, both of which show the influ-ence of Western norms: first, "social recognition of the legitimacy of indi-vidual as well as group aspirations for financial and status enhancement" and second, "acceptance, even encouragement of social mobility to improve one's economic and social position" (Bennett 1967, 412). The contrast with the nationalistic asceticism in vogue during the war years could hardly have been more pronounced.

Such a sharp switch in the focus of standards, along with the physical aftermath of the war, was naturally accompanied by structural innova-tion. However, the way in which the Japanese actualized standards like equality and democracy showed from the outset the culture's propensity for absorption and adaptation rather than conversion. The overall Japa-nese social structure that emerged during this period, while distinctly dif-ferent from the sharply stratified Japan of the war, has more often been described as "homogeneous" than "equal" in the American sense. Ameri-can democracy, with its focus on equality of rights—including, perhaps especially, the right to nonconformity—was redirected in postwar Japanese culture to emphasize equality of circumstances. One widespread structural change resulting from this version of equality was the burgeoning of middle-class values. In 1950, 72 percent of the Japanese population claimed they belonged to the middle class; by 1967 the figure had reached an overwhelming 88 percent (Yoshino 1967, 40).

This change in the stratification of Japanese society could not have occurred without an underlying economic support. Such support was provided in part by the country's large corporate enterprises, which absorbed more and more of the labor force in the years following the war and created a huge structural niche for salaried, middle-class employees. Eventually the example of these large companies and their workers became an almost universal model for the "typical" Japanese lifestyle. According to Patrick, "as large firms employed a larger part of the labor force, the life style of enterprise workers became dominant, particularly as it became the model for most workers, blue and white collar" (Patrick 1967, 43).

Emergence of Lifetime Employment as a Norm

This model was strikingly different from the entrepreneurialism of the immediate postwar years. As Japanese society recovered from the effects of war and entered a phase of rapid industrial growth, individualism and high mobility became less necessary and less attractive to the Japanese executive. Part of the normative salaryman lifestyle was—as we have seen—assumption of lifetime commitment to a single organization, a situation that had always characterized periods of economic growth in Japan. Fruin writes that "persistency of employment apparently improved" during this period "as general economic conditions picked up and were translocated into better wage benefits" (Fruin 1983, 227).

Crawcour lists four structural factors that encouraged the predominance of lifetime employment in the years following the immediate postwar period: (1) the shrinking of agriculture and small business as the "modern sector" of large enterprises absorbed more and more of the labor force, (2) increasing wages and plentiful opportunities for promotion resulting from the rapid growth of large companies, (3) the continuance of the solidarity between firms that had characterized wartime Japan, and (4) the conservative government of the Liberal Democratic Party (Crawcour 1978, 242–244). Although the ideological standards that had maintained lifetime employment as an ideal during the war were changed by its outcome, the new standards worked well with these postwar structural and economic realities to preserve the system after the war.

During the postwar period, as much as ever, social sanctions acted as a mediator between the intellectual formulation of standards and the observable reality of structure. As philosophical innovations began to influence Japanese attitudes, observers noticed a change in typical patterns of social control. In keeping with a loyalty ethic that had changed its emphasis from hierarchy to equality, the elements of friendship and affection became more important relative to sheer duty as dominant sanctions. Yoshino noted this transition in the Japanese family after World War II.

> The relationships among family members can no longer be characterized as authoritarian domination and absolute submission. These relationships have taken on a cooperative and democratic character. No longer is authoritarian filial piety considered a virtue. Affection has replaced obligation in governing relationships within the family. (Yoshino 1967, 2)

This change in sanctions was not limited to the family. It extended into many aspects of postwar Japanese society, and the expanding corporate sector was no exception. Personal connections became more important than ever for securing a good job and favorable career opportunities. In a period when plentiful jobs minimized the need for careful selection of employees, these personal relationships often replaced other qualifications as the key criterion in hiring decisions. Thus in the mid-1950s a college student who had failed a qualifying exam described how he had obtained a job simply by submitting a letter of recommendation from his professor (Koyama 1956, 10–39).

In this and less drastic situations, personal friendship was more and more characterized in Japanese business relationships following the war. Even when the motivations for executive action might seem to be economic, there was considerable social pressure to conduct business as if it were based on mutual respect and liking. The positive sanctions surrounding the development of friendship networks were complemented by the discouragement of individualistic business ventures. John Cornell, studying the stability of groups in postwar Japan, found that his Japanese interview subjects expressed strong surprise and disapproval when one of their neighbors set out on a "lone wolf" entrepreneurial venture (Cornell 1963, 113–125). Cornell's subjects emphasized that this unconscionable individualism could never have succeeded if the man in question had not been very wealthy in the first place.

Postwar Growth Period

By the mid-1950s Japan was emerging from the period of basic recovery that followed the war. Japanese industry was no longer struggling to pick up the pieces of a shattered economy, but rather to establish itself as a legitimate force in the world market. The object was no longer to rebuild Japan internally, but to catch up to the rest of the industrialized world. The economic, political, and social structures that made Japan's recovery rapid were equally serviceable to the goal of attaining a position of power. These structures, like many of the innovations of the Meiji period, had not merely evolved from Japanese tradition but had been carefully constructed from a combination of native and foreign institutions and practices. Their efficiency and effectiveness having been tested and proven in the reconstruction effort, these structures continued to flourish as Japan continued its economic climb. Structural change in Japanese industry from the mid-1950s to the mid-1970s consisted mainly of rapid growth.

This expansion made it possible for almost every ambitious college graduate to find a job in business and to expect steady promotion, even though the number of applicants rose rapidly as the postwar "baby boomers" matured. Even those who had not attended college could find jobs in this era of labor shortage; demand for junior and senior high school students surpassed supply by three or four times during the early 1960s (Yoshino 1967, 115). However, a university degree was still the surest ticket to a comfortable job with a paternalistic "lifetime employer." The degree was far more than a certification of education and ability. It was documentary evidence of an acquaintanceship network that served as the true basis of the graduate's business success. This made the college one had attended a much more compelling qualification than what one had learned there. Of 1,150 company presidents surveyed in 1967, well over a quarter had attended Tokyo University. Keio University came in a distant second, producing about 8 percent of the presidents. Kyoto and Hitotsubashi universities followed at 7.3 percent and 6.5 percent respectively (*Gendai Shachō* 1966). Occasionally a Japanese could circumnavigate the "top college" route to business by relying on family ties. In one instance, when a youthful preoccupation with sports kept one Hiroshi Anzai from gaining admittance to Tokyo University, Anzai redeemed his career by marrying the daughter of the chief engineer at Tokyo Gas. He became president of the company in 1967 and chairman in 1972 (Cooper 1976, 16). Nevertheless, as a general rule it was understood, as Nakane observed during this time, that "education creates more effective relationships than kinship . . . a common educational background comes next to institution or place of work in degree of function and is more effective than either family or local background" (Nakane 1970, 128). A job applicant's college connections operated both to make him desirable to companies and to make a given company desirable to him, since both the student and his parents usually placed implicit trust in the advice of professors about which firm he should join (Takagi 1985, 40).

Civil service and trading firms were the most popular choices for a new graduate because they were known to be secure, and as one official from the Ministry of International Trade and Industry (MITI) put it, new recruits "believe that they will be safe as long as their employer does not go broke. This amounts to absolute trust in lifetime employment" (Taichi 1981, 23). Graduates were cautious about where they placed this trust, since they fully expected their commitment to the corporation to be equally absolute. Ideologically, lifetime employment was more than ever in the ascendant. Changing jobs, whether viewed from the employee's or the company's perspective, came to be seen more and more as a morally deviant act. "Given the moral implications of joining and leaving company employment," writes Wanous, "quitting and firing [subjected] both management and employees to the suspicion of being defective" (Hanke and Saxberg 1985, 236). Corporate standards of this period reemphasize the intensely emotional, as well as economic, involvement "lifetime employees" experienced within their organizations. Throughout the postwar decades, fully 80 percent of the Japanese continued to believe that employers are responsible for offering "personal advice to the worker if requested." Ninety-five percent felt that employers have the right to involve themselves in employees' marriage decisions (70 percent of Americans object to such involvement) (Takezawa and Whitehall 1981, 119). Between the mid-1950s and mid-1970s, structural constraints such as extremely high growth and the need for technical expertise within firms occasionally led to midcareer job changes for Japanese employees, but this was seen as a last resort (Yoshino 1967, 230–231). Overall, the standard of corporate loyalty grew with the economy.

During this period of expanding industry, the typical Japanese salaryman was not likely to encounter either reduced career opportunities within his company or any better prospects outside it. Since there was little in the employment structure to interfere with the ideology of lifetime loyalty to one's firm, this ideology was imposed with untroubled enthusiasm by social sanctions. Cole noted that "Japanese leaders were adept, on both a conscious and unconscious level, at using traditional symbols to secure the legitimation of the new institutional arrangements associated with permanent employment" (Cole 1978, 262). Sazo Idemitsu, founder of Idemitsu Kosan, put it more bluntly: "In America, able managers are baited with high salaries like fish and change from one company to another. In Japan such a man would be considered a traitor and an immoral and mean fellow" (Idemitsu 1971, 200). Hirschmeier and Yui point out the ways in which economic reliance and emotional commitment combine to form a relationship that subjects the Japanese employee to a very thorough form of social control. "As people identify themselves with some institution which is caring for them," the authors state, "they in turn must be careful not to bring any shame on that school or company or other group to which they belong by unruly behavior" (Hirschmeier and Yui 1981, 369). By the mid-1950s the corporation was becoming more and more firmly institutionalized as the locus of community for the Japanese executive (Hazama 1976, 44–45). Within this community, deviations from the ideal of lifetime employment elicited immediate and powerful negative sanctions. Not surprisingly, the great majority of individuals and organizations conformed to this ideal.

Historical Patterns

From the premodern splendor of the Tokugawa courts to the modern boardroom, loyalty has been the ethic by which Japanese elites claim to determine their employment choices. The constancy of this standard as expressed in popular and official media—*Chūshingura,* the Mitsui House Code, the nineteenth-century philosophies of Ninomiya, World War II propaganda, television documentaries—has led many Westerners to conclude that the Japanese have always been imbued by their culture with a capacity for loyalty that makes lifetime employment practically inevitable. But a closer look at history brings out the enigmatic character of Japanese loyalty. Unlike the complex of attitudes and behaviors Westerners refer to when they use this word, the Japanese virtue of loyalty appears to contain aspects of a rational calculus that makes it contractual and contingent as well as emotionally absolute. It can therefore switch its focus with a suddenness and totality baffling to a Westerner. If the lifetime employment contract is seen as the exchange of the employee's whole life for the return of that life—in terms of economic and emotional well-being—the historical patterns of change in employee loyalty begin to make logical sense.

The outstanding historical regularity in Japanese employment decisions is essentially this: that in periods of rapid economic growth employees have always shown a high rate of job persistency. This persistency has broken down, historically, in the face of two related structural phenomena: the slowing of economic growth (not necessarily a downturn) and the emergence of opportunities outside an employee's original organization. This pattern holds true in the case of a single firm, such as Kikkoman, and on a broader national scale. The periods of high employee turnover that have occurred since Tokugawa—early Meiji and the aftermath of World War II—have also been characterized by a surge in internationalization and exposure to Western technologies and ideologies.

During such periods, the emphasis in public standards has switched from the individual's duty to his or her superior and to his or her duty to the nation. The sanctions that dictate personal behavior seem sensitive to conditions in the individual's life that reflect on a small scale the major historical switches in public ideology. Indefinite devotion to an employer is expected of individuals, but no less strictly than indefinite care is expected from the organization. Economic growth creates a happy cycle in which the company is able to offer the employee secure income and steady rise in status (by promotion) throughout a lifelong career, thus enlisting the unmitigated devotion of the employee to the organization and helping to optimize the organization's chances for continued growth. Slowed growth, while it may have little immediate effect on the employee's status, clouds the horizon with the possibility that the individual might not get a fair return on the "investment" of total loyalty. Under such conditions, it becomes almost imperative for survival to switch loyalty to a superordinate who can offer a fair return for the commitment of a lifetime. The loyal retainers of *Chūshingura,* once robbed of their provider and with no other master to turn to, were doomed men. When cultural change and innovation were combined with new opportunities, however, more alternatives existed. The loss of one lifetime commitment might presage the establishment of a new one. Thus it became possible for individuals to direct their loyalties to their own best advantage; the probability that they would do so increased when the economic future of the organizations they worked for began to dim and the prospect of new types of employment brightened.

These patterns are particularly interesting in light of the current status of Japan's employment system. The nation is at the apex of world economic achievement, a fact attributed by many scholars in part to the institution of lifetime employment itself. Almost all observers are impressed by Japan's permanent employment, and many advocate that it be emulated by other societies. But historical evidence suggests that lifetime employment is more than a cultural standard: it is also an economic arrangement that can be causally influenced by factors in the larger economic sphere. Japan is presently undergoing precisely the kinds of changes that in the past have changed the character of employment decisions for its executive work force. The flexibility with which Japan has accommodated such changes has been as much a part of its historical economic climb as the constancy of the society's normative themes. In light of the structural realities of present history, we might be able to see whether job-changing patterns in Japan do in fact rely on traditional continuities or whether they change as an adaptive response to altered structural realities.

CHAPTER THREE

The Lifetime Employment System in Equilibrium

WESTERN AND Japanese scholars have focused a great deal of attention on the lifetime employment system over the past two or three decades, particularly since 1958. In that year, James Abegglen published a description of employment policies in Japanese factories, which differed significantly from normal practice in the West. Abegglen, like most other writers who were to discuss this topic during the 1960s (see Ballon 1969, 123–166; Bennett and Ishino, 1963; Whitehill and Takezawa 1961), contended that the Japanese form of employment was a cultural throwback to the premodern Tokugawa period. Abegglen predicted that as Japan modernized, its labor market would come to resemble more closely the external labor market present in developed Western countries.

Contrary to these expectations, during the 1970s the Japanese continued (very successfully) to utilize lifetime employment policies. As the decade progressed, many scholars became more and more convinced that the Japanese system may indeed have a place of its own in a modern economy. Ronald Dore suggested that other countries may actually converge to a "later-developer" Japanese model of employment. In the late 1970s and early 1980s, as it became more obvious that Japan was fast developing the most successful economy in the world, Western scholars began to publish books urging Americans to heed the example of Japanese institutions. Works that explained Japan's success (with the implication that Western companies should imitate Japanese management practices) became increasingly popular in the United States, reaching an audience of academics and businesspeople alike.

Our brief history of lifetime employment in chapter 2 showed that the interaction between the environment and the persistency of employment was significant throughout the period of Japan's modernization. But during the 1960s and 1970s, Japan's employment system for the managerial elites reached a state relatively close to equilibrium. By equilibrium, we mean a stasis in which some change does take place, but the alteration is minor by comparison to changes in the system in previous historical periods. A visitor to Japan in the mid-1980s would probably not have taken exception to descriptions of the lifetime employment system written in the 1950s or 1960s.

In this chapter we examine the state of the employment system for the managerial elite between the mid-1950s and the mid-1980s, focusing in particular on the values and world view that arise from the cultural and historical context of lifetime employment. Next we describe the structures of the lifetime employment system and the behaviors of its participants, organizing this discussion around the typical life course of an employee from recruitment into the firm to retirement. For the purposes of this discussion we will rely heavily on such authors as Dore, Vogel, and Rohlen, who described this system for readers in the West. These authors planted in our Western minds an image of an unwavering system of employment in Japan. It seemed a valid image, for during the thirty years following the postwar establishment of lifetime employment for elite employees, this employment system had been a structural reality of Japanese economic life.

Japan's Social Imperative toward Equilibrium

As we mentioned briefly in chapter 2, many of the values and beliefs that have historically surrounded the country's business elite appear to have existed in Japan at least since the Tokugawa period. The primacy of the human group—the idea that the individual is subjected and loyal to the group—is one of the keys to understanding modern Japanese society. There are many ways that this norm can be enacted, but the submission of individuals to group norms in lieu of personal desires has long been extolled as an especially important virtue in Japan. Part of the Japanese people's social solidarity is based on the interdependence of an isolated population occupying an "island nation." As Dore pointed out in his discussion of Japanese political action:

> The Argentinian newspaper editor in danger of arrest or assassination could slip across the river to Montevideo and still find himself a home, amid familiar sounds and faces and familiar books, easily able to find friends and a new job. . . . But to all but a tiny fraction of Japanese only one place has ever been home. (Dore 1964, 238)

Historically, these conditions have influenced not only wide-scale political behavior but also the most minor interactions of Japanese daily life. Any deviation from norms set up by the society or the groups therein could bring about severe consequences. The Japanese traditionally lived in villages, where residents knew each other for whole lifetimes. Only that social group—the village and the family in the context of the village —defined the individual. To be cut off from village and family, therefore, was to be cut off from one's personal identity and connectedness. It is little wonder then that the most extreme institutionalized reaction to "improper" behavior was traditional *mura hachibu*. In this ritualized action, usually initiated by the community leaders, a troublemaker who could not learn to live by group rules was cast out of the village to live a solitary life. In premodern Japan, being forced to cut ties with the village meant that the deviant would never be able to form a human nexus within "proper" society. Village dwellers in other parts of the country knew that anyone who came without an introduction from his or her own village was probably an outcast.

As Japan modernized, the number of possible primary groups—the family, company, neighborhood, religious group—into which an individual might fit increased significantly. A person cast out from one group today could probably find haven with another. For this reason, *mura hachibu*, which in its modified modern form does not involve a literal casting out, is not considered as severe a punishment as in the past. It is still generally true, however, that

> refusal to abide by group norms will cause isolation for the individual—
> a highly undesirable situation. Because the Japanese derives his worth
> through an intimate relationship with a group, beginning with his fam-
> ily and continued in the work group, he has a high need for dependence.
> (Hanke and Saxberg 1985, 236)

In fact, as Vogel has noted, because most groups in Japan are stable and long lasting, members learn to recognize and send subtle signals to signify that they or others are acting in an unacceptable manner. To be overt or heavy-handed in exercising social control would be considered "crude and unnecessary" (Hanke and Saxberg 1985, 236).

Dore defined and discussed six sanctions used to control deviant behavior in modern Japan: (1) actions designed to elicit shame from one person, (2) actions designed to elicit shame from family or we-group, (3) punishments for breaking the law, (4) "the displeasure of particular individuals resulting from failure to perform obligations toward those individuals," (5) "the displeasure of particular individuals for failing in other respects to live up to certain standards of conduct which those individuals had enjoined on him," and (6) guilt that an individual feels for failing to live up to her or his own standards (Dore 1958, 382–383). Interestingly, only one of these six is internally motivated, and only one is a legal action by a broader societal entity. All of the other forms of sanction Dore lists are as subtle as "shame" and "displeasure," and five of the six emanate from the primary group. The Japanese chart their courses in life by the constellation of family members, schoolmates, and co-workers (for men, neighbors for women). These primary groups, into which each person is socialized early in life, become the universe in which the individual will be allowed to function. Those who are obviously trying to rise above the group will receive its disapprobation, or as a Japanese proverb bluntly puts it, "The nail that sticks out will be pounded down." Thus most Japanese do not aspire to change their positions in life radically. Instead they are content to function within the group or in other groups to which they have been introduced by members of their primary group (see Vogel 1963, 261).[1]

In a society with these kinds of social sanctions, it is not surprising that personal interests are ancillary to the interests of the group. Even if the individual were to honestly feel *(honne)* that one set of behaviors would be "best," behaviors *(tatemae),* and therefore apparent attitudes, all must show deference to the group. In Japanese society, the strong pressure to ostensibly give priority to the group can take a number of different forms. For example, from the perspective of Western norms a shopkeeper might reasonably be expected to run his or her business with the objective of making a living. However, in Japan the shopkeeper who desires to maintain a reputation as a decent person must appear uninterested in such crass material objectives. Hirschmeier points out that throughout Japanese modern history, "work and cooperation toward the group are felt as strong ethical imperatives quite independent of pay; to work only for money appears somehow morally base, something to be ashamed of" (Hirschmeier 1970, 35). The only way for a shopkeeper to remain a respected member of the community, then, is to appear to focus more on the relationship with the customer than on the process of "doing business." The Japanese system of morality allows only for duties and responsibilities, not for rights (Vogel 1963, 147).

Vogel notes that the modern corporate employee is tied up in this contradiction between working for money and working to add social value to the society:

> The salary man, however, does not see himself as looking out primarily for his own interests. When he enters the company, he receives a low salary, much less than he deserves by straight economic calculations. Since his salary is regular and determined more by seniority than his good work, he feels he is doing good work not out of his own interest, but out of his devotion to the firm. He receives a bonus not on the basis of his individual contribution to the firm, but on the basis of the success of the firm. By being committed to the firm for life and receiving many benefits

for his long-term service, he, in fact, ordinarily feels loyalty and is genuinely interested in the firm's welfare. Thus the salary man has solid grounds for self-respect in his basic value system. He sees his own long-term interests as fully identified with the company's interests but because of his devoted service to the firm, he cannot be accused of putting his own interests first. (Vogel 1963, 160)

The more an individual internalizes the classic Japanese system of the primacy of the group, follows the norms, and tries to encourage others to follow the norms, the more loyalty that individual is likely to show to the group. As each act of social control invoked by a specific social standard engenders more loyalty toward the group, the cycle of control forms an ever-tightening spiral. In the minds of many Japanese these concepts—standards, control, and loyalty—have been wound together so tightly that the differences have become almost impossible to tease apart.

The centrality of loyalty in Japanese society was still unquestioned in the 1960s, when Vogel wrote that "loyalty of the individual to the group remains the most important attribute of the respected person" (Vogel 1963, 147). During the Tokugawa era this loyalty had principally been exacted in familial relationships, but the corporations soon learned to adopt this rhetoric to create loyalty within their ranks. Rohlen's description of Uedagin Bank carries with it a flavor of Buddhist connectedness that was originally intended only for family members.

> According to the ideology of the bank, the present membership is duty bound to repay their debt to the past by working to advance Uedagin for the benefit of future generations. Conceptually, the present generation stands in an intermediate position between the past and the future Uedagin. This relationship, one that stretches over time and interlocks different generations, is fundamental to the bank's sense of history, institutional continuity, and social morality. (Rohlen 1974, 48)

But it was not only the corporations that managed to convince the worker of this equivalency between family and company. Japanese society as a whole was willing to buy into the idea that it was natural for a man, once he became a man, to gain status and prestige not from his family, neighborhood, or even profession, but from the organization to which he belonged and owed his homage.

In postwar Japan, the sense of belonging that flowed from membership in a large organization seemed to justify and empower the corporation man in his daily endeavors. The size of the organization appeared to be a very important determiner of its employees' status, a fact that may have echoed the prestige afforded to bureaucrats during the Meiji period. At that time government intervention was seen as the only means by which Japan would be able to pull itself up by the proverbial bootstraps to become a modern country. After World War II, however, the role of government was limited, and economic institutions became the means by which Japan expected to rebuild its war torn infrastructure and damaged pride. As Yoshino noted, "In postwar Japan, a managerial career in a large corporation . . . carried as much or greater prestige than governmental service or professional activities, and it attract[ed] the most capable graduates from Japan's leading universities" (Yoshino 1967, 91).

Following World War II, everyone in Japanese society seemed bent on obtaining a job as a salaryman. Vogel, in his book *Japan's New Middle Class,* maintains that the education system was "dominated by the spirit of the salary man" (Vogel 1963, 267). Young women aspired to marry salarymen, and fathers and mothers rejoiced when their sons decided to join a company and become one of this honored breed. The executive's stable if monotonous career owed much of its allure to the risk aversion of a society stunned by military defeat. As Vogel put it,

> In the context of the pessimism of the smaller traditional enterprises, the salary man represents for most Japanese the "bright new life." The salary man's career is not a rapid and glorious rise to such great heights that it appears beyond their reach, but a secure path to moderate success. (Vogel 1963, 9)

The similarity between traditional forms of security and the security associated with the employment system that came into being after the war contributed even more luster to the salaryman's job in the modern era. Writing in the 1960s, Vogel saw clear connections between the cultural history of Japan and the appeal of lifetime employment.

> Although the search for security has rational components, as mentioned before, it has been heightened by the many upheavals in the lifetime of the average adult and by the difficulty which the contemporary urban parent had in finding a long-term livelihood when he was young. For the urban resident, a job in a large corporation is as close as one can come to the security that country relatives have by belonging to a household firmly attached to land and the local community. Just as obtaining land is thought to secure the future of a family even in the next generation, so does a job in a large corporation provide long-range security and insure that one's children can be given a proper position in life. (Vogel 1963, 42)

In light of these conditions, it is understandable that the life of a salaryman had such a tremendous appeal in early postwar Japan—to the extent that to obtain it, individuals were willing to forgo the pleasures of family life, the freedom of individual volition, and even the "need to make personal moral choices" (Yoshino 1967, 227). The security, prestige, and confidence accrued by the salaryman through service and loyalty to the organization has held the lifetime employment system in place during the four decades since World War II.

Part of the reason that salarymen in present-day Japan are willing to forgo many personal freedoms to devote their time and efforts to the company is that the firm occupies an overwhelmingly important position in such an employee's life once he is hired. Dore has described the process of joining a company as "the handing over by a group (school, family) to another group (the firm) of one of its members—much as a traditional marriage involves the transfer of a girl from one family to another" (Dore 1973, 72). In the United States it is possible for an individual to belong to a number of different groups. In Japan, in contrast, "one can belong to only one *habatsu* [a clique or group]—the *habatsu* demands of its members permanent and total commitment" (Yoshino 1967, 209). This is why many Japanese, in contrast to most Westerners, feel that devotion to the company is a more important virtue than "devotion to the immediate family" (OECD 1977, 28). In a survey of youth conducted by the Prime Minister's Office in 1972, 28 percent of Japan's young people (under twenty years old) listed "work" as the fundamental goal of their lives—compared with 13.3 percent, 8.9 percent, and 8.8 percent of the respondents in England, the United States, and France respectively (Sengoku 1985, 120).

The effect of Japan's relatively recent shift in loyalties from kin to company is that throughout their careers, Japanese employees devote less and less attention to family life, at least when they are embedded in the context of work. In other words, family and company work in very different spheres of control. The relationship between the two aspects of life is reciprocal but not overlapping: the company takes care of one's family through salary and other benefits, but the family is, in turn, obligated not to place any demands on the company. Vogel writes that

> the effective isolation of the family from contact with the husband's place of work insures that work considerations are separated from family considerations. Similarly the separation of the husband from participation in the wife's neighborhood activities insures that he will not interfere with her group. Each group has virtually complete autonomy, and the opportunity for family loyalties to conflict with other group loyalties is minimized. (Vogel 1963, 140–141)

The surprising lack of conflict of interest between family and company can be seen in a national character survey conducted by a Tokyo institute in the early 1970s. The respondents were asked to imagine that they were the president of a company in which only one post was to be filled. The runner-up on an entrance examination is a relative, and the section chief indicated he would be happy to take either of the candidates. The question posed in the survey was: "Would you be willing to exert pressure to see that the relative is employed?" Only 18 percent of the respondents answered that they would (cited in Dore 1973, 212).[2]

The company—or, more accurately, the individuals in the work world —might eventually take over roles in a Japanese employee's life that would be reserved only for the family in the West. As we noted in chapter 2, 70 percent of Americans think that a company superior should not be involved in any way in an employee's marriage decision. Only 5 percent of the Japanese see no role for a boss in that decision. Eighty percent of Japanese think that superiors should be willing to offer all kinds of "personal advice to the worker if requested" (Takezawa and Whitehall 1981, 119). These responses were constant over two separate surveys conducted in 1960 and 1976.

This is not to say that the influence of the Japanese company on family life is a one-way street. The family can play a very important role in creating and maintaining a member's corporate loyalties. Most obvious is the example of a natal family pressuring a son to join one company or another and to succeed in the job he chooses. For instance, Noboru Inui, the president of Sumitomo Metals in the 1970s, decided to join Sumitomo because he was the only son and his family wanted him to settle down near his home town in Kobe. He had attended Tokyo University and had always planned to join the civil service, but that would probably have meant living in Tokyo. Since Sumitomo's headquarters are in the Kansai region near his home, he decided to join that company (Cooper 1976, 68–69).

Of course, while stories like Inui's may be interesting illustrations of employment practices in modern Japan, every individual salaryman's experience is different. Nevertheless, the intense pressure on many members of the Japanese business elite to act in a consistent, normative manner makes generalities about the "typical" career course of a Japanese salaryman more than usually justifiable. Most participants in the country's lifetime employment system experience a series of career events that, from a Western perspective, are astonishingly predictable. A description of the "typical" elite salaryman's career path, then, is helpful in understanding the system of lifetime employment from a cultural and even social-psychological point of view.

The Structure of Lifetime Employment: Recruitment to Retirement

THE RECRUITING PROCEDURE

The first and most important step in the process that will eventually replace the salaryman's family ties with company ties is the recruiting process. Especially among the corporate elite in Japan, the senior year of college and the one following are pivotal years in determining a young man's life course. It is during this time that college students who have had no real vocational training try to match their interests and personalities with opportunities available in various organizations. And it is also during this time that organizations spend huge amounts of time and money ferreting out the new employees who will be most successful over a lifetime. As Yoshino put it in the late 1960s, "Only at the time of college graduation can one choose his lifelong career without undue disadvantage. At the time of entry into the firm, both firm and employee make a permanent and irrevocable commitment to one another" (Yoshino 1967, 229).

The first steps in making this "permanent and irrevocable commitment"—the recruiting and socialization processes—are motivated by the company's interest in appraising and developing new employees. On one hand, in a system of lifetime employment, both the organization and the individual need to feel that the new recruit has the necessary skills and abilities to remain with the company for a lifetime. A large contributor to the social prestige of the salaryman's life in modern Japan is the sense of confidence this rigorous selection process instills in successful candidates. Anyone who has been admitted to one of the large corporations in Japan knows that he has passed tests of intellect and social savoir faire that many of his peers have failed. "Everyone in the organization is considered to have at least a minimum of ability so that he is not threatened with the possibility of discharge" (Vogel 1963, 161).

On the other hand, part of the sense of pride new recruits feel is based on the hyperbolic descriptions they receive from the recruiters and the company employees about their very special skills and place in the Japanese corporate hierarchy. There is not any part of the rites of entry into a Japanese firm that does not have elements of both the practical evaluative process and the almost ceremonial "efforts to socialize members to the ways of the group and the organization" (Hanke and Saxberg 1985, 239).

Dore described four steps in the recruitment process at Hitachi. According to his account, these are conducted in the following order: "1. universities' appointment bureaux are contacted and invited to recommend up to a given quota of suitable students to take Hitachi's tests; 2. test—includes special subject, personality test, translation from English; 3. screen by interview; and 4. personal check" (Dore 1973, p. 49). Dore's concise labels deserve some elaboration and comment here.

The first step Dore describes in the recruitment process—contacting university appointment bureaus—is typical of a culture in which human relationships and friendship networks dictate the direction an individual might take in many aspects of life. As we mentioned above, one of the most devastating implications of the traditional penalty of *mura hachibu* was that the outcast, lacking an introduction from his or her old village, would probably never be permitted to join a new one. This emphasis on obtaining introductions to new groups through contacts and recommendations carried over into job placement in traditional Japan. If an employer knew that an individual's family background was good, and especially if he had a personal involvement with that family, the employer had access to more forms of social control to use in bringing the new employee into line with the rest of the company.

In modern Japan, by contrast, very few hires seem to be based on connections. In Rohlen's Uedagin Bank, "of the 120 incoming men, only three or four of the high school graduates (less than 10 percent) and eight or nine of the university graduates (about 20 percent) were observed to have connections" (Rohlen 1974, 68).

A small bank like Uedagin would be just the kind of organization in which one might expect to find a high percentage of personal contacts. In larger banks or manufacturing firms, the number of employees who have personal ties with potential hires and the large number of new employees each year make a recruiting evaluation based on personal connections impossible (Vogel 1963, 41).

Personal connections have been formalized in the recruiting process, however, through school ties. The recommendation of a teacher is widely recognized as the primary basis for a candidate's selection (Rohlen 1974, 68). Because of their desire to have an inside track on recruiting, many companies maintain very close relationships with professors. In some ways, especially in the sciences, a college professor who has trained a student in his senior seminar acts much like a matchmaker in a marriage. The student looks to the professor for advice about what he should expect in a good company. The company consults with the professor to find his most talented students. And the parents are reassured by the professor that the fit between student and company is right (Takagi 1985, 40). If both the student and the company agree with the professor's assessment, a match is made.

Alumni are also an important link between the new recruit and a company. Seniors are prohibited from engaging in formal interviews in companies until the middle of August each year. But most companies have found a way to circumvent that regulation, and many top students have job offers in hand before the formal recruiting period begins. One of the most common routes used to sidestep the formal interview rule is informal recruitment by alumni. Recent graduates return to their alma maters in droves during the summer months to wine and dine groups of college seniors, who for their part are eager to find out more about the companies in which these alumni work. What would not be obvious to the casual observer is that these *senpai* ("seniors" or "elders"—used in contradistinction to *kōhai*—"juniors" or "youngers") are usually on a two- or three-month assignment in their companies' personnel departments. In this capacity they have formal evaluative responsibilities. Hosting and having avuncular chats with the potential hires is often the recent employee's only job during these months.

Clearly, educational ties are in many ways more important in the recruitment process than are family ties. Vogel has noted that "being admitted to a given university becomes, in effect, a basis of ascription which provides fairly clear limits to one's later mobility" (Vogel 1963, 43). Some companies are more likely to recruit at a particular university than others. Thus, the likelihood of entering a particular company is greatly affected by the university one attends. The hierarchy of status among universities is very carefully delimited in Japan, however, and universities that sit at the top of this hierarchy can place their graduates in just about any company in the country.

Be that as it may, a graduate of Keio University with aspirations to climb the corporate ladder would probably be wary of a company in which all of the top officials hailed from Tokyo University. The *gaku-batsu* (school cliques) in companies are usually a topic of great concern among college seniors. There is reason for concern about common college background on the part of the the individual and the organization. As Chie Nakane has recounted, "Education creates more effective relationships than kinship . . . common educational background comes next to institution or place of work in degree of function and is more effective than either family or local background" (Nakane 1970, 128). Most people in Japanese society readily admit that the education acquired in Japanese colleges is not the main reason for attending school. It is the human nexus that is formed in school that matters. Even Kikuichi Iwao, president of Daiwa Securities, who himself did not attend college, admits to "some regret" when it comes to the issue of human relations and college experience. "By going through the educational process," he said, "you might acquire many different friends who might be helpful in many ways in business or in private life" (Cooper 1976, 130).

A job candidate who has made it past the initial screen of alumni review—the first step noted by Dore in the recruitment process—will be invited by the company to take the second step. This consists of an entrance examination. The average Japanese college graduate in the mid-1970s took three company exams (van Helvoort 1979, 62). Usually the graduating senior has already decided to take a job with a certain firm before taking its test, but the threat of failing the written examination causes the candidate to keep his or her options open until after the examination is completed.

The entrance examination is in almost all cases a perfunctory step in the recruiting process, one that serves little purpose except to reassure the company that their new employees can all perform at a basic level in math and written expression. Especially in the managerial class,

> the usual selection procedures are not so much geared towards judging a specific kind of aptitude, skill or proficiency but rather towards finding out personality traits, the ability to associate and get along with others, learning potential and conformism. (van Helvoort 1979, 61)

The third step in the recruitment of new salarymen, the interviews, are normally conducted with company officers at various levels. Many large companies boast that recruits must pass interviews with director-level executives in order to join the firm. Some even involve the president of the firm in all final hiring decisions. Here, as with the exam, if lower-level employees support hiring a particular student, it is unlikely that that decision will be vetoed by higher-ups. The formal interview is more an opportunity for a new recruit to feel that he has been approved by the top brass than for the top brass to seriously involve themselves in hiring decisions.

The fourth and final step in the recruiting process is one quite foreign to the American system. In fact, it is prohibited by American legal restrictions concerning rights to privacy and equal opportunity.[3] This is the dreaded "personal check." In some companies the background check necessarily involves a personnel officer's visit to the new recruit's parents. Rohlen noted that during this interview the officer would observe the following matters:

1. Health of family members
2. Cleanliness and order of the house
3. Nature of family relationships
4. Expectation that the son will (or will not) eventually succeed to his father's position
5. Parents' character
6. Parents' attitude toward employment in the company
7. Father's social reputation
8. Religious affiliation (a bias against those who adhere to "new religions")
9. Applicant's and his parents' political views
10. Parents' religious behavior
11. Candidate's dating habits (Rohlen 1974, 71–73)

Rohlen observed that all of the above issues relate to three basic criteria: "character, involvement in other institutions, and family reputation" (Rohlen 1974, 71–73). A candidate with any black marks in these areas —even one who has been acceptable through the interview stage—might be deemed unsuitable for the job.

In some cases the personnel department relinquishes its responsibility for conducting background checks to a private investigator. A single investigation for a new employee can cost between ¥60,000 and ¥150,000 (Nevins 1984, 47). While this is much more expensive than a personnel officer's visit to a family's home and neighborhood, the private investigator can often uncover information that a family could have concealed from a company official. Vogel reports that the salarymen in the neighborhood he studied in 1963 were convinced that "if two young men of roughly equal qualifications [were] seeking employment, one whose home include[d] a father and one whose home [did] not, the job would go to the boy with a father" (Vogel 1963, 17). The company would be likely to assume that the boy without a father would be "more apt to be dishonest, for his greater need for money might tempt him to embezzle or in some way cheat the company for personal and family needs" (Vogel 1963, 18). This threat of a lost job opportunity may be reason enough for some families to try to deceive the personnel officers.

During the course of our research, we saw the pressure exerted on one college student by the fear of the personal check. Yuichi was graduating at the top of his class in the law faculty at Waseda University. He spoke flawless English and had been a contender to be on the Olympic basketball team in 1984. All those around him knew that he would have his pick of any nonscience job in any company in the country. Nevertheless, the topic of *shūshoku,* or finding a job, hung like a low-lying fog around his head. Whenever the topic came up, he quickly dismissed it, saying he had plenty of time to think about that.

Yuichi had told all his friends that he wanted a career in the private sector. A large bank or high-tech manufacturing firm were his first choices. But his parents were pressuring him to join the civil service. No one understood his parents' attitude until the day he announced that he had given up his dreams for a corporate job. He was not even planning to talk to any of the corporate recruiters. The fatal flaw in Yuichi's record was at last made public, and Yuichi's associates finally understood his family's hesitancy to put their only son through a futile job search.

The "dirty" truth was that Yuichi's mother had high blood pressure. She had been known to have fainting spells because of it. Worse yet, Yuichi had been warned by his doctor that he might at some point develop similar health problems. He knew that alcohol and lack of sleep aggravated the condition for his mother, and so he was careful to avoid these if possible. No matter what precautions he took, however, Yuichi knew that if a background check were done into family, the corporate recruiters would find out about the "family secret." He, his parents, and friends with whom he had discussed this problem were convinced that none of the top corporations would be willing to chance a lifetime employment commitment on a flawed specimen. Yuichi spoke bitterly about his decision:

> They have all the best students at all the best universities to choose from. There are a lot of students as good as me. Why should they choose someone who will not be able to drink a lot at *tsukiai* [get-togethers, almost always involving alcohol consumption, in which interpersonal bonds are created and re-created], who is careful about his sleep schedule, or who might have a fainting spell on the job? They have no reason.[4]

Japanese companies expend much time and effort on the four steps of recruiting, trying to attract just the right kind of employee to the firm. One estimate put the number of work-hours a large trading company puts into recruiting just one new employee at more than two hundred hours.[5] Nor is the search inexpensive: the entire recruiting process is not handled by the lowest-paid employees in the firm. High-level executives in the company are involved at various points, identifying and wooing elite college graduates.

SOCIALIZATION INTO THE COMPANY

After recruitment, the next stage in the career of the salaryman is a kind of initiatory phase that might be best described as the "socialization" period. Once the student has determined which company to join, has graduated from school and spent a month of vacation (probably the last month-long vacation until retirement), he or she is inducted into the company. The formal ceremonies and training programs surrounding this event are tremendous by Western standards. The first month or two of most initiation programs involves speech after speech by corporate dignitaries, who impart to the new graduates general information about the company's history, its line of businesses, and the proper attire and attitude of a salaryman in that company. According to the official description of the induction course at Hitachi, the purpose of the course is

> to enable new graduates to grasp the history of the company and of its separate establishments; further it seeks to develop within them the spirit and attitudes appropriate to Hitachi men, and, while imparting certain basic knowledge and skills relevant to their professional status as technologists and managers, to promote the development of character and of their general education. (Dore 1973, 50)

At the end of the two-month induction course, new employees receive their first job assignments. These assignments could take them to any part of the world, doing almost any kind of work. The only distinction drawn in most companies is between students with liberal arts degrees and those with science degrees. Anyone with a science degree is as likely as anyone else on that track to have a first job as, for example, a quality control engineer in a small plant in Shikoku. Or the science graduate may stay at headquarters and assist in the research and development of a new product. Those with liberal arts degrees may begin in sales, personnel, finance, or accounting, no matter what their specific degrees within that arts education happened to be.

New recruits have traditionally had little or no input into the decision-making process that assigns hundreds of new employees to rather small and unimportant jobs around the company. A sense of discouragement often accompanies hearing one's first assignment. After a senior year filled with companies clamoring to welcome the potential employee into their folds, a graduation from a top university in Japan which accredits the recruit as one of the nation's elite, an induction ceremony in which the recruit is told over and over again that he or she personally represents Japan and one of the greatest companies in Japan, it is an understandable let-down to be assigned to a first job in Aizu-Wakamatsu riding a bicycle from one mom-and-pop store to another collecting loan repayments. The thought that this assignment could last four or five years is a difficult one for any new employee fresh out of college to entertain.

Dore describes the initial assignments of all college graduates at Hitachi as "humble," with nontechnical managers spending their first years with the firm in accounting departments and employees with technical degrees working as draftsmen. According to Dore's account of the Hitachi factories, however, there appears to be some wisdom in providing such humble beginnings for the managerial employee.

> The senior managers who designed this policy doubtless had in mind the thought that they had come up the hard way and it did them good. It does ensure, however, that later in their careers managers have a reasonably intimate knowledge of the actual work of those whom they supervise. (Dore 1973, 53)

All of the induction exercises, even the plebeian first assignment, have the purpose of socializing and creating loyalty within the new employee. But the socialization and obligation-building process does not end after the initial six-month probationary period (van Helvoort 1979, 66).[6] Even after the *seiyakusho* (formal contract of employment) is signed, and the employee is considered a *seishain* (regular employee), the ties that socialize and bind the employee to the firm are only beginning to be established.

A number of temporal benefits offered employees of any large enterprise in Japan help bind them to the organization. These include company housing for the unmarried single or young married couple. After his family has reached a size and age that makes it appropriate for the employee to buy or build a home, the company offers low-interest loans for the purpose. "For example, in 1974 a large manufacturing firm was reported to grant loans of between 3 and 6.5 million yen [to] employees at least thirty years old or of at least ten years of seniority; interest rates were very favorable and repayment had to be completed within 15 years" (van Helvoort 1979, 101). In addition to housing loans for the family, the company may offer educational loans for employees' children; Hitachi even maintained a dormitory in Tokyo for children of employees attending university or *yobikō* (cram schools to prepare for university entrance exams) (Dore 1973, 209).

In addition to benefits designed especially for the family, there are many perquisites that profit the individual employee. Memberships to sports clubs and golf courses, use of a company resort near a mountain hot spring, and a lavish expense account for more senior management staff are all structural incentives that tie an employee to the firm. It is interesting to note that these benefits for the individual all operate in the context of a company group. Japanese corporation elite go to sports clubs and company resorts together with their co-workers. Part of a top manager's expense account is used to wine and dine customers, but the rest is to be used on his *buka* or subordinates. Thus even the new recruit benefits from the expense account of his *senpai* in the firm.

The importance of doing things together with co-workers is evident in the value system and the activities of employees in a firm. In the first years of employment with a firm, the company sponsors a number of retreats to various resorts for the new recruits and their bosses (van Helvoort 1979, 65). It is especially at these times, and in the after-work *tsukiai*, that the values of loyalty and devotion are instilled in new recruits (Vogel 1963, 103–104).[7]

To facilitate the development of strong interpersonal relationships between the new employee and other company personnel in the early years of employment, a new recruit will often be assigned a *senpai* who has been in the work force only two or three years himself. This *senpai* is normally from the same university, if not the same department, as his *kōhai*.

It is assumed that those who attended a certain university (and sometimes even a certain department within a university) will feel mutual loyalty and share similar attitudes, making it possible for them to work together harmoniously despite differences of opinion and temperament. (Vogel 1963, 44)

It is the company's hope that the ties of loyalty already established between the new graduate and his or her university will be transferred to same-school employees in the company and finally to the company itself.

The ultimate goal of this socialization process seems to be to train new employees out of their previous affiliation to other institutions and even overall ideologies, replacing them with a feeling of belonging to the company (Vogel 1963, 153). This goal can best be achieved by demonstrating to employees that the company cares about them and about their previous primary groups. Once employees identify themselves with the company "which is caring for them," they know that "they in turn must be careful not to bring any shame [on the company] by unruly behavior" (Hirschmeier and Yui 1981, 369). When the firm has become the standard by which individuals direct their behavior, even when associating with other groups, the company is placed as the primary group in the employees' lives. The company's requirements therefore supersede demands on the salaryman's time made by all other reference groups. The most obvious of these "company" requirements is simply hard work.

The success of Japanese companies in gaining the loyalty of employees and in instilling an ethic of diligence among them can be seen in the "miracle" of Japan's postwar economy. Even more direct evidence can be found in the behaviors and attitudes that people display in relationship to their work. For example, companies are required by law to allow each employee a specified number of vacation days a year, yet very few Japanese use their whole vacation period because anyone who took the whole vacation time would be considered "selfish and disloyal by his co-workers and by his superiors" (Vogel 1963, 35).

The sanctions that enforce a standard of hard work in Japanese companies are not all negative. Somehow the socialization process through which Japanese youth are put in a company produces more highly motivated employees than can typically be found in the United States. In the survey of youth in 1972, American and Japanese high school students, college students, and young workers were asked whether they would prefer to be idle or working. In the United States the percentage choosing to be idle increased from 8.4 percent in high school to 21.1 percent in young workers. In Japan the responses were reversed. In high school (a very stress-filled part of any Japanese youth's life) 27.3 percent of the respondents said they would choose idleness over work. That percentage dropped to 19.4 percent among young workers. (79.9 percent of Japanese young workers said they would choose work compared to 75.5 percent of the Americans in the sample.) In other words, the Japanese corporation is doing a better job of motivating its workers than American firms. It is not just that Japanese are naturally more motivated to work; it is something that happens to them during the period of being socialized into a company (Sengoku 1985, 123).[8]

SALARY

In the United States, the role company socialization might play in motivating employees to work is small compared to the overwhelming role of the dollar in that process. In Japan, however, money does not appear to be such a major factor in deciding how hard to or even where to work. The Japanese executive's life is extremely predictable where salary is concerned. Within any particular company, it is easy to forecast how much a person will be making in ten or twenty years (Vogel 1963, 168). Even in the labor market as a whole, merely knowing an employee's age and educational background and the industry in which he or she works constitutes reasonably adequate grounds for predicting the employee's salary. The accepted understanding in postwar Japan was that the corporate elite were not motivated by the money they would receive for their work. Yoshino reports that executives earned only between $20,000 and $50,000 in 1968 exchange rates (Yoshino 1967, 92). Even top executives usually lived in small homes an hour or two removed from their offices. If it were financial compensation that motivated these salarymen, they would have started their own companies or joined the ranks of the "independent professional."

These findings are not surprising, for salary has not historically been the primary motivation for the Japanese executive. Rather, the corporate employee was interested in the security and the prestige of working for a big firm. The security came not from large pay raises or high absolute income but from confidence that the modest salary would provide for the family's needs. Yoshino reports that children's educations, buying a home, and saving for retirement were the three major expenses for which a salaryman had to prepare (Yoshino 1967, 74–78). Everyday expenses were met by everyday salary; these big-ticket expenses were covered by biannual bonuses. Sometimes these bonuses, paid at year's end and in the summer, could total as much as six months of the regular salary of the corporate employee. The family would learn to live day-to-day on the regular salary, and the big bonuses could then be safely stashed away in savings accounts. It is not hard to understand why Japan's personal savings rate has been the highest in the world throughout the postwar period.

PROMOTION

Yozo Ishizuka, president of Pioneer Electronic Corporation during the high growth 1960s and 1970s, summed up the normative view of financial success during that period when he said: "Naturally, financial reward is very important. But for me achievement, or accomplishment, is more important" (Cooper 1976, 77). And what better way to gauge achievement or accomplishment for a salaryman than advancement or promotion within the firm? Financial success itself was inextricably tied to one's position in the company, but this was only one factor that made promotion a major motivator and source of social prestige in Japanese economic bureaucracy.

The difficulty with gauging one's success on the rise through the ranks of a Japanese corporation is that range of variation tends to be very narrow. Promotions have historically been based almost completely on the employee's date of entry into a firm. Most members of each entering class are promoted to each level within a few years of each other. The competition comes in receiving one of the early promotions. Those who receive the early promotions at any stage are most likely to advance to the next highest level. An elite-track employee who falls behind even one year is unlikely to ever again be numbered among the early promotions. Because of this, the salaryman "will be bitterly disappointed if he receives even a small promotion only a year later than he had originally expected" (Vogel 1963, 33).

The typical promotion structure for large enterprises in Japan is one of the reasons that so much prestige has been attached to landing a job in these firms. Almost all employees with college degrees obtained promotions to the first and second levels in their firms (*kakarichō* and *kachō*). Dore's data on Hitachi in the late 1960s support this view. He found that the youngest age by which someone in the Hitachi company was promoted to *kachō* was thirty-two; 80 percent of college graduates were *kachō* by age thirty-six; and almost all were given that rank by age forty (Dore 1973, 68). Not all college graduates fared as well as those in the top companies. A Japan Productivity Center poll in *President* magazine in 1977 showed that only about 10 percent of college graduates nationwide ever reach the level of *kachō*. Less than 3 percent of these college graduates ever become *buchō*.[9] The differences in advancement opportunities in large Japanese firms, as opposed to their smaller counterparts, is a major contributor to the tremendous pressure on Japanese youth to enter the right high schools and colleges as a road to employment with big enterprises.

The motivational powers of promotion in Japanese firms are even more clear in light of the vertical nature of Japanese society. Chie Nakane, a University of Tokyo professor, found that one of the greatest differences between her country and others she visited was that in Japan, vertical relationships—between older and younger people or those higher and lower in an organizational hierarchy—formed the basis of society

(Nakane 1970). As Rohlen noted, in Japanese society, where an individual's vertical relationship to associates is of great importance, the "titles of rank appended to last names is the dominant mode of reference" (Rohlen 1974, 27). This use of titles both in and out of the workplace is one of the most obvious forms of status identification in modern Japan. The pervasive use of business cards in all professions reflects the obsession that Japanese have with status. The most important pieces of information on a Japanese business card are not the address and phone number, but the company name and the individual's title of rank.[10] Every businessperson is familiar with the various nuances of rank titles. For example, to be the president *(shachō)* of a small company carries with it some prestige, but not as much as being a general manager *(buchō)* of a large multinational firm. In Japanese companies, where workers and executives alike wear the same uniform, eat in the same cafeteria, and park in the same parking lot, the rank title is one of the only signals of status (Rohlen 1974, 27). In a society that has a preoccupation with status, this fact makes promotion a prime incentive for hard work and corporate loyalty.

Promotion decisions are centralized in personnel departments. Dore describes the "extensive dossiers and records of earlier merit ratings of each of the possible candidates for a foremanship" maintained by Hitachi's personnel department. These records are vital to an employee's climb up the corporate ladder. Promotion decisions are not based only on the "recommendations of the immediate shop superintendents and department managers" but can be "checked and possibly questioned at a higher management level before appointments are made" (Dore 1973, 67). Although Dore was discussing the promotion decision for a foreman's position, the system of record keeping he described does not differ greatly from that at Dentsu (Japan's, and now in joint venture with Young & Rubicam, the world's largest advertising firm). The personnel department maintains large computer files on each college graduate employed by the firm. In these files are contained the individual's employment history and performance records since the date of induction into the firm. Of particular interest in making promotion decisions, according to one informant, are the black marks on an employee's record.

> There are not many positive remarks by former supervisors that will change one's rise through the ranks. It is the negative remarks that are carefully weighed by the personnel manager and employee's current supervisor, and that can slow one's advancement.[11]

In addition to the files (computerized or not) that are kept on all employees, the personnel department uses the informal networks within organizations to make decisions on promotions. In fact, van Helvoort asserts that with the "powerful informal organizational structure in Japanese firms . . . personnel officials would rather rely on the signals obtained via this network than through any kind of more 'objective' method for formulating promotion decisions about employees" (van Helvoort 1979, 82).

Even though black marks and informal networks seem to figure so prominently in promotion decisions in Japanese firms, the mere fact that the decision-making power is centralized in the personnel department apparently makes the system appear more fair to employees than the promotion systems used by some other countries. Dore compared the attitudes of workers in Japanese firms with those in British firms and found that the average Japanese worker thought that he or she had a better chance at promotion and was less likely to be discriminated against by an unjust system than his or her British counterpart (Dore 1973, 67).[12]

The promotion decision itself is based on both structural and attitudinal factors. Hirschmeier and Yui, in their review of business history in Japan, found that four qualifications were most important to promotion. These were seniority, learning and achievement, cooperation, and dedication (Hirschmeier and Yui 1981, 351). Noda's findings were in agreement with the basic findings of Hirschmeier and Yui. He, however, included chance, personality, school background, and personal connections on the list (Noda 1960, 55). Many of these factors are quite similar to the criteria for promotion in the West. The two most dramatic departures from a Western model can be seen in the importance of cooperation and personality.

One general manager in a semiconductor factory in Osaka described his objective in developing the executive human resources in his plant as "creating *kintarōame.*" *Kintarōame* is a long roll of hard candy, popular with children in Japan. Running from one end of the cylinder to the other is the face of a fairy-tale hero, Kintaro. Wherever one cuts the roll of candy, the same smiling Kintaro face appears. The Osaka manager saw the creation of a group of identical, smiling Kintaro faces to be the goal of management development in his company.[13]

With this kind of attitude pervading Japan's business traditions, it is understandable that personality and cooperation are major criteria for evolutionary selection in the Japanese firm. In a study of middle managers in twelve nations, Rosenstein found that cooperation leads to faster rates of advancement in Japan and Scandinavia, has no effect on promotion in the United Kingdom and the Netherlands, and actually slows rates of advancement in all of the other countries studied (Rosenstein 1985, 1–21). Moreover, the Japanese salaryman must do more than perform cooperative actions. His entire personality must seem to fit into the organization if he is to be positively evaluated in promotion decisions. Nakane believes that in job evaluations the Japanese tend to "pay more attention to and find greater interest in personality than capability" (Nakane 1970, 123).

The most difficult part about the promotion process from the perspective of the employee is that the promotion criteria are fuzzy descriptions like cooperation, dedication, personality, and achievement. Because there is no job description in the typical Japanese job, employees end up devoting their whole lives to the company, rather than simply sharpening their work skills, in order to prove their worthiness for a promotion. As van Helvoort describes it, "each individual's maximum capacity provides the standard against which he will be evaluated" (van Helvoort 1979, 80).

RETIREMENT

The criteria for advancement are not the only parts of the employment structure that motivate Japanese to work hard throughout their lives. The retirement system in Japanese companies is set up in such a way that most managerial employees face early retirement, at age fifty-five or sixty. For most of the postwar era the life expectancy for Japanese men has been more than seventy years, and the ten or fifteen years between retirement and death have not been easy ones. Vogel has described this as the period in which the salaryman would experience the "greatest financial difficulty."

> His company will provide some retirement benefits, either in the form of a lump sum or pension, but generally these are small, barely enough for minimum subsistence. [After retirement,] to supplement his company's retirement benefits, [the salaryman] must turn to his savings, supplementary income, or his children, although sometimes his company will help him find a part-time job after retirement. (Vogel 1963, 34)

Usually the part-time jobs that are found for employees after retirement are not on the same pay scale as the jobs they had prior to age fifty-five. Pay rates drop, in many cases, to levels earned by teenagers in fast-food restaurants. Rohlen has described this change to a new job as a "bitter experience" for most of the white-collar workers in the bank he studied. "The new job almost invariably represents a step down in life" (Rohlen 1974, 77). Bigger companies, especially banks, are able to lean on subsidiaries and transfer some of their best retirees into important management positions in these related firms through a system called *amakudari,* literally "descent of angels."[14] This is not the only advantage big companies have over small companies in the area of retirement. In a survey done by the Ministry of Labor in 1975, workers from large companies (more than three hundred employees) retiring with forty years' tenure were offered 43.1 months' retirement pay. Those from smaller companies—companies with one hundred to three hundred employees and companies with fewer than one hundred employees—were able to offer only 31.6 months and 27.5 months' retirement respectively (van Helvoort 1979, 51).

The only way to effectively mitigate the harshness of an early retirement in the Japanese corporation is to be made a director. Directors of the firm are allowed to stay on after the mandatory retirement age. This is the only instance in which most Japanese college graduates over the age of fifty-five are allowed to earn a higher salary than employees who are below retirement age. But even in the case of directors there is a hitch. They are only allowed to remain as directors as long as they are younger than the current company president. When a new president is installed in the company, all directors in the company who are older than the president are expected to turn in their resignations with the assurance that the resignations will be accepted.[15] Only if a director is made president of the company will he be able to remain employed until death or voluntary retirement.

The motivating power of the Japanese promotion system, coupled with early retirement for those who do not make it to the top of an organization, can hardly be overestimated. There are enough—very few but enough—examples of executives who have been "resurrected" from late promotion at one rank to join with the first promotion at the next level to make Japanese corporate elites believe that no matter when they have been promoted they still have a chance at becoming *yakuin* (president or director) of their companies. This outside chance of being able to weather early retirement has been a major motivator to Japanese employees with college degrees. As Nevins put it:

> Surveys of young Japanese employees indicate that a surprisingly large percentage of them feel that they have a chance of being president of a company. . . . Japanese management has mastered the art of keeping all young employees working at peak capacity in hopes of gaining a high management position or perhaps a spot on the board of directors of a firm. (Nevins 1984, 290)

Primacy of the Lifetime Employment System

No analysis of the typical course of elite corporate employment in Japan could overlook the overriding importance of the *shūshin koyō seido* in every elite salaryman's life. All of the elements of the system described above—recruitment, socialization, salaries, promotion, and retirement

—are integrally linked with this system. The remainder of this chapter discusses the postwar system in broader statistical terms, considers some of the pressures that might have worked against the system, and suggests some reasons for the impressive stability of *shūshin koyō seido* during the period from the 1950s through the 1980s.

The best comparative works describing permanent employment have been conducted by Cole and Dore. Both found that rates of turnover were greater in the West (in Britain and the United States) than in Japan. Cole compared the labor pools in the cities of Yokohama and Detroit and found that 34.9 percent of his subjects in Yokohama had been with the same employer throughout their entire careers. This compared with 13.5 percent of the Detroit sample who claimed to have held only one job (Cole 1979, 64). Dore found that the turnover rate of Hitachi factory workers (both manual and nonmanual) was about 10 percent per year, which compared with 20–25 percent turnover rates for male manual workers and 10 percent for nonmanual workers in Britain (Dore 1973, 34). While the turnover rate between Japanese manual and nonmanual workers did not seem to differ greatly in Dore's analysis, it is important to remember that both Dore's and Cole's statistics emphasize blue-collar or non-college graduate employees.

The rate of turnover for elite employees in Japanese firms appears to be smaller than that for lower-level workers. While there are no national statistics on which to base this conclusion, studies that have been conducted over the past twenty years seem to indicate that turnover rates for corporate elite have been extremely low. Rohlen's study of white-collar workers at Uedagin Bank found that the turnover rate was about 1.5 percent annually. That included ten to fifteen men who quit the bank to take other jobs and twenty to thirty women who quit without marrying (Rohlen 1974, 82). Takagi's study at Tokyo Electric Company found an even lower rate of "about 1% of the headquarters-based employees [who] resigned annually in the first ten years after recruitment" (Takagi 1985, 32).

A larger survey of professional managers in 250 manufacturing and 125 nonmanufacturing firms found that 46 percent of the 1,410 respondents had spent their whole lives with one company. Of those who had moved, 19 percent had previously worked in financial institutions and 9 percent in government. (It is very likely then that this 28 percent were either *amakudari* or on *shukkō*—a system of transferring employees between related companies to give them experience outside their own organization that will be discussed in chapter 6) (Aonuma 1965, 140–141). An even larger study of 5,000 company presidents conducted by the Nihon Keizai Shinbun (Japanese Economic Journal) organization in 1979 showed that 51 percent of the presidents had never worked outside their own organizations. Of the nearly half who had been employed by more than one firm, over 32 percent were transferred into the presidency from a related company; the other 31 percent had come from a bank or government office (Hirschmeier and Yui 1981, 347).

The timing of an employee's job change is an important issue in understanding lifetime employment. Takagi observed that the 1 percent turnover rate was applicable only for the first ten years of any cohort's tenure in the firm: "Resignation after the ten-year mark was very rare" (Takagi 1985, 32). Rohlen's anthropological study confirms Takagi's data. He quotes a saying, popular in the Uedagin Bank, that "if a young man is going to quit he is most likely to do it after three days, three months, or three years." He finds that "quitting for men over thirty is almost unheard of" (Rohlen 1974, 82). This is especially true before the one other period during which job changes are fairly common—around retirement, when top personnel forced out of one organization sometimes join a smaller organization in a position where they can still wield some power and prestige.

The statistics presented above, which show the number of professional managers and company presidents who have been employed by more than one firm, might seem to contradict claims about the universality of lifetime employment for successful corporate elites. In fact, the apparent anomaly shows a cohort effect resulting from the freedom executives had to change jobs in the period around World War II. Gary Cooper, a reporter for the *Japan Economic Journal,* conducted interviews with many of Japan's top executives in the mid-1970s. The life histories of many corporation presidents and chairmen he interviewed show job changes linked to economic and political instability surrounding the war. For instance, Seisi Kato, president of Toyota Motor Sales, entered the labor market in 1930, when only about 20 percent of college graduates found employment immediately after graduation. He worked temporarily for a foreign company, General Motors, and then joined Toyota seven years later (Cooper 1976, 106). Katsuji Kawamata, chairman of Nissan Motors, changed companies as a result of postwar war criminal purgings. He had been working at Industrial Bank of Japan for seventeen years when Nissan's managing director of finance was purged and Kawamata was asked to fill the vacancy (Cooper 1976, 113).

During the postwar period, top executives who have made job changes later in life have usually done so through socially acceptable methods like *amakudari* and *shukkō*. One example of *amakudari* is Shizuo Asada, chairman of Japan Airlines, who left a post as administrative vice-minister of transportation to start JAL. The first president of JAL was also an "alumnus of the LDP [Liberal Democratic Party] cabinet" (Cooper 1976, 20–21). Other examples can still be found on the board of directors of almost any company in the country.

Only two examples are given in Cooper's interviews of executives who had changed jobs in midcareer because of personal preference alone. In both cases, an engineer at Toshiba left to join a smaller company with more flexibility. Yozo Ishizuka, president of Pioneer Electric, joined that firm at age forty-seven after working at Toshiba for twenty-five years. He explains that he joined Pioneer Electric because the founder was a "personal friend" who had asked him to manage the business (Cooper 1976, 77). Katsutaro Kataoka left Toshiba earlier in his career. His best friend and mentor died unexpectedly after he had been with the firm for eight years. He decided that he should go his own way and later became president of Alps Electric Company (Cooper 1976, 101–102).

Japanese who stay with their firms seem to stay for the same reasons that Americans do—"cumulative pay, rank, seniority, and status" (Marsh and Mannari 1971, 798). Those who leave Uedagin Bank, according to Rohlen, also appear to go for fairly universal reasons. He ranked the reasons for leaving in order:

1. Dreams of a more interesting or more exciting life and work
2. Bad relations with one's superiors
3. A general sense of unsuitability for banking work
4. Loneliness
5. A special opportunity for advancement elsewhere
6. Unsatisfactory social relations (Rohlen 1974, 83)

These reasons for leaving companies are about the same as those frequently found in the West. Most Japanese feel these pressures, realize that changing jobs might be one way to escape them, and even go so far as to "consider it seriously enough to speak to others about it" (Rohlen 1974, 82). Nevertheless, comparatively few Japanese employees leave their firms or even honestly think they will ever change jobs. Dore's study found that of Japanese workers under age thirty-five, 92 percent thought that they would be with the same company in five years. In two British firms, 61 percent had the same expectation (Dore 1973, 35). Takezawa and Whitehill, in a survey of seven hundred Japanese and seven hundred American workers, found that only 5 percent of Japanese—but 23–26 percent of Americans—said they would "leave the company and take a job with a more prosperous company" (Takezawa and Whitehall 1981, 129).

It would appear that structural and attitudinal obstacles alike hinder a Japanese employee's joining another firm. Whether from tradition or design, structural barriers that inhibit a job changer from rising to the top of a company are strong. Even in Cooper's study, only sixteen of fifty company presidents or chairmen had worked for more than one company.[16] More evidence for the stability of the lifetime employment system can be seen in that of Hitachi's twenty directors in 1969, fifteen joined the firm (or another subsequently absorbed by Hitachi) immediately after graduating from a university or from one of the technical high schools which before the war had quasi-university status. All except one of the others joined within four years of graduating. (Some may have been waiting for an opening since there was a good deal of graduate unemployment in the twenties.) . . . The exception was a former banker who left his bank directorship to enter Hitachi as a director at the age of 52. (Dore 1973, 217)

The pervasiveness of lifetime employment and its respected position among Japanese institutions have led modern college graduates to seek their first jobs in reliable organizations such as trading firms or the civil service. Largely because of their absolute faith in permanent employment, employees "believe that they will be safe as long as their employer does not go broke." Because of the high growth of trading companies during the 1960s and 1970s, jobs in these companies, perhaps more than any other organization in the private business sector, were those most sought after by security-conscious nontechnical college graduates who did not want to join the civil service (Taichi 1981, 23).

The social forms that held the Japanese lifetime employment system in place emanated from both sides of the employment contract. Like a vice, if either side of the clamp had been allowed to move, the system would have failed miserably. Dore describes the relationship he found at Hitachi:

It takes two parties to make an employment contract, and it takes certain attitudes on both sides to make for stability of employment of the Hitachi type. On the worker's side is the expectation that he *will* be able to stay with his chosen firm, and the intention to do so, an intention which is conditioned by the fact that staying is the norm of Japanese occupational life and is bolstered by the knowledge that he has a good deal financially to gain by staying on. On the employer's side is an expectation that (provided he offers "standard" wages and conditions of employment) the workers will *wish* to stay. This expectation is combined with a sense of obligation to provide work for them as long as they do so—an obligation conditioned by the fact that it is one normally assumed by Japanese employers, and sanctioned by the employer's knowledge that he stands to meet tough union resistance and to lose a great deal in work motivation if he departs from the norm. (Dore 1973, 35)

Rohlen, who studied a white-collar organization, emphasized the extent to which social norms and attitudes affected the mobility of elite labor in postwar Japan. Rohlen suggested that the feeling of obligation Dore described emerging from the organization was actually present in the worker, the employer, and Japanese society as a whole. Rohlen claimed that the loss of face that resulted to both sides of a broken employment contract kept the on-going work relationship alive.

> When someone quits or is fired there is the strong implication that the relationship has failed. A general feeling exists that both parties must share responsibility for its failure. As a rule, both suffer some loss of reputation because of it. Irregular departures are embarrassing and unhappy affairs similar in atmosphere to marital divorce. Although in a few cases gains could be calculated by one side or the other (e.g., a better job, or the loss of a poor worker), it is usual for both sides to experience a sense of failure as parties to an important relationship that collapsed. The expectation of continuity and the emphasis on the integrity of the company-member relationship establish this. (Rohlen 1974, 74)

At the societal level, then, many analysts have noted a strong feeling in Japan that "quitting and firing subjects both management and employees to a suspicion of being defective" (Hanke and Saxberg 1985, 236). Both sides are responsible for making the relationship a permanent one. Companies who fire employees are thought to be untrustworthy and are often subject to careful review of union and government rules.

A study of eleven business firms in Kanazawa City showed that employees will be fired only in the "most extreme of cases." None of the officials interviewed said that low productivity or poor work was a reason to dismiss someone. "Only reasons such as embezzlement, public dishonoring of the firm, violation of written rules, or possibly frequent absences" qualified as excuses for letting someone go (Endo 1974, 23). Rohlen describes the only two dismissals from Uedagin during 1969 as being for "theft or its approximation." He explains that under the postwar system of permanent employment, observed so scrupulously in white-collar organizations, "incompetency . . . is no excuse for firing someone. People unable to do their jobs are normally transferred to posts of little responsibility" (Rohlen 1974, 79).

A company having difficulties with cash flow or profitability would not be forgiven for treating workers as variable costs, asking "Whom can we do without?" In Japan, such a company would inevitably lose not only its ability to recruit new employees, but also the goodwill of customers and suppliers.[17] Companies trying to increase profitability must therefore ask themselves "What new markets or product lines can we open up so that we can fully employ our workers?" (Dore 1973, 38). Methods of dealing with redundant employees include using temporary workers and depending on subcontractors to minimize the number of regular employees who are eligible for lifetime employment. Once regular employees become redundant (as many of them appeared to be in the

1970s[18]), companies must adopt methods of using them flexibly. Such measures include moving employees to different jobs, moving employees from factory to factory based on need, sending employees off to other firms with "semi-dependent sub-contracting relations," and retraining employees (Dore 1973, 38–40). Vogel concluded that a salaryman's best interests were not served by midcareer job change "because his salary and benefits rise sharply with the number of years of service" (Vogel 1963, 33). Besides that, in the early 1960s the "typical salary man never receive[d] an offer from another firm," so the onus of deciding to stay or leave was never placed on him.

During the years of Japan's rapid growth following World War II, it appeared that the lifetime employment system served the interests of management to a greater extent than it served the interests of the elite corporate employee. Managers tended to discriminate as to rank and salary against midcareer recruits when compared with lifetime employees of comparable education and age. Yoshino found that this discrimination resulted from the "strong suspicion of outsiders" and the "worry that newcomers won't fit [in]" (Yoshino 1967, 232). Considerable scorn was leveled by Japanese businessmen at the shoddy morals of employment systems more flexible than Japan's. Sazo Idemitsu described the U.S. system of employment mobility as one in which "able managers are baited with high salaries like fish and change from one company to another" (Idemitsu 1971, 220). The lifetime employment system thus seems to be treasured by at least some of the management side of Japanese society; nevertheless, the reduction of freedom it created for workers was interpreted by a number of Japanese and Western intellectuals from a Marxist perspective. In many ways the Japanese employee was handcuffed to his company of first choice. It is not surprising, then, that Cole and Tominaga referred to permanent employment not as a system but as the "dominant management *ideology* that has pervaded much of the Japanese industrialization in the twentieth century" (Cole and Tominaga 1976, 88).

Summary

The Japanese lifetime employment system is a modern phenomenon couched in centuries of cultural precedent. Throughout Japan's recorded history, the value given to human relationships, social rank, and organizational loyalty presaged the emergence of "permanent employment" in the industrial and postindustrial era. From these venerable underpinnings sprang a system within which Japanese white-collar elites follow a predictable course—from the glories and terrors of the recruitment process, to the drudgery of the new employee's menial duties, up through the fiercely contested promotional ranks, and on to an often disappointing and anticlimactic retirement. This system, perhaps because of its solid grounding in the Japanese world view and tradition, has maintained its existence and integrity over the three decades since it first became clearly defined. In so doing, it has drawn the attention of social analysts all over the world and been recognized as one of the pillars of Japan's postwar economic miracle.

CHAPTER FOUR

Continuity and Change in the Lifetime Employment System

THE JAPANESE employment system described in the last chapter should be impressive to anyone who has been involved in or studied business in the West. "Permanent" employment has remained a relatively changeless fixture of Japanese business throughout a thirty-year period of rapid transformation in Japan's economic environment. This chapter discusses the reasons for the resiliency of the lifetime employment system. It considers some of the pressures that might have been expected to drastically alter, if not demolish, Japan's employment practices and explains why and how permanent employment withstood these pressures for the three decades following World War II. However, the sturdiness of the lifetime employment system is not absolute: in the late 1980s the system began to show subtle but significant signs of breaking down. A discussion of these changes concludes this chapter.

Pressures on the Lifetime Employment System, Mid-1950s to Mid-1980s

The "management ideology" of lifetime employment has survived through most of the postwar era despite its being the first period in Japanese history during which "freedom to change jobs and to change residence in order to improve the individual's social and economic position [was] accepted and even encouraged" (Bennett 1967, 412). During the 1960s, high economic growth in the country and the need for technical expertise fueled a small boom in midcareer hiring in companies experiencing much higher growth than average. Even in these companies midcareer hiring was used carefully, and only as a "last resort" (Yoshino

1967, 230–231). A study of twenty-five Japanese companies by Ballon in 1969 showed that only one had hired "a number of middle management personnel from the outside labor market" (Ballon 1969). This was the fastest growing company in the sample.[1]

This midcareer hiring by expanding companies was encouraged by the labor shortage. Yoshino describes this labor shortage as being so severe that demand for junior and senior high school students surpassed supply by three or four times between 1961 and 1967 (Yoshino 1967, 115). Dore noted that in 1969 Hitachi tried to hire 1,100 college graduates for new positions in the firm but was able to attract only 623 (Dore 1973, 50). Vogel's preface to the second edition (1969) of his 1963 book on salarymen questioned whether or not the employment system could continue to thrive under the pressures of the labor shortage: "in the last few years, since the labor shortage has caused some large businesses to look to the smaller enterprises for employees, there have been signs that the double structure might begin to break down" (Vogel 1963, 8).

Japanese enterprises responded to this labor shortage by trying to recruit on the open labor market. Large corporations turned to small companies for needed expertise, but not to the extent that young, growing companies tried to scout talented and frustrated employees from the large firms. One of the most dysfunctional parts of the lifetime employment system is that in every large corporation there are employees who are not climbing the corporate hierarchy, whose talents, for political reasons, are not being fully used. During this period in Japan, such employees had often been assigned to jobs they did not enjoy or, for one reason or another, had been assigned to desks that were out of the main flow of everyday business—usually along the window side of the office.[2] It was these employees that small firms seeking technical expertise or big-company contacts tried to "poach" from large enterprises.

Dore found that among the working class at Hitachi the group of employees hired in midcareer was "a mixed bunch." Many were earning below the minimum wage for Hitachi employees based on their age and experience. But there were also a number of "skilled men" to whom the company was paying higher wages "than the maxima for home-bred" (Dore 1973, 101). The higher wage for technically skilled employees was not only to get them away from other firms: it was also to keep them. It appears that the smaller companies were driving the wage rates in Japan during this period when skilled labor was in short supply. Dore notes that "able youths would still come to Hitachi for 85% of the starting wage at small firms with less prestige and less attractive prospects, but still the differential could not be allowed to become too great" (Dore 1973, 107).

Hitachi reacted to some of this wage pressure by readjusting promotion schedules to allow some "high-flyers" to move to higher ranks than their age would justify so that they could receive the salary at that level. The company concentrated especially on twenty-one- to twenty-six-year-old technical workers, who were in great demand and who were likely to move during this "most footloose period of life." Hitachi personnel managers said that the biggest reason for the altered promotion schedule was that "they were worried about the general effect on the morale of these workers if they saw themselves as seriously under-appreciated in comparison with others of their age and skill" (Dore 1973, 100).

The response that Dore noted in Hitachi became more formalized and structured in the 1970s. The *shikaku seido* (literally, "competence system") uncoupled the systems of ranks and wages. Part of the problem with Hitachi's experimental promoting of "high-flyers" more quickly than others was that promotions given to provide increased wages necessarily also brought supervisory responsibilities. In Japan's hierarchical society, very few people are managed by people younger than they. The Hitachi method of early promotion flew in the face of this tradition. In contrast, *shikaku seido* allowed for talented employees to receive higher wages without having to move into higher management positions. As van Helvoort put it, the new system allowed companies to "utilize and reward excellent performance and capacity, while at the same time seniority rights and steady 'status' progress can be at least partially maintained as a stimulus for continued loyalty" (van Helvoort 1979, 79).

By the late 1970s Japanese companies were much more willing to accept systems like *shikaku seido,* partly because the national mind set was more open to these systems. In 1958 the Teachers' Union fought strenuously against any system of merit ratings. By 1976, however, these systems were not only in place, but were being praised by many teachers (Takezawa and Whitehall 1981, 91). While the adoption of merit ratings by the Teachers' Union may be seen as a special, politically motivated case, the attitudinal changes of many teachers were indicative of alterations that were sweeping the country. Vogel noted these changes in the Japanese middle class between the late 1950s and 1969. They were not drastic alterations of behavior or structure, but subtle adjustments of attitudes and outlooks.

> Ten years ago, to be employed by a large company was considered highly desirable by most of these families [in the Mamachi section of Tokyo], as well as by most of the other people in Japan. . . . By now all these aspirations for security, material possession, and regular hours have been realized not only by the salary man, but by most the population of Japan. The models and visions that were provided by the salary man a decade ago have been essentially achieved already.
>
> This very success has led the Mamachi citizen to raise new questions

about his life, to question assumptions that a decade ago were taken for granted. Why should one sacrifice for the good of the company? Why should one labor so assiduously for so many years at the same place? Are there not other, more interesting things to do? Why should the youth study so hard to be admitted to the good colleges and the good firms? Are there not other values of greater importance? . . . they remain salary men, but they wonder if this is still so desirable. (Vogel 1969, 272)

Vogel was not the only observer who noticed a change in attitudes over time in Japan. A survey by the Japan Research Center noted that "with growing affluence and labor shortage the strong commitment of regular male employees to large firms is being reduced because of a greater concern with the work one is doing" (1972; cited in Patrick 1967, 87). Another survey by the Morale Survey Center in Japan found that of fourteen attitudinal variables they had been tracking through social surveys between 1956 and 1972, the most "dramatic change" occurred with the variable of "loyalty to one's employer. Specifically there has been a drastic decline in the value over the last 16 years" (Mizutani 1972; cited in Cole 1976, 205). Yoshino commented that senior executives in late 1960s Japan "deplore[d] the privatized pettiness of their younger subordinates" (Yoshino 1967, 222).

Vogel tried to describe this "privatized pettiness" in terms of modern changes in the value of loyalty in Japan. He found that, compared to previous generations, younger Japanese in the 1960s "placed increasing importance on the ties with equals as opposed to the ties between superiors and inferiors." Furthermore there was a "narrowing range of loyalty" in the country. Rather than focusing on the nation or the broader society as an object of loyalty, middle-class Japanese were increasingly limiting that devotion to the "nuclear family and the immediate work group." A third trend Vogel observed was an "easing of rigidity with which loyalty is demanded" (Vogel 1963, 150–153). All of these changes were taking place in a society in which, as Dore asserts, "managers can and do operate on the assumption that workers fully accept the values and goals of the firm" (compared to Britain, where "managers operate on the assumption that their workers' commitment is a very limited one") (Dore 1973, 240).

Attitudes of self-interest and corporate structures of lifetime employment have often been at odds. The conflicts between them seem to contribute to a build-up of pressure in the labor market. One illustration of this phenomenon can be seen in the explosion of interest in Sony's advertisement for midcareer openings in the late 1960s. Twelve hundred employees, many from "large, prestigious firms" applied for the forty positions Sony sought to fill (Yoshino 1967, 233). Nor was the Sony incident an isolated event. According to one source at a major surveying company in Japan, any time a respectable company attempts to make midcareer hires from other large companies, the outpouring of interest from elite executives has been tremendous.[3] Vogel, after revisiting his Mamachi salarymen in the late 1960s, noted that while lifetime employment practices "remained firmly institutionalized for most salary men," "in areas of labor shortage or where a high degree of technical skill is required," the length of time "the low mobility between firms and the primary commitment to the firm rather than to occupational specialty will continue is an open question" (Vogel 1969, 265).

Marsh and Mannari underscored Vogel's suspicions of change in the lifetime employment system in their 1972 article "A New Look at 'Lifetime Commitment' in Japanese Industry." They noted that "the labor shortage, the shift from seniority to job classification systems, visibility of job ads in newspapers, differential attractiveness of employment in large versus small firms, etc." would be major factors in the "long run" in the waning of the "lifetime commitment patterns . . . in Japanese industrial organizations" (Marsh and Mannari 1972, 611–630). Following the oil shock in 1974, a number of articles put forth very different reasons for the impending downfall of the lifetime employment system. Cole posited that aging and slower economic growth would lead to an end of permanent employment (Cole 1976); Haitani added an increase in the tertiary sector to Cole's factors as influencing the employment system (Haitani 1978, 1029–1045). Finally, articles in business magazines and newspapers popularized the notion that the lifetime employment system in Japan was an endangered institution.[4] Even the Japanese executives were becoming involved in the doomsday soothsaying during the period following the first oil shock. In a survey of corporate presidents by Nikkei Business in July 1976, 71 percent of the respondents thought that the system of *nenkō* (seniority) wages would change. Fifty-six percent foresaw the eventual end of the lifetime employment system.

In the early 1980s, following the successful publication of books like *Japan as Number One* (Vogel 1979) and *Theory Z* (Ouchi 1981), the tone of articles on Japan's employment system changed. Suddenly it was fashionable again to suggest that the Japanese system could be expected to last indefinitely (Rohlen 1979, 58; Martin 1982). By this time the permanent employment system had weathered not only the storms of labor shortage and a gradual shift to the use of *shikaku seido* (see chapter 6), it also seemed to have survived two oil shocks and the resulting slower economic growth. How the aging population would affect the situation was still an open question, but as of the early 1980s, Linda Martin suggested that

Japanese labor force institutions are more flexible than most Western observers have thought, and appropriate response to the changing demographic situation has already begun. The Japanese government and private enterprises are devising innovative policies for accommodating an older labor force. (Martin 1982, 19)

The employment system, by all accounts, appeared to be adapting to all these attitudinal and structural changes without major variations in its original design.

The Persistence of Lifetime Employment

It is obvious even at a glance that postwar Japan has sustained economic, demographic, technological, and globalization pressures that might in themselves seem adequate to crumble any employment system. Since Western economists have shown that the bulk of the explanation for turnover variation is grounded in macroeconomic shifts in labor markets, one would expect to find that the employment system in Japan has changed with the alterations in the economic and social environment. That this was a period of unabated economic growth in Japan and that the system was stable during this period fit the historical trends presented in our second chapter, in which prosperity tended to lead to an increase in the ethic of employee loyalty. Nevertheless, the combination of the oil crisis, the slowed growth of Japan's economy, an aging population, rapid technological change, and an increasing role in the global economy would seem enough to justify predictions of chaos in the postwar lifetime employment system no matter what the historical precedent. By the early 1980s, however, many of the theorists who had predicted that Japan's employment system would necessarily break down under these pressures were forced to admit that the "Japanese system" appeared to be here to stay. In this section, we examine the apparent lack of change in Japanese employment practices through the mid-1980s and propose some explanations for the impressive stability of the lifetime employment system.

Michael Godet is one of a number of social scientists who have warned Westerners about the potential hazards of accepting Japanese "permanent employment" at face value. In his 1987 article Godet proposed that Westerners have at least ten preconceived ideas about Japan, ideas that must be either "reappraised or put into perspective." Among these is the collage of misconceptions concerning "lifetime employment and consensus within a Japanese firm" (Godet 1987, 371), which Godet claimed presents a simplistic and inaccurate image of permanent employment. A Westerner hearing the story of one Japanese job changer might conclude that such an occurrence is a unique and unprecedented break from a universal tradition. Godet pointed out that such isolated instances of job changing have always existed in Japan. In an interview we conducted at the National Institute of Employment and Vocational Research in Tokyo, a Mr. Kameyama agreed with Godet's claim that there has been no widespread alteration in career patterns among Japan's white-collar elite. He pointed out that the real term for the system in Japan should have been *chōki koyō seido,* or "long-term employment system."[5] The uninitiated observer's belief in the universality of this system, and in the absolute adherence to it by all Japanese, has never been grounded in fact. Throughout the heyday of the lifetime employment system, famous Japanese companies have actively participated in midcareer hiring. Without the ability to poach engineers, designers, and managers, for example, Sony and Honda would never have been able to reach their present worldwide status. Contrary to the ideas of many Westerners, Mr. Kameyama assured us, there has been some evidence of a midcareer external labor market throughout the period of employment stability that produced the phrase "lifetime employment."

Japan's Economic Planning Agency published a report on the mobility of labor among engineers in 1986 that concurred with Kameyama's conclusions, although their reasoning was different from his. Mr. Kameyama reported that levels of job changing in Japan have always been as high as they are currently. The Economic Planning Agency agreed that when "all of the research is gathered concerning job changing [among engineers in Japan], there is not much of it happening" (Keizai Kikakuchō 1986, 74). However, they based this claim on the belief that most of the increase in job changing in this field (which they acknowledge to be higher than in the past) is a result of employees' returning to the university to pursue a pet research project. They also claim that the level of scouting in Japan has not and will not change a great deal.

Other adherents of the "unchanging Japan" theory have focused their attacks at the level of culture, particularly at the myths that have come to surround the Japanese employee. David Plath, in his book *Work and Lifecourse in Japan,* warns the Westerner not to assume the absoluteness of Japanese groupism and self-sacrifice. Plath's work disentangles the conflation of Western and Japanese ideas of loyalty in much the same way we have done in chapter 2 of this book. He points out that the physician who is said to have such a "deep attachment" to his or her hospital or his or her university is not simply acting out "some culturally absolute group affiliation"; rather these "are loyalties which serve his own career" (Plath 1983, 113). In the public corporation, also, loyalty is not simply a cultural norm that employees blindly follow. Plath found that employees don't fit the mold of the supposedly passive Japanese worker who can direct his attention to productivity without being over concerned about promotions. Most employees are actively involved in efforts to shape their own work careers. (Plath 1983, 70)

According to Michael Godet, Mr. Kameyama, and Dr. Plath, then, we must be careful to view job-hopping activities of Japanese employees today in the context of a system that has always allowed for a certain level of job changing. Westerners who hear of one person changing jobs should not assume that this in itself is evidence of unprecedented evolutionary trends in Japanese-style management.

The scholars mentioned above represent only a few of the analysts who have criticized the idea that Japan may be evolving toward a replication of Western employment practices. Their point that this prediction represents a simplistic response to current data, based on inadequate understanding of Japanese culture and institutions, is well-grounded enough to cast serious doubt on the idea that the lifetime employment system will disappear. Such experts base their belief that permanent employment is likely to continue on their familiarity with the intense social pressures that often tie individuals to jobs for a lifetime in Japan.

If the mass of Japan's elite salarymen are known for staying in one job for their entire careers, it is not necessarily because the Japanese are either less picky or more placid than executives from other cultures. There is a great deal of variation among individual Japanese college graduates' reactions to a given job, just as there would be among individuals of any other nation. However, until the very recent past virtually every Japanese executive who might have been dissatisfied with his job faced a phalanx of social pressures more solid and pervasive than those that discourage job hopping in most other countries. Because social nuance and the preservation of interpersonal harmony are trademarks of the Japanese culture, these pressures are all the more intense. One young electronics engineer insisted that all the people in their twenties in his company "would move to a different firm if they could, but about two-thirds of them cannot because of social obligations."[6]

The social obligations that tied these young employees to their jobs came primarily from parents, who would be disappointed at best—more probably outraged—by a son's decision to change jobs. As employees age beyond their twenties, this obligation to parents expands into a broader network of social ties. Relationships with wife and children, extended family members, neighbors, co-workers, superiors, and subordinates combine to ensure that older workers are even more tightly bound to their jobs than are their younger colleagues. A survey exploring the reasons for middle managers' hesitancy to change jobs found that the most important reason was career related, but all of the subsequent reasons concerned human relations (Figure 1).

The heavy investment of an elite salaryman's family in the success of his career makes family involvement in a decision about changing jobs particularly important. Mr. Murakami of TMT informed us that, in persuading an executive to change jobs in midcareer, it is fundamental to convince family members that such a change is advisable. He even recommended "mak[ing] it sound like there is no choice."[7] Those unfamiliar with Japanese society may consider this technique extreme. However, after some experience with the type and extent of pressure a potential job-changer in Japan may receive from his family, even the most liberal Westerner might come to agree that Mr. Murakami's method may be the only effective (if not necessarily desirable) way to afford an executive the social "space" to change jobs.

Mr. Sato was one potential job-changer with whom one of the authors had contact as a headhunter during the summer of 1987. Although Mr. Sato disliked his job and seemed enthusiastic about moving to another company, he explained to the headhunter that his wife seemed less than overjoyed by his comments on the subject. The headhunter discussed

Figure 1

Reasons for Hesitance in Job Changing

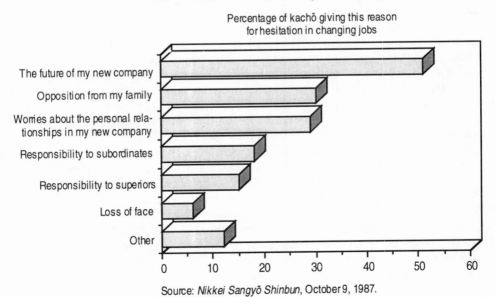

Percentage of kachō giving this reason
for hesitation in changing jobs

Source: *Nikkei Sangyō Shinbun*, October 9, 1987.

some ideas Mr. Sato might present to soften his wife's resistance, and the next week Mr. Sato called to inform the headhunter that she had been persuaded by his arguments. Soon after this conversation the headhunter needed to arrange a meeting between Mr. Sato and the company that wanted to hire him. Following a surreptitious tradition of executive search firms, the headhunter called Sato in the evening at home rather than risk his being "found out" at the office. Mrs. Sato answered and informed the caller that her husband was not home. When the headhunter left a message including his name, company, and phone number, he suddenly found himself experiencing Japanese social pressure at a level of authenticity rarely attained by Westerners. A sample of the almost thirty-minute conversation is transcribed below:

Mrs. Sato: Are you from that headhunting company?
Headhunter: Yes.
Mrs. Sato: My husband told me that he had told you to stop bothering him. Why are you still calling him? You should leave him alone. You are confusing him.
Headhunter: He'd told us that he was still interested in . . .
Mrs. Sato: I'll tell you what he is interested in. He is interested in taking care of his family. He has done that for twenty-five years and has done a good job of it. You know we work together, as a family, for his company. We've been doing that for twenty-five years, too! He has made great sacrifices for the company. He is out all night long working for the company. He does not even take vacations so that he can work for the company. That company has paid for our food and housing; it has sent our children to college. They have been very good to us. My husband has a bright future with the company. Even if he did not, it is not his decision to change jobs. We have worked together for the company, and I have a right to be involved in the decision. He does not realize how hard it will be to succeed in a new company. You know all of his friends are in the old one. He has people there who would do anything for him. He has subordinates who sacrifice for him and superiors in the company who take good care of him.[8]

The rest of the conversation is adequately represented by this comparatively short diatribe, during which Mrs. Sato touched upon all the main arguments against a salaryman's changing jobs in Japan today. Mr. Sato had undoubtedly considered all these objections before seeking a new job; perhaps he thought he could overcome them; in the end, however, family resistance proved too strong. The day following this conversation the headhunter received a call from Mr. Sato, who had decided to withdraw from the search process.

Even if family members acquiesce to the household head's leaving a position with one company, it is still necessary to gain their support for the new job. One man who joined an American firm after twenty years with a Japanese enterprise found that the difference in working hours was of great concern to his wife and children. While working for the Japanese company, this salaryman had returned home from work every night at close to midnight. The American firm, he said, "made me work harder during office hours, but I was expected to leave the office by seven o'clock."[9] His family decided that his job change had been a great mistake because the new company had no real need for their breadwinner. If he had been filling a truly important role, he would have been busier than he had been in the previous job. It took a phone call from the president of the foreign subsidiary to this man's wife to convince her that everyone in the American firm returned home in the early evening and that her husband was making a very valuable contribution to his new company.

The line between family- and company-related responsibility has always been less distinct in Japan than in the West, and companies themselves often use tactics to discourage job changing not unlike the social pressures the executive encounters at home. Indeed, companies do not appear to have been averse to forming a direct alliance with a mutinous executive's relatives to keep him in his job. The story of Ken'ichi Takahashi, the salaryman turned sushi seller, presented in the introductory chapter, was not unusual even in the very recent past. If a salaryman announced to someone in his company that he was thinking about changing jobs, both corporate and domestic forces would immediately be rallied to convince the man of the folly of his ways. The president of the company and other top executives might contact the man's co-workers and family members to deliver the news that this employee was considering a move that could destroy his life.[10] Phone calls would pour in from relatives and friends around the country. Superiors would explain to the job-changer that his lot would not be easy if he left the comfort of the company community. The man's friends, who would usually all be members of the same company, might threaten to end their friendship if he decided to leave the firm. Worried parents, in-laws, and more distant relatives, who put the words *tenshoku* (job changing) and *chūtosaiyō* (mid-career hiring) in the same category with *hannin* (criminal) and *uragiri* (betrayal), might threaten to disown the traitor if he carried out his plan to shame the family by leaving his present position. Under this barrage of threats and criticisms, only the most stubborn and determined salaryman would actually carry through with a job change.

If he repented of his wild and misguided intentions by remaining with his original firm, the wayward executive would become a prime target for another type of social pressure characteristic of Japanese culture. Japanese businesses, like most other institutions in the society, are adept at engendering obligation *(giri)* in the members of the social group. The corporations of Japan have elevated the creation of *giri* in their employees to an art and then refined it to a science. Until very recently, part of the socialization system in a Japanese firm has always been the process of convincing employees that the company has forgiven their mistakes, and so they must forgive the mistakes of the company. Superiors have placed themselves in the position of benevolent caretakers whom an employee would not care, nor indeed dare, to betray. As Yoshino and Lifson put it:

> When an employee who makes an error observes that his boss or colleagues forgive him and unite in overcoming the consequences of his mistake . . . he incurs a feeling of obligation. This serves as a very powerful motivating factor for hard work in the future. . . . For example, the head of a soybean section estimated that the mistakes made by a soybean commodity trader in the training may cumulatively cost as much as $200,000. But, *given the assurance that the employee will stay with the company,* and that a mistake especially in the earlier stages of an employee's career will make him very strongly motivated and also more seasoned and self-confident, the cost of a mistake may well appear to be a justifiable investment. (Yoshino and Lifson 1986, 186)

This managerial tactic—forgiving a subordinate for errors and taking his side in correcting them—is extraordinarily effective in eliciting a high degree of loyalty from employees. The authors can personally testify to the intensity of obligation that is felt by subordinates in such a situation. We spent the summer of 1983 working as systems analysts in the U.S. embassy in Tokyo. One of our superiors was a Japanese citizen by the name of Itoh, a man of modest demeanor and diligent habits. We noticed immediately that Mr. Itoh never reported any of our mistakes, which were many since neither of us was familiar with the embassy's computer system. We were grateful to Itoh for "covering up" for beginners, but his behavior did not seem terribly out of keeping with what a rather kindly American might do in similar circumstances.

We had no idea how far Mr. Itoh's protective blanket extended until the day that a Korean Airlines passenger aircraft was shot down by Soviet fighter jets just north of Hokkaido. The event caused a huge international uproar. All during the night after the jet was downed, Japanese rescue crews worked feverishly, searching the cold northern sea for bodies and clues as to what had actually happened. The information they retrieved, bit by bit, was telephoned immediately to reporters waiting in Tokyo. They reported the information in the Japanese press, and the news was immediately snatched up by translators at the American embassy in Tokyo. We had gone to work very early that day and locked ourselves into the main computer center, determined to "learn the system" once and for all. We spent the morning busily pushing buttons and commenting to each other on the results, blissfully unaware of the furious work transpiring in the translation section. One of those buttons, apparently, was the wrong one. We were roused from our efforts by the frantic knocking of Mr. Itoh, who rushed past us into the room when we opened the door. He sat down at the computer and typed furiously at the computer for several minutes. It was no use. All the translated data regarding the KAL crisis had been blipped into oblivion by our experimentation.

The boom fell hard for this misdeed, but it did not fall on us. As our *senpai*, Mr. Itoh immediately went to his superior and claimed full responsibility for losing the translators' data. The reader may recall that the American press criticized Ronald Reagan, then the U.S. president, for responding slowly to the KAL incident. Although the authors argued at length with embassy personnel that this slowness was our fault and not Mr. Itoh's, the criticism we received was softened immeasurably by Mr. Itoh's continued claims of personal responsibility. We will not attempt to describe the feelings of indebtedness generated in us by his actions. Suffice it to say that the Japanese workers' fidelity to their superiors has never seemed quite as inexplicable to us since the infamous KAL incident.

Because of the kindness they receive from the company early in their careers, employees of Japanese firms typically carry a keen sense of obligation, making them unwilling to desert the company and the superiors who have dealt so liberally with them. Yoshino and Lifson pointed out in 1986 that companies rely heavily on this sense of loyalty in their employees. The company leaders "know that no one who owes them an obligation will unexpectedly leave the firm, leaving behind an unfulfilled debt that will have to go uncollected" (Yoshino and Lifson 1986, 203).

If informal social obligations proved insufficient to end an employee's consideration of a job change, a Japanese company might resort to more formal measures. In many companies, work rules required that an employee have the permission of his immediate superior to leave the company "prematurely" (Wysocki 1985). This rule meant that the superior was entitled to badger an employee unmercifully if there was any serious indication that the subordinate was considering leaving the firm.

One young man told of being locked in an empty room in his office for two days while other employees in the company—from the president on down—were paraded into the room one by one to try to shame or entice or threaten or humor him into changing his mind. He changed jobs anyway, and has since received letters, occasionally threatening, from company and family members repudiating him for his disgusting behavior.[11]

Something salarymen have claimed bothers them even more than this in-firm opposition to a job change is the fear that powerful people in their original company will try to besmirch the job hopper's reputation (and protect that of the firm) by spreading a rumor that the employee was fired, when the truth is that he changed jobs by choice.[12] One way many job-changers have avoided the worst consequences of this stigmatization has been to change jobs to a different industry as well as a different company. This tactic would minimize the negative effects of job changing not only for the individual, but for the hiring company, since companies who lost personnel to another firm within the same industry tend to discriminate against that firm in business dealings. In particular, if a new employee were assigned to work on a deal involving his former employer, the deal is unlikely to succeed. By changing jobs to a new industry the employee would not be as likely to have contact with his previous company where recriminations for "disloyal" behavior might hurt his standing in the new company.

Another common practice in the lifetime employment system has been for the president of a potential job-changer's company to call the president of the company to which the employee expects to move to talk the second president out of hiring the new employee. Once word gets out that a salaryman intends to betray his firm by moving to a competitor, these "discussions" between corporate higher-ups have often prevented the move. More was at stake than courtesy and personal relations: if the job change took place despite the protestations of the company president, the hiring firm may have encountered difficulty in dealing with the old company from that time forward. As one Mitsubishi Bank employee put it: "Japanese corporate society is actually very small. If I change jobs, I will still probably have to work with Mitsubishi Bank in the future. I have to worry about that relationship."[13]

Why have companies, co-workers, and families acted so strenuously to keep elite executives faithful to Japan's lifetime employment system? For the companies, one important reason has been the prestige and reputation associated with retaining all the employees who initially joined the company. Recruiters for new college graduates have feared that if the word were to get out to college seniors that many employees were leaving the recruiter's company, the effects on their college recruiting efforts could be devastating. In addition, the disloyalty of a subordinate could mark the end of the climb up the company hierarchy of the immediate supervisor of a job-changer. An upwardly mobile career in a large Japanese corporation can survive only so many black marks, and

> losing a valued employee is a black mark. . . . Supervisors rarely can offer their people big raises in return for staying, since that would disrupt tightly controlled pay scales. So they yell at departing subordinates. They lock them in rooms and badger them. Sometimes they even appeal directly to the employee's family. (Browning 1986)

The reasons for the family's likelihood to support the aims of the employer even over their kinsman are, if anything, even clearer than those behind companies' reluctance to let an elite employee go. To the family of a Japanese executive, the breadwinner's changing jobs has traditionally meant downward mobility. In the past, it was virtually impossible to move from a job in one highly respected firm to another such company. This meant that if it occurred, a job change was the first downward turn in the lives of most Japanese college graduates. Its impact would be felt by every member of the salaryman's family. Parents who had paid for *juku* (after-school cram schools), supported their child's education at one of the best universities, watched as he entered a top company, and bragged to neighbors about his promotions in the firm would perceive their son's job change as a terrible loss of face. To parents who had beamed with pride as their daughter married an NEC or Fujitsu or Mitsui or Mitsubishi man, talk of a job change was something to be squelched as unthinkable, almost as if the original terms of their daughter's marriage were about to be irrationally altered—the groom who changed jobs would become damaged goods. To the wife and children who had felt as much of the "corporate family" as the salaryman, his job switch would necessitate a drastic change in their identity, not only as members of another corporation but as co-conspirators in an action that was distinctly non-Japanese. Mr. Murakami of TMT Consulting in Tokyo (the proponent of "no alternative" persuasion techniques) mentioned that of all the family members affected by a Japanese executive's job change, the wife is often the hardest to convince. "Women are usually more conservative than men—they don't like risk. They want a secure life."[14] This attitude, and those of the people who depend on even the most dissatisfied Japanese executive, is understandable in light of the repercussions that have surrounded the associates of a job-changer during the heyday of the lifetime employment system. Wives, children, aging parents, and other family members may have no other source of social and economic sustenance than the salaryman's "permanent" job. Equally understandable is the individual's decision to live with his job rather than swim upstream against a such a powerful current of social sanctions.

Companies try in every way possible to maintain the loyalty of workers. It is upon this loyalty that Japan's postwar miracle was established. Edwards has argued that Japan's lifetime employment has in some ways been a "conspiracy" of the managerial class against the freedom of the working class. By subjugating the working class to long work hours and allowing little or no employment mobility, these classes were unable to rise up in Marxist-style revolution against the rulers (Edwards 1986). One of the problems with this interpretation of historical events is the strength with which the managerial class had adopted these norms into their own lives. So deeply ingrained are the organizational attitudes and structures holding Japanese managers in the lifetime employment system that even companies that try diligently to incorporate some more relaxed standards toward mobility run into serious obstacles in the workplace. Sumitomo Trust is one company that has made a concerted effort to put policies in place that will allow midcareer hires to feel as much a part of the organization as lifetime employees. In interviews with Sumitomo's midcareer employees we found no evidence of structural discrimination against them. But even in this company, executives who have recently made midcareer job changes into the firm claimed that they sense some distrust from employees who have been with the firm since their college graduation.

In the past Japanese firms have emphasized personality rather than knowledge and experience when hiring and promoting employees. In the internationalizing, mobile labor market of the mid-1980s, it has become necessary to emphasize knowledge and experience over personality. Some employees express concern that the added stress placed on workers by this attention to performance over seniority could lead to even more "tension and animosity inside Japanese corporations, which despite all the emphasis placed on harmony, are often [already] hotbeds of factionalism and turf battles" (*WSJ*, November 14, 1988, R14).

Another social problem is the age-old dichotomy of the insider *(uchi)* versus the outsider *(soto)* in Japanese society. The pervasive sense in Japanese society is that when a man has spent a number of years with one firm (especially his early, formative years), he absorbs the culture of that organization and can never be changed. All of the big conglomerates in Japan possess their own distinct cultures, which are often referred to in terms of Tokugawa imagery—Hitachi is the field warrior, Mitsui the lord, Toshiba the samurai, Mitsubishi the merchant, and Sumitomo the new merchant.[15] The problem that many midcareer recruits face is that they are labeled according to their former employer. It is difficult to dissuade many Japanese from the belief that "a Hitachi man is a Hitachi man from top to bottom."[16]

Related to the problem of cultural labeling is the company's fear that a midcareer recruit would not understand the subtle cultural aspects of communication in his new firm after having been "trained" in a very different system.

> Japan is what one anthropologist has called an "endogamous society," implying that the inhabitants share so many aspects of consciousness and experience that explanations via the medium of language become unnecessary in many situations. Rather than saying something outright, one might merely have to supply a nuance.
>
> This ability to communicate meaning indirectly or nonverbally has been reinforced and developed by . . . groupism and the primacy of vertical relations. Because groups are so important, potential clashes of will —especially clashes between subordinate and superior—have to be avoided. If relations between two people in a group are allowed to become sour, it can easily affect the harmonious functioning of the entire group. Given the importance of the group commitment, really fundamental clashes can have serious and lasting consequences for many people. . . . The importance of these shared understandings is one reason why most Japanese companies hire only fresh graduates and shun the hiring of people from other companies. (Yoshino and Lifson 1986, 98–100)

New managers who are brought in to oversee new operations in diversifying companies face a great deal of opposition. These executives often find themselves managing lifetime employees who have been plucked from their comfortable jobs in an industry they understood and forced to learn new skills under "foreign" management. When the Hayashibara Group in Okayama diversified from the base food and confectionery business into biotechnology, new and old workers alike were forced to grapple with the issues of insiders versus outsiders.

> "Sure there was some resistance from the other workers when I first came in here," said one manager who was hired from outside and placed above long-time Hayashibara employees. "They saw that opening as the only chance they would have to be promoted. But we made it clear that I would be in the department for a few years, and then move elsewhere. And we are all working cooperatively now." (LAT, July 9, 1988)

Another social problem encountered by some companies who are attempting to do midcareer recruiting is the issue of relationships with other industry firms whose employees they are hiring. A number of executives from banks that are not participating in midcareer hiring point to the problems Mitsubishi Bank has had to deal with in hiring job-changers. When the bank announced that it would begin midcareer recruiting, it received more than 560 applications for 100 positions. Many applicants were interviewed, but in the end the company was able to hire only twenty new employees. The problem was an *enmantaishoku* (smooth or harmonious resignation) clause in the Mitsubishi Bank contract. New employees had to show that they still had a good relationship with the company they were leaving. "Very few candidates could meet this condition" (*AS,* March 11, 1987). Either the new recruit was not willing to go to his superiors and negotiate with them a harmonious resignation, or when he did the top brass in his former company would give Mitsubishi Bank officials a call and threaten to remove business if any poaching took place. Other banks, including Mitsui and Sumitomo Trust, encourage good feelings when an employee leaves another firm for theirs, but they do not contractualize it. Thus even though Sumitomo Trust has had to delay one person's hiring for a year to "make sure relations with the previous company were good," these companies have had no trouble hiring as many people as they wanted (Esaka 1988, 172).

One of the most significant problems accompanying the recent increase in midcareer hiring is the worry that midcareer employees (or even the idea of midcareer job changes as a possibility) will taint the lifetime employees in the firm. How do you keep lifetime employees motivated when some of the higher-level slots they expect to fill have been given to "turncoats" from another company? Balancing the need for midcareer expertise and the motivation of regular employees is one of the most difficult juggling acts with which top managers are faced these days.

The powerful normative stance against deviation from traditional job or lifestyle patterns in Japan is strikingly illustrated by the case of Japanese who have moved—if only temporarily—into foreign cultures. One of the most difficult challenges that Japanese returning from abroad have is in overcoming the discrimination leveled by their fellow countrymen against anyone "tainted with foreignness." School children are taunted by their classmates, housewives are avoided by their neighbors, and even the husband may find that there is no easy social niche to fit back into once he has started to think a little more like a foreigner. The fear of this discrimination (and the fear that foreign schools—even Japanese schools—will not give their children the education necessary to pass the difficult entrance examinations into Japanese universities) motivates many Japanese businessmen to leave their wives and children in Japan while they travel on two- or three-year assignments abroad.

American and European companies in Japan often claim that this fear of being tainted by foreignness is one of the major reasons it is difficult for them to hire qualified and competent Japanese staff members. In one instance, Bolt Beranek and Newman, a Massachusetts software firm, was trying to establish an office in Tokyo. They hired a headhunter to find "the right person for the top job there." After five months of waiting, the headhunter had not identified one candidate for the job who was willing to be interviewed (Browning 1986). Finally BBN had to hire a top manager away from another foreign firm in Tokyo—an employee who had already been "tainted" and was willing to think about their offer in terms of the job and not the social implications.

Another illustration comes from Motorola, which set up operations in Japan as a wholly owned subsidiary in 1975. Since then the company has grown quickly to become one of the most successful foreign technology firms in the country. Even with the reputation that Nippon Motorola has among engineers in the country, however, the company still found it difficult to recruit qualified personnel in the mid-1980s. According to one manager who is very familiar with recruiting at the Japanese operation, "If a Japanese middle manager will talk to us, something is wrong with him. It is our job to figure out what that something is, and if we can live with it." The "something wrong" may be as innocuous as a desire to spend evenings after 6 or 7 o'clock at home with his family (which an executive normally could not do in a Japanese firm). More often it is that the manager in question is not going anywhere in his present company.[17]

The apprehension and suspicion involving a potential job-changer and a foreign firm in Japan is not a one-way street. It also acts as a barrier against Japanese considering changing jobs to a Western firm where they might expect to avoid the stigma attached to job hopping in Japanese firms. The Japanese executive being recruited by a foreign firm has heard his whole life about the mercurial temperaments of Western managers. He probably wonders why this new company is interested in him: "Why couldn't they find anyone better?" "When they do find someone better, will he replace me?" The Western company, in most cases, has no personnel system in place; it has no well-trodden career path. It is little wonder, then, that the potential job-changer to a foreign firm in Japan expects an attractive compensation package. Although he probably does not conceptualize his demands as clearly as the economist, he expects a higher discount rate for risk factors.

The myriad attitudinal and structural constraints placed on the corporate elite in Japan at the societal, organization, and familial levels are part of the reason for Japan's continuing low rates of turnover. There is evidence to suggest that very little increase in Japanese turnover rates has occurred in recent history. Recently the *Asahi Shinbun* reported that between 1965 and 1974, the overall turnover rate in companies in Japan was consistently over 10 percent. Between 1975 and 1984, the rate dropped below 10 percent, and in 1985 and 1986, the turnover rate dipped below 8 percent (*AS*, August 26, 1986). In elite corporations, moreover, the turnover rate is far below the national norm. One large manufacturing firm reported an annual turnover rate of 0.7 percent between 1985 and 1987, with only 31 of 4,600 college graduates leaving the firm before retirement in 1986.[18] The large trading firms *(sōgō shōsha)* reported similar statistics. Yoshino and Lifson reported that between twenty and forty "core staff members might leave a firm before retirement" (Yoshino and Lifson 1986, 137). Yoshino and Lifson gathered their data in the late 1970s and early 1980s, and the rate of turnover they reported seems to have gone unchanged through the mid-1980s. The data in table 1 were gathered from one of the large *sōgō shōsha*.[19]

These kinds of data, which can almost always be traced back to company reports, have been enough to convince many analysts that Japan's lifetime employment system is stronger than ever. However, it is inadvisable to rely on company information alone. In the first place, it must be remembered that company data are limited and subject to reporting bias. Rohlen maintained that information on a company's labor or management turnover is perhaps the most sensitive in the company (Rohlen 1974, 82).

Many Western and Japanese analysts familiar with the intense sociocultural pressures against job changing in Japan see the lifetime system as virtually impervious to the many forces that would appear to be working against it. We have attempted to present this perspective fairly, and we readily acknowledge that the idea of a changeless Japanese employment system is well supported by a variety of data. However, we also think that Japanese culture itself contains a strong attitudinal bias against acknowledging the existence of increased change in the country's employment practices. The use of company data to support the idea of a "changeless Japan" is one example of how such pervasive cultural bias may obscure trends in the Japanese system. The next section discusses a newly emerging body of arguments that have recently begun to challenge the notion that permanent employment is itself a permanent system.

Change in the System

In the previous chapter and in the first part of this chapter, we have shown some of the plentiful evidence that Japan's employment system

Table 1
Job-changes in one major Japanese firm

Job-Changers	1981	1982	1983	1984	1985	1986
Through grade three (age 37 or so)	11	10	10	10	12	11
Voluntary retirement (age 45–52)	14	4	5	15	15	8
Involuntary retirement (age 53–56)			5 to 15 each year			

Source: Interview, Summer 1987.

has changed very little since it was first instituted following World War II. However, the late 1980s saw the rise of contradictory evidence as well. This final section of this chapter discusses the changes in Japan during the years following 1985, offers some explanations about why such changes may have been downplayed in some analyses of Japanese employment patterns, and describes ways in which Japan's corporate actors may be changing both their beliefs and their behaviors in regard to job hopping.

Anyone who has followed the Japanese press since the mid-1980s has probably noticed the coverage given to tales of successful job-changers. Almost every day, Japanese newspapers seem to contain another article about one more executive who has left his traditional career track to join a foreign firm or a diversifying Japanese company. Some of the more popular stories in Japan in recent years have included the tales of Eiji Wakabayashi, Yukio Imada, Sousuke Yamane, and Youichi Watanabe. Wakabayashi left the Bank of Tokyo's New York branch to head up Nihon Kangyo Kakumaru's securities operations in New York. It is reported that his salary is one billion yen (more than US$8 million). Imada left Mitsubishi Chemicals to become the team manager of Nippon Kokkan's Bioproject. Yamane left a post at Nike Japan to become Adidas Japan's office manager. And Watanabe, at the age of fifty-nine—practically doddering by traditional Japanese standards—left Teijin, the textile company where he was a director, to become the director in charge of international business at Suntory, the beer maker (Takita 1987, 334–346).

These stories and the increasing number of others like them are significant in at least two ways. First, they may be indicative of widespread trends toward job changing; this is a claim often made in the articles, although it cannot be assumed on the basis of anecdotal evidence alone. Second, media coverage shows the interest of the public in changes in the lifetime employment system generally, and the positive tone of many stories may actually encourage the emergence of attitudes favorable toward job changing. The interrelationship of behaviors and attitudes is of course so complex as to make the two almost inextricable. This is particularly true in considering the individual's decision to leave or stay at a job.

INCREASES IN JOB CHANGING

By the mid-1980s, when the predictions of Japan-watchers that the country's demographic, economic, and attitudinal changes would topple the lifetime employment system were still unfulfilled, many analysts decided that the system would never change. However, current data suggest that this conclusion might have been premature. Information produced in the late 1980s showed more definite signs of a trend toward increased mobility among Japan's work force than had been evident even a short time earlier. Some 1,900,000 people changed jobs between 1984 and 1985, up 10.6 percent from the year before (*AS*, August 25, 1985). The Ministry of Labor reported that more people in Japan changed jobs in 1987 than in any year since 1956.[20] In 1988 the number increased by another 17.4 percent over the previous year to 2.47 million job-changers.[21] And by 1990 the number of job-changers had climbed to 2.57 million or 4.2 percent of the total work force.[22] While much of this increase can be accounted for by the larger number of women in the work force and higher turnover rates among part-time employees, it was still the highest turnover rate for men in general since the oil crisis year of 1974.

The change in attitudes toward job changing and in actual turnover is even more impressive when the analysis is limited to corporate elites—the segment of the population in which lifetime employment has been most significant. Recruit Jinzai Center, which helps young Japanese executive-track employees find new jobs, placed 104 job-jumpers in 1978, its first year of business. In 1987 it filled 2,306 jobs.[23] A recent survey of Japanese managers working in large corporations found that more than 70 percent would consider changing jobs. Five years earlier, a similar survey had found that fewer than 30 percent would even consider a job change.[24]

These changes in stated attitudes appear to be legitimate indicators of actual behavior toward job changing in Japan. Broad-gauge statistics published by the Ministry of Labor show a dramatic increase in turnover rates among employees with college degrees in 1985 through 1989 over previous years (Figure 2). With the exception of the year following the first oil crisis, Japanese companies have hired about 1.4 college graduates with no work experience for every college graduate with experience. In 1985 and 1986 that number dropped to parity.

Figure 3 indicates that the largest increases in male turnover during the past decade have not been in the traditionally largest sectors of production/transport/communication workers and craftsmen. In these sectors the number of job-changers actually decreased. Rather, job changing increased most quickly in the managerial and professional sectors. During the decade of the 1980s, the number of engineers, professionals, managers, and official employees who changed jobs grew at an annual rate of more than 10 percent.[25]

Another survey by the Ministry of Labor shows that 27.4 percent of the entire work force has changed jobs at least once in their career and that that percentage climbs to more than 50 percent when the analysis is

Figure 2

College Graduate Male Experienced Hires vs
New Nonexperienced Graduate Hires, 1967–1989

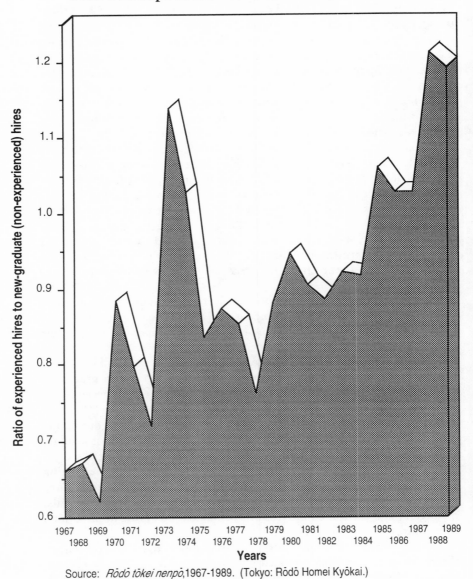

Source: *Rōdō tōkei nenpō*,1967-1989. (Tokyo: Rōdō Homei Kyōkai.)

Figure 3

Rates of Job Changing
by Occupation, 1968–1987

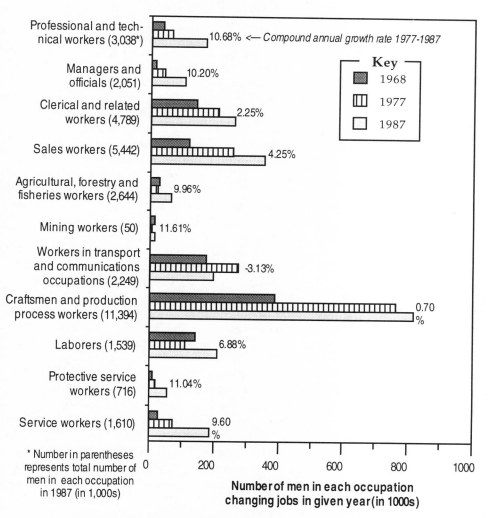

Source: Statistics Bureau, *1987 Employment Status Survey*, pp. 74 and 540 (Tokyo), and related charts in 1977 and 1968 reports.

limited to workers under age thirty (Ribeiro 1988, 28). Ministry of Labor data yield similar findings when statistics are limited to corporate elites.

At times company and government data appear to be contradictory. For instance, personnel managers at one bank informed us that only one employee had left that firm to join another company during the previous year. However, employee informants at the same bank mentioned seven or eight job-changers in the previous year—most of whom had gone to foreign companies. In Japan, the differences between company and government data may indicate bias on the part of job-changers when dealing with their companies rather than any misrepresentation of facts by the companies themselves. Companies base their information on what they are told by departing employees; those who leave the firm for reasons other than a job change are not considered job-changers. Yoshino and Lifson report that most preretirement job leavers from *sōgō shōsha*—by definition elite college graduates—"leave for personal or health reasons" (Yoshino and Lifson 1986, 137), and these are still the reasons personnel directors give for most of the job changes in their companies today. However, it is evident that more and more executive-track employees are finding "personal or health reasons" for leaving one firm to join another.

It must also be noted that even fairly recent findings showing low rates of turnover in Japan might not accurately portray present conditions and trends. To focus on corporate elites, we designed and administered a questionnaire survey to 157 college graduates in the Tokyo area in August 1988. Our survey indicated interesting changes that seem to have taken place only in the very recent past (figure 4). It showed that young people—those under forty—have changed jobs to a much greater extent than their elders. Some 37.5 percent of respondents in their twenties and 28.3 percent of respondents in their thirties had changed jobs at least once, compared to much lower percentages for forty- and fifty-year-olds. The survey revealed that most of this job changing had occurred just before the survey. Fifty-five percent of those who have ever changed jobs in their lives had done so in the past three years. More than three-fourths of the job changing had taken place within the six years before the survey. These findings suggest that surveys completed even one or two years before this may be somewhat outdated in capturing the full extent of job changing in Japan.[26]

Data from Westphal's 1991 study of trading companies seem to corroborate the notion that significant midcareer job changing and midcareer hiring are taking place. Interviews indicated that in the 1990 recruiting year, C. Itoh hired 200 university graduates, of whom 50 were midcareer job changers. Nippon Steel claimed that 125 of 575 new hires with college degrees were employed elsewhere before. And Sumitomo

Figure 4

Timing of Job Changing

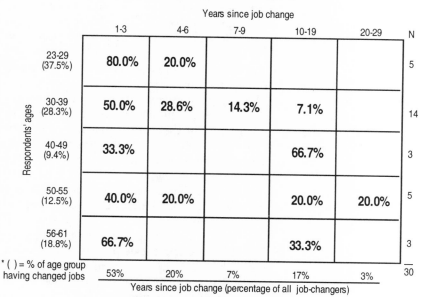

Years since job change

Respondents' ages	1-3	4-6	7-9	10-19	20-29	N
23-29 (37.5%)	80.0%	20.0%				5
30-39 (28.3%)	50.0%	28.6%	14.3%	7.1%		14
40-49 (9.4%)	33.3%			66.7%		3
50-55 (12.5%)	40.0%	20.0%		20.0%	20.0%	5
56-61 (18.8%)	66.7%			33.3%		3
* ( ) = % of age group having changed jobs	53%	20%	7%	17%	3%	30

Years since job change (percentage of all job-changers)

Source: Survey of 157 college graduates in Tokyo area, 1988.

Metals said that half of its 600 new hires were experienced workers (Westphal 1991, 63). The same study showed that 30–50 percent of *sōgō shōsha*'s subsidiary managers were midcareer recruits who brought with them necessary technical expertise to guide the trading companies' diversification moves (Westphal 1991, 49). Westphal noted that "all cases" of the midcareer job changing he described "were a phenomenon of the 1980s" (Westphal 1991, 63).

Statistics that purport to show changes in Japanese executives' actual behavior in regard to job hopping are thus hard to come by and even harder to interpret. However, there is less confusion and more evidence about change in *attitudes* toward job changing among Japan's elite employees. Registry *(tōroku)* companies, to which Japanese (in particular young people) are flocking to sign up for an opportunity to change jobs to a good company, have been extremely successful in recent years. Both attitudes and behaviors toward scouts and headhunters also seem to be changing. One headhunter said that when he approached Japanese corporate elites about the possibility of a job change in the late 1970s, they showed very little interest, and only about fifteen or twenty executives per year inquired at his company about the possibility of changing companies. In 1987 this man's office handled more than two hundred inquiries from Japanese executives about the likelihood of being able to change jobs.[27] Another headhunter said that in 1987 about four or five of every ten executives approached indicated interest in changing companies. This was a far cry from the almost negligible interest shown by salarymen in the late 1970s.[28]

The increased contact that headhunters have with corporate elites and the number of articles about headhunting and job mobility appearing in the Japanese media have led many Japanese executives to be more amenable to the idea of changing jobs. A recent survey showed that one of every three executive-track engineers in the Tokyo area has been contacted by headhunters (*BT*, May 1987, 40). Another survey showed that 21 percent of a randomly selected sample of section managers had been approached by headhunters. The word "headhunter," while a moniker that executive search firms try to avoid, has been part of business jargon in Japan since the mid-1980s. In 1987, fully 79 percent of the *kachō*-level employees who had been approached by a scout or headhunter had immediately rejected these advances. When asked about the future, however, only 47 percent of the total sample said they would rebuff a similar inquiry (*AS*, October 9, 1987). The results of another survey of forty- to forty-five-year-old managers by the Hitotsubashi University Personnel Management Research Division yielded the results in table 2. More than 40 percent of Japanese who listed themselves as "satisfied" with their jobs reported that they would at least consider a job change, while fully three-

Table 2
Would you listen to what a headhunter had to say?

	Percentage
People who are working hard and satisfied with their present jobs:	
Would enthusiastically listen to what the headhunter had to say	5.4
Would listen if the conditions sounded right for me	36.8
Would listen, but would not consider a job change	46.6
Would not listen	11.2
People who are not very passionate about their present jobs:	
Would enthusiastically listen to what the headhunter had to say	25.0
Would listen if the conditions sounded right for me	50.0
Would listen, but would not consider a job change	12.5
Would not listen	12.5

Source: Tanaka Yoshihiro and Itō Momoko, Tenshoku jidai—Ima ya "Issha kenmei" [Isshōkenmei] wa owatta, *Shūkan Tōyō Keizai*, July 27, 1987, pp. 4–17.

fourths of those who were not "very passionate" about their jobs said they would consider a headhunter's proposition.

Other statistics show that the expression of these attitudes toward job changing is not merely the casually liberal response of survey respondents considering a hypothetical situation. If that were true, surveys on attitudes toward job changing would not change significantly over time. However, statistics do show a definite change in Japanese attitudes toward job hopping in the recent past. As might be expected, this attitudinal change seems to have begun somewhat earlier than the behavior that manifests it. As mentioned earlier, a 1981 survey of Japanese managers in one "large corporation" revealed that roughly 30 percent would "consider a job change": five years later, a similar survey found that more than 70 percent of the respondents would do so.[29] A broader survey of white-collar workers in eleven large companies in 1985 showed that 38.9 percent of the workers asked would change jobs "to any company if the money and position were right." Another 25.7 percent were more finicky, saying that they would change jobs, but they would "decide based on the specific job offer" (Takita 1987, 346).

Besides asking direct questions, another way of understanding the attitudes of Japanese executives toward lifetime employment is to inquire how they would advise a colleague concerning a job change. In 1985, Recruit Research asked respondents how they would react if a friend expressed interest in changing jobs. Fourteen percent said that they would definitely encourage their friend to leave his present company for another opportunity. The other 86 percent said that they would suggest that their friend try changing jobs, but only if the conditions were right. Not one of the respondents felt that a friend should definitely *not* consider changing jobs (*AS*, March 20, 1985). Although job changing is still considered risky by most Japanese salarymen, attitudes in Japan seem to have evolved to the point where job changing is no longer considered a universally inappropriate behavior. One observer of Japanese job changing behavior described the way most Japanese seem to feel about changing jobs: "It is a racy, thrilling, but nasty thing to do."[30]

THE SHINJINRUI GENERATION

Shinjinrui is a term modern Japanese use to describe a new, young cohort of their population. The term means "new human race," and it accurately conveys the vast difference older Japanese perceive between themselves and their juniors. Whether one is looking at behavior or attitudes, the younger generation of Japanese elites have been the most likely to change jobs since the mid-1980s. Figure 4 showed that almost 35 percent of surveyed employees in their twenties and thirties had already changed jobs. An earlier survey by *Asahi Shinbun* showed that 30 percent of those up to

thirty years of age had changed jobs; and 30 percent of those had
changed jobs more than once (*AS*, July 28, 1986). A 1986 survey of Japanese adolescents (aged ten to nineteen) showed that 47 percent preferred
an "employment changing job environment to a single lifetime employer"
(Wysocki 1986). When new recruits were surveyed at the time of their
nyūshashiki (celebration of joining a company), 60 percent thought that
they might "job hop" sometime in their careers (Kanabayashi 1988). Age
appears to have a significant impact on two measures of employment stability. Figures 5 and 6 show the percentage of respondents who have
claimed to be considering job changes and those exhibiting various levels
of organizational commitment. It is significant that in the former, in no
age group does the percentage of respondents thinking about quitting
their present job drop below 20 percent. It is even more important that
the twenty-year-olds exhibit such a high propensity for considering job
changes. This discontinuity with other age groups[31] is partly due to the
fact, discussed in chapter 2, that since World War II job changing in
Japan traditionally took place (if it happened at all) before the employee's
twenty-fifth birthday. For most of the postwar period, employees were

Figure 5

Consideration of Job Hopping by Age

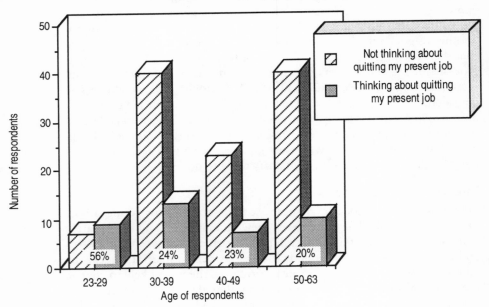

Source: Job Changing Survey, 1988.

Figure 6

Levels of Organizational Commitment by Age

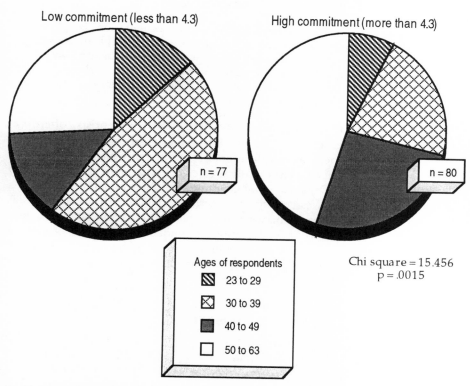

Low commitment (less than 4.3)

High commitment (more than 4.3)

n = 77

n = 80

Ages of respondents

- 23 to 29
- 30 to 39
- 40 to 49
- 50 to 63

Chi square = 15.456
p = .0015

Source: Job Changing Survey, 1988.

considered, like Christmas cakes, no good after the twenty-fifth. (More recently the age limit on changing jobs has been rolled back from age twenty-five to age thirty to coincide with the age at which a man is expected to get married and settle down.) Considering this social context and the impact social obligations play in the individual Japanese executive's decision about changing jobs, it is not surprising that the number of people even considering job changing drops off precipitously after the thirtieth birthday. Nevertheless, the change in attitudes of younger workers in today's Japan cannot be completely explained by the "Christmas cake effect." Masahiro Miki, a marketing and public relations official at Texas Instruments Japan, summed up the responses we heard from most informants about the attitude of the *shinjinrui* toward job hopping. "My friends and I don't think of it in the same way our parents did. It used to be that people would look down on you if you changed jobs" (*LAT,* July 9, 1988). Mizobuchi, chief of Recruit Jinzai Center, elaborated further on this theme of intergenerational differences:

> Changing jobs used to have a very negative connotation. People who changed jobs were regarded as dropouts or seemed unable to cooperate with others, or sometimes people thought [the job changer] was not patient enough to stick with one company. . . . That's changing because of the American influence. Younger people have begun to think it's not too bad. (*LAT,* July 9, 1988)

A variable that, according to Western turnover theorists, often precedes conscious consideration of a job change is an employee's organizational commitment. If organizational commitment wanes, the probability of a job change is purportedly greater. This variable, as measured by the fifteen-item Organizational Commitment Questionnaire (OCQ), is a standard term in Western turnover literature. Figure 6 shows that there is a significant difference between the organizational commitment exhibited by older and younger Japanese respondents. Almost 60 percent of those with low organizational commitment are under forty, while more than 71 percent of those with high organizational commitment are over forty years of age.

Summary

This chapter has considered the recently emerging body of evidence that supports the notion that Japan's employment system is in transition. Behavioral changes in the country's elite executive corps have been increasingly noted in the Japanese press and popular literature. This anecdotal evidence may be indicative of actual changes that have been masked by reporting bias from companies and individuals who find themselves involved in job changing. While such biases make behavioral changes difficult to trace, there is no doubt that recent years have seen a pronounced change in attitudes toward job hopping, especially among younger Japanese workers. Finally, responses to increasing demographic pressures and demand for new talent has led many of Japan's corporations to adopt unprecedented measures for moving superfluous employees out of their firms.

All of these factors indicate a growing Japanese awareness, whether implicit or explicit, that the lifetime employment system is under pressure. The inclination for individuals and companies in Japan to accept or even encourage job hopping appears to be growing with the aging of the work force and the demands of internationalization. In other words, it is becoming increasingly less difficult to establish that Japan's lifetime employment system might be undergoing significant changes. The following chapter considers some of the macroeconomic reasons why labor mobility among the executive classes in Japan is much more prevalent in the late 1980s than it was in the two decades before.

CHAPTER FIVE

The Rise in Elite Job Mobility

THE INCREASING success and extent of midcareer recruiting in Japan would not exist if this departure from traditional societal norms did not carry with it some fairly powerful advantages. We believe that the advantages of higher job mobility in the elite Japanese work force are becoming more compelling as Japan's economy undergoes broad environmental pressures that are altering the nature of the nation's business organizations. Among such contingencies are the rapidly aging population of Japan, lower economic growth rates, the related need to move out of stagnant markets into new high growth markets, and Japan's deregulation of domestic industries in an attempt to better integrate into the international marketplace. This chapter briefly describes these factors and discusses some of the implications they seem to be having on the lifetime employment system.

Aging

Since the beginning of World War II, the population of Japan has undergone some of the most dramatic demographic shifts ever experienced by any society. War-caused deaths (which were more numerous among Japanese men than other groups), the postwar "baby boom" and current "baby bust," and the impressive increase in the average Japanese life span all combine to mean that the number of male employees moving through Japan's corporate world has been far from constant. At present, the demographic trend that looms most ominously on the horizon for Japanese society and economic organizations is the tremendous increase in the proportion of elderly. The general aging of the work force is already exacerbating the discontents some younger and middle-aged Japanese salarymen feel in their lifetime career paths. Predictions for future trends in Japan's population would lead one to expect these problems to grow rather than diminish in the years ahead.

The effects engendered by Japan's aging population had not been significantly tested in 1982, when Linda Martin wrote her article in the *Population Research and Policy Report*.[1] At that time the percentage of Japanese over age sixty-five was just over 9 percent. Today that percentage has climbed to 11 percent, and it is expected to top 15 percent by the year 2000 (Statistics Bureau 1983, 25). When Martin published her article, Japan still had a relatively low percentage of elderly compared to the United States and West Germany (with 11.9 percent and 15 percent respectively). All developed nations are facing an increase in the percentage of elderly. The difference between Western countries and Japan is the precipitous climb that Japan will take to become the nation with the oldest population among all industrialized nations by 2025.[2] The share of Japan's elderly population is expected to double from 7 percent to 14 percent in just 26 years. In the United States this doubling is expected to take 70 years, while in France it will take 130 years. This fact led the International Monetary Fund to conclude that "the impact of the demographic change on the Japanese economy is likely to be the most extreme among the Group of Seven" (quoted in Jones 1987).

The cause of Japan's rapidly aging population is a combination of high longevity rates and a decrease in the birth rate. In 1947 the average life expectancy was only fifty years for men and fifty-four for women (Jones 1987). By 1986 Japan had surpassed Sweden and Norway in terms of the longevity of its population, and the Japanese boasted the longest average life expectancy in the world. Japanese men born in that year were expected to live 75.2 years, and women 80.93 years.[3] The increase in the percentage of elderly forecast by this increased life span is augmented by the fact that fewer Japanese babies are being born each year than ever before in the country's history. In 1985, the birth rate fell to 11.9 births per 1,000 persons.

> The drop is attributed to the smaller number of women in their 20s, the prime child-bearing age group, as well as a decline in the fertility rate (the average number of births per woman in her lifetime) from 3.65 in 1950 to 1.8 in 1983. Since this is below the 2.1 rate necessary for a stable population, the Health and Welfare Ministry expects the population to begin declining in the year 2013 after hitting a peak of 136.25 million. (Jones 1987)

The demographic problems created by high longevity and a low birth rate are even further complicated by a postwar baby boom. Between 1947 and 1950 almost 10.5 million children were born. That figure equaled almost 14 percent of the 1946 population (Statistics Bureau

1986, 24). This baby boom began creating special problems for employers in the late 1980s. Most of these problems had not even begun to surface when Martin wrote her article in the early 1980s. In Japan's seniority system, employees have traditionally expected to be promoted constantly until the retirement years. In the four decades following World War II such expectations posed no problem. The high number of male deaths in the war and low number of births during the war meant that almost all executive-track employees in a firm were able to assume leadership positions over the large number of employees who were born just after the war and who started joining companies in the mid-1960s. Now the baby-boomers are reaching the age when they expect to gain titles of *kachō* and *buchō,* but there aren't enough junior employees for them to supervise. Employers are thus being forced to limit the number of management positions they can make available to their older workers (see chapter 6).

The government, too, is worried by the number of older people in the population. In prewar Japan, families traditionally assumed the burden of caring for their elderly parents and grandparents. In 1953, 81 percent of those over sixty-five years of age lived with their children (Vogel 1979, 196). By 1970 this percentage had dropped only slightly, to 77 percent. But during the following decade, a decrease to 69 percent suggested important changes in Japanese society (*Economist,* May 1983, 95). A recent poll by the Prime Minister's Office in Japan showed that only 56 percent of the total population feels that old parents should live with their children. It is significant that the percentage drops below 50 percent for respondents under forty years of age (table 3).

During the 1960s, a growing array of social safety nets were put into place to help ease the strain of Japan's aging population. Many influential Japanese publicized the notion that too much emphasis had been placed on

> the amount of return from investment. Expenditures for social welfare, which do not produce material benefits and are not directly connected with increasing production capacity, are made reluctantly. This has been the traditional course always followed by Japan. To overcome the lack of concern and awareness implicit in the traditional course is the only hope of building a society to be proud of. (Fukutake 1974, 156)

In accordance with this philosophy, during the 1970s the benefits of social programs instituted in the 1960s, particularly pensions programs, were "ratcheted upwards." By 1983 Japanese pensioners were receiving 60 percent of their base salary after thirty years of contributing to the plan. This figure appears to be comparable to or perhaps even higher than the average American or Western European percentage, until the

Table 3
Where do you want to live when you get older?
(answers in percentage)

	With My Children	By Myself	Not Sure
Total	56	21	23
By population			
11 biggest cities	40	30	30
Population > 1 million	52	23	25
Population < 1 million	65	18	17
Rural area	66	14	20
By sex			
Men	61	16	23
Women	51	25	24
By age			
20–29 years old	49	21	30
30–39 years old	45	28	27
40–49 years old	53	22	25
50–59 years old	62	18	20
60–69 years old	66	19	15
70+ years old	73	9	18

Source: Prime Minister's Office, *Seron Chōsa*, May 1983, p. 20.

Japanese semiannual bonuses are taken into account. Bonuses included, the pension drops to 44.2 percent of salary, which corresponds "roughly to the levels in the US and Western Europe" during the same period (Thayer 1969, 50). Even though the levels of social security benefits have been similar, a comparison of social security expenditures to gross domestic product (GDP) or per capita governmental expenditure shows Japan to have been less a "welfare state" than any of its Western counterparts (figure 7). The reason for this seeming discrepancy is readily evident.

In the early 1980s the population of Japan was still relatively young. Figure 8 exhibits one of the reasons why Japanese government expenditures increased while expenditures of the other Western "welfare states" (with the exception of Sweden) have leveled off.

An article in the *Far Eastern Economic Review* in April 1983 noted some alarming statistics and quoted government and business leaders who found the numbers worrisome. In 1983 the insured-to-beneficiary ratio in Japan was about 15 percent (compared to 30 percent in West Germany, France, and Switzerland). That ratio is expected to rise to 25 percent by 2000, to 37 percent by 2015. Tadaharu Matsukawa of the

Figure 7

Social Expenditures by Country

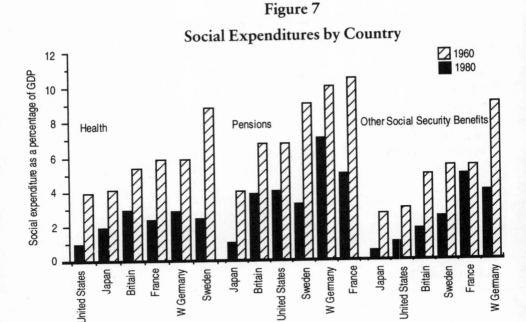

Source: OECD, as quoted in "The Aging of Japanese Social Security" in *The Economist*,
May 14, 1983.

Health and Welfare Ministry concluded that "we cannot pay the amount
we are now paying. We should decrease the amount of pension or we will
become like other countries (in the West)." If the present trend continues,
"working people in the year 2000 may be forced to pay 30–40% of their
salaries to keep the system solvent." This worries business leaders like
Kazuo Tange, an official of Nikkeiren: "If this situation arises, a company's competitive power will slacken and the Japanese economy will be
damaged. In order to cope with the problem the amount of pensions
should be controlled." Noriyuki Takayama, associate professor at Hitotsubashi University, concludes that unless some action is taken,

> at the turn of the century, when the baby-boom generation begins to
> retire, our present system could become bankrupt. Intergenerational
> wars might arise, along with labour disincentives and an underground
> economy. The high level of social security benefits will cause pension
> fascism. (*FEER*, April 1983, 51)

It is little wonder, then, that the government is encouraging companies
to push back the mandatory retirement age in firms from the traditional
age of fifty-five to sixty or sixty-five. To facilitate such moves on the

Figure 8

Aging in Industrialized Countries, 1900–2025

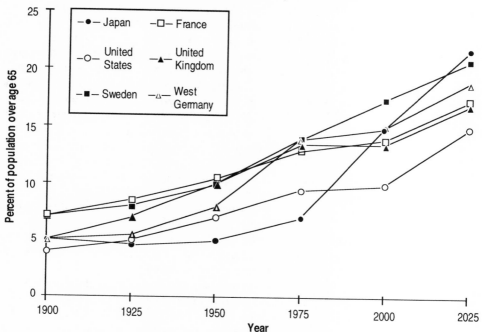

Source: Economic Planning Agency, *Japan and the Year 2000* (Tokyo: Japan Times, 1983)

parts of employers and to gain employee support for such systems, the National Pension Plan's payment schedule has been revised to begin only after an employee reaches his or her sixty-fifth birthday.[4]

While the aging problem is one understood by almost all Japanese, it has not yet impinged on most of their lives. In fact, according to a January 4, 1987 report in the *Asahi Shinbun,* only 16 percent of personnel directors surveyed in 1987 responded that they felt the aging of the population was a problem in their company at that time. Another 60 percent, however, responded that they expected the rise in the number of Japanese elderly to become a problem. It is premature to rule out the negative effects that an aging society will have on Japan's employment system simply because those effects have not yet become obvious. The coming decade, which will see the baby-boomers pass through their final years of corporate life and approach retirement, should bring the influences of Japan's changing demographic structure into glaring prominence. Already in companies across Japan the effects of the change are becoming more evident, as personnel planners develop programs to deal with the effects of a rapidly aging employee base.

The complaint of a personnel planner in a large *sōgō shōsha* expressed the dilemma of his counterparts in other industries: "Our organization is no longer shaped like a pyramid, it's a diamond. Middle management and above rankings now account for 46 percent of our managerial and staff members, and we fully expect it to reach 50 percent" (Yoshino and Lifson 1986, 153). Figure 9 shows the age structure of one large company in Japan. The problem with this kind of organizational structure in the context of the Japanese employment system is that employees have made tremendous wage and effort sacrifices during their younger years in anticipation of managerial position and high salaries later in life. During the growth years of Japan's economy every employee knew that he would rise through the ranks at least to the *kachō* level. This promotion brought with it considerable social prestige and an entertainment expense account that all lower employees would envy.

The extent of cutbacks in hiring following the first oil shock is evident in figure 9. These cutbacks, coupled with the huge bulge of baby-boomers pushing through the middle management ranks of organizations, mean that there are simply not enough lower-level employees for each of the older employees to be made a manager. Most company leaders agree, whether they admit this publicly or not, that the only way to turn the corporate age-structure diamonds back into pyramids is to take some off the top and add more to the bottom of the age-structure. The president of Nippon Steel, one of the largest firms in Japan, was quoted as saying that he would like to terminate four thousand people at the top of the company and hire three thousand others at lower levels in the organization (Brender 1986, 26).

The belief that midcareer recruiting is part of this corporate response to an aging population is borne out by the fact that such recruiting is directed mainly at younger workers. Removing older employees from the top half of an organization brings the shape of the age distribution closer to the ideal pyramid. If removing older employees from the enterprise is supplemented by adding workers at the lower levels, the age-distribution shape more quickly begins to resemble a pyramid. The system of midcareer recruiting in Japan, then, is focused almost exclusively on employees in their twenties or thiries. Some job advertisements reach into the young forties, but midcareer recruiting is almost never targeted at anyone over forty-five.

Although midcareer recruiting is one response to the problem of Japan's aging work force, readjusting the age structure of a company in Japan is not as simple as merely hiring young workers and firing old ones. Japanese companies do feel a sense of obligation to their employees

Figure 9

Age Structure of Major Trading Company in Japan

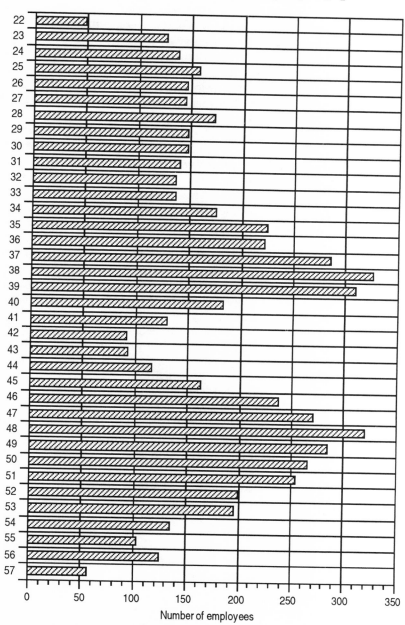

Source: Internal Company Records

—especially older employees. After years of preaching that these people should be loyal to the company, most large companies that have been part of the lifetime employment system try to come up with some kind of senior post to which they can promote their workers. In many cases they can fulfill their obligations by offering these employees jobs as project team leaders or specialists. If they cannot create some kind of position within the company for their employees, they may spend considerable time and effort in trying to help those employees relocate outside the company.

Some of the increased diversification that has been taking place in Japanese firms has been a response to the need for firms to create promotion opportunities for middle-aged employees who expect to move up. Nippon Steel has explicitly set up "new ventures for its thousands of redundant workers" (Wysocki 1986). These new businesses include a security-guard company and a futon-cleaning service. Hitachi Heavy Industries, which was a premier shipbuilding company a little over a decade ago, is closing down its shipbuilding operations. Now some of the shipyard buildings are used for other businesses such as fish farming. Mamoru Murakami, age fifty-one, worked for many years as a marine architect for Hitachi. Now, as the president of a four-member fish-farming operation, Murakami raises flounder for market. He supervises ten ponds, each eighteen feet in diameter, each holding some thirty-six hundred flounder (Wysocki, 1986). According to Murakami, "My wife complains that I spend all my time studying fish. But the ship industry is in such a state, while fisheries have some kind of future. So I took the job even though it wasn't what I wanted" (Wysocki 1986).

Some employees of Hitachi take a more pessimistic view of the companies that are spun off to employ older workers. Yukiharu Miyaji, a forty-two-year-old executive, declared: "Hitachi set up those small companies merely to keep people employed. After three or four years they will probably go bankrupt, and if I am out of a job at that age it will be that much harder to be hired."

At present, Japanese companies have little comfort to offer in response to such apprehensions. Firms established in the demographic situation of the early postwar era, when the Japanese male population itself formed a tidy "age pyramid," are not structurally adapted to satisfying the expectations of a very different population. The very makeup of Japan's population is forcing those firms to deal with difficulties in the lifetime employment system that have only recently come to seem like pressing issues. It remains to be seen what strategies will finally emerge to confront this dilemma. In the meantime, an aging population is not the only stumbling block cluttering the smooth road of lifetime employment in Japan.

Slower Growth

The abundance of corporate positions open to the relatively small pool of employees available for hire at the beginning of Japan's reconstruction was augmented by the tremendously high growth rates of Japanese firms throughout the first decades of the postwar era. Under these conditions of intensive demand for labor, lifetime employment was a satisfying and workable strategy for corporations and employees alike. In the past several years, however, the breakneck speed of Japan's economic growth has slowed. The advantages of permanent hiring have become correspondingly smaller for many of the country's businesses. Slowed growth, as well as an aging work force, is increasing the pressure on Japanese firms to modify the traditional lifetime employment system.

During the period from 1955 to 1970 (the Japanese "economic renaissance") annual economic growth rates in Japan averaged more than 10 percent. Domestically, economic growth was fueled by a society eager to rebuild following the war. During the war 4.2 million homes had been destroyed, leaving only 16.4 million homes intact in 1950 (Fukutake 1974, 130). The years that followed have been characterized as a period of "my-home-ism" *(mai hōmu shugi)* in Japan. Nationalistic pride in the nation's military unity and ascetic self-sacrifice gradually shifted to a greater emphasis on possessing creature comforts—particularly a home. Six hundred thousand housing units were built in 1960; in 1973 this number had climbed to 1.35 million. By 1980 more than 34 million homes existed in Japan (Statistics Bureau 1986, 47).

Once people had homes, they became interested in finding things to put inside them. In the early 1960s Japanese sought the "three sacred treasures"—a refrigerator, a washing machine, and a vacuum cleaner (Fukutake 1974, 40). When these treasures were obtained, attention turned to the 3 Cs (car, color TV, and cooler [air conditioner]) and later to the 3 Ds (dish washer, [garbage] disposal, and [clothes] drier). This internal consumer market, combined with a developing export policy, drove the high growth of the postwar era.

The oversupply of labor that had existed in Japan immediately following defeat in World War II was quickly absorbed by companies growing at tremendous rates. So intense was the rate of hiring in the 1960s that the labor surplus was replaced by shortage during the late 1960s and early 1970s. Companies, particularly manufacturers, continually added capacity to meet the demands of a consuming public that was entranced with gaining the good things of life. The trading companies were the favorite employers for elite college graduates during this period. As Yoshino and Lifson describe it:

During each of the high-growth years, every sogo shosha aggressively recruited a large number of new graduates. The leading five sogo shosha together hired 799 young men as management trainees in 1968, and between 1970 and 1974 the five companies took on over a thousand college graduates each year. In 1971, the peak year, the number reached 1,400. (Yoshino and Lifson 1986, 247)

Following the 1974 OPEC oil embargo, however, hiring dropped off sharply in the *sōgō shōsha* as it did in other sectors of the economy. As a result of the oil shock, Japanese growth figures, which had been galloping along at an annual rate of 12.2 percent during the years from 1966 and 1970, slowed to a mere 5.1 percent during the 1971 to 1975 period (Kosai 1986, 4). Following that period Japanese gross national product (GNP) growth never climbed much over 5 percent per year, and in the 1980s it hovered around 4 percent annually (Lincoln 1988, 39). The aggregate sales of nine *sōgō shōsha* remained flat between 1976 and 1979. Although sales did rebound in 1980 and increased 30 percent between 1980 and 1983, "profit levels remained virtually unchanged" (Yoshino and Lifson 1986, 247).

During the periods of high growth, university and high school graduates alike were able to find jobs with Japan's top companies (generally, those listed on the first section of the Tokyo Stock Exchange.) By 1983 only 27.5 percent of the estimated 229,000 university students seeking jobs after graduation were able to find jobs in any of the 1,743 companies listed on the Tokyo, Osaka, or other stock exchanges in Japan.

It was not just that companies had reduced their hiring in the period of slower growth. Because of the demographic changes described above, employers were eager to slough off some of the older employees in their firms. A personnel manager at Nissan explained that during the period of high growth the seniority system was "rational, since companies could hire many young workers and pay them lower wages. As the average age of their work forces increased, however, companies [had] to pay all these older employees higher wages" (*FEER*, December 1983, 50).

Slower economic growth and the competition from developing countries meant that Japan's steel and shipbuilding industries were forced to consider layoffs and other forms of rationalizing their human resource structures (see chapter 6). In the summer of 1987, spokesmen for the five largest firms in the steel industry reported that by 1991, 44,000 permanent employees were expected to be cut from their combined forces of 150,000 workers (*Maclean's*, June 8, 1987, 42). Other firms tried innovative ways to reduce their work force without actually laying off employees. Nippon Steel announced a "rotational" system whereby 6.5 percent of employees (both blue- and white-collar) "will be laid off for several days before returning to work. While on furlough, they will get

70% of their normal pay, paid partly by the government. In effect, they will take a 30% pay cut for about a week. Then a new group will go on furlough" (Wysocki 1986). Companies who resorted to layoffs were roundly criticized for the decision to dismiss workers. In one instance, a city councilman in Inoshima (pop. 37,000) berated a Hitachi Shipbuilding representative for the company's "lack of social responsibility" in a decision to suspend a thousand of its twelve hundred employees in that town. The manager responded "that things had reached the point at which 'keeping the company running is our No. 1 social responsibility' " (Wysocki 1986). It is important to note that while heavy industries were the most likely to announce layoffs, the "rust bowl" industries were not alone in having to deal with employees made redundant by slower growth. A Sanwa Research Institute study found that there were as many as nine hundred thousand unnecessary employees in the electronics industry alone (Ribeiro 1988, 27).

The Hitachi manager's comment that the survival of his enterprise supersedes the company's responsibility to maintain workers permanently is a sign of the new position lifetime employment occupies in an environment of slower economic growth. When the present system of permanent employment was instigated, high growth rates made the survival of companies and the long-term retention of workers compatible if not synonymous. In the past few years, however, more and more companies have been finding these two goals increasingly at odds. Slower growth and the aging of Japan's work force are two of the forces that have brought about this change.

Diversification

A third cause for the decline in commitment to permanent employment is the increasing emphasis of many of Japan's corporations on diversification. Among the top ten companies in the first section of the Tokyo Stock Exchange in 1979, almost 87 percent of the revenues came from their main business. In 1986, this figure had dropped to 80 percent, with the other 20 percent of revenue coming from related businesses. If the revenues of the parent company are combined with subsidiary revenues, the percentage of revenues accounted for by main business interests drops to 60 percent (AS, February 2, 1988).

We have mentioned the diversification efforts of some companies that are trying to make room at the top for aging salarymen on an increasingly crowded corporate career ladder. Slower growth has also led many firms to diversify in an effort to keep growth rates high. Another reason for diversification is the emergence of new technologies associated with established industries. Undertaking such new technologies requires more

than simply removing current lifetime employees into new branches of
the firm. Technologically driven diversification often requires hiring new
employees with skills in new areas of production.

Much of the "new-skill" hiring driven by attempts to diversify has
taken place in industries or segments requiring "ABC *jinzai*" (ABC
human resources): "A" for artificial intelligence, "B" for biology and
banking, and "C" for computers and communications (Tanaka and Ito
1987, 4–17). The need for midcareer hiring seems most pressing in companies diversifying into areas requiring these kinds of specialists. For
example, Nissan's entry into automotive electronics was a "related"
diversification, based less on a lack of profitability in the base business
than on the assumption that the electronic content of automobiles will
increase tremendously over the coming years.[5] The company's decision
to enter the automotive electronic business, rather than leaving the development and production of electronic parts to its subsidiary firms, com-
pelled them to announce in January of 1988 that the firm was planning
to hire more than three hundred midcareer employees during the following three years. By June of 1988, more than five hundred people had
applied for the jobs offered. Forty of these applicants were offered jobs
during the first six months of recruiting (Koyama 1988, 8–9).

Some diversified offshoots of parent companies try to draw much of
their necessary talent from other divisions within the parent company.
Mitsubishi Corporation's Communications Services Division attempted
to use this approach when the division was formed in 1986. Twenty-five
of the thirty-one original employees in the group came from the Aero-
space and Computer Equipment divisions. Still, six employees had to be
hired from the outside to bring necessary skills not extant within the
company. Those employees came from such big-name firms as Toshiba,
Kawasaki Heavy, and three Mitsubishi group firms—Mitsubishi Electric, Mitsubishi Petrochemical, and Mitsubishi Research Institute.[6]

Japanese companies increasingly found themselves needing to develop
new products, diversify, and internationalize (figure 10). Firms that
stressed diversification and product development were likely to place relatively little emphasis on finding "loyal" employees (figure 11). It seems
probable that the necessity of hiring specialists (often in midcareer) to
manage the production of new technologies works against the traditional
norms of absolute corporate fidelity that underlie the lifetime employment system. Of course, other business conditions besides the emergence
of new technologies may also serve to encourage diversification and midcareer hiring. Some Japanese companies are recruiting their employees in
midcareer because of poorly performing base businesses and a desire to
diversify into areas in which there is little or no skill currently available in
the company. Mitsui Metals had to hire thirty-three midcareer employees

Figure 10

Importance of Past and Future Key Strategies
in Japanese Corporations

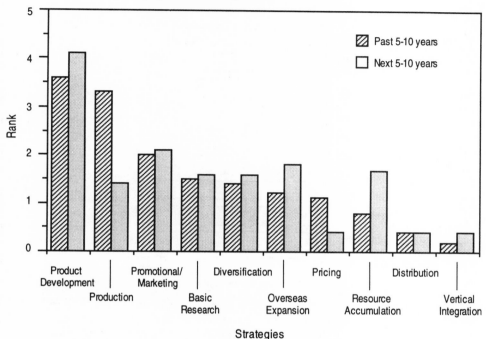

Source: Monitor Company reports, 1989.

in 1986, after the strong yen forced them to close some of their mines abroad. A diversification plan at the firm necessarily included midcareer hiring as a way to bring new talent into the company (Esaka 1988, 169).

One of the best examples of a company in Japan undertaking a strategy of diversification is Nippon Steel, whose desire to cut three thousand people from the top of the firm and add four thousand more at the bottom of the firm we have already mentioned. This need for restructuring the company was largely motivated by a need to diversify into new areas. Through the early 1980s Nippon Steel was renowned as one of the great companies in the world. When it came to producers of steel and steel-related products, the company was unsurpassed, claiming world dominance over companies like US Steel. Today the story is quite different. As Atsuhiko Tateuchi of Drake Beam Morin–Japan (an outplacement consulting firm) put it:

Figure 11

Emphasis on "Loyalty" in Companies with a Variety of Corporate Strategies

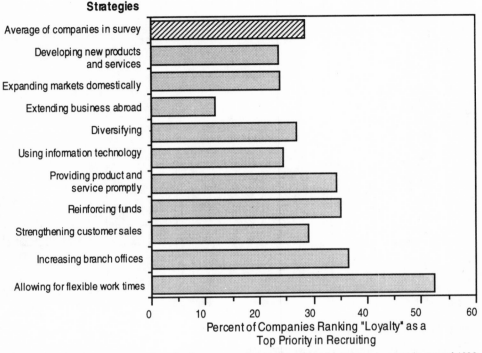

Source: Ministry of Labor, Survey of trends of management strategy and its effect on employment (survey of 4000 Japanese service firms), *Rōdō Tōkei Nenpō*, 1985, p. 53. (Tokyo: Rōdō Hōmei Kyōkai)

Because of competition from Korea and elsewhere, the steel industry is no good. Now Nippon Steel has to do something—perhaps go into the plastics area or the ceramics area. But they don't have engineers in ceramics and plastics—not old engineering people. The time is quite different. (Brender 1986, 26)

The February 1988 *Japan Economic Journal* reported that "Nippon Steel hopes to give greater momentum to its planned expansion of non-steel sectors"—areas like electronics, biotechnology, and new materials (19). The problem with expansion into these new areas is that it involves hiring engineers with these skills. The company estimated that thirty midcareer personnel would have to be hired in addition to forty or fifty college graduates with skills in areas not traditionally associated with steel companies.

The large trading firms are also significantly involved in diversification in the Japanese market. As of 1990 Sumitomo Corporation, for instance, had approximately two hundred subsidiaries. It plans to increase that number by more than one hundred during the decade of the 1990s, each subsidiary with a capitalization of about $2 million (Westphal 1991, 51). Table 4 shows a list of other large Japanese firms and their diversification plans for the 1990s. For all of these new subsidiaries specialists will need to be trained or hired. "If the new company does not have sufficient human resources in chemical areas, which is generally the case as it is a typically young company, outside personnel will be hired away from other companies" (Westphal 1991, 49).

To compete, perhaps even to survive, in an ever-expanding global market, Japanese firms are feeling both technological and economic pressures to diversify. Ironically, while some companies have used diversification as one way to cope with an aging work force and slower growth without defying the social norms of lifetime employment, many have dis-

Table 4
Selected Japanese diversification activities

Company	Activity
Asahi Chemical	25 percent of revenues from new businesses in construction materials
Fuji Heavy Industries (Subaru automobiles)	Aerospace components
Japan Airlines	50 percent of revenues from restaurants and clothing by 1992
Kawasaki Heavy Industries (shipbuilding/machinery)	50 percent of revenues from nonsteel by 1995; semiconductors and biotechnology
Kobe Steel	50 percent of revenues from nonsteel by 1995; semiconductors and microprocessors
Kubota (machinery/pipe)	$158.1-million investment in eight biotech and electronic ventures
Matsushita	Entry into movie production through $8 billion acquisition of MCA
Mitsubishi Chemicals	Biotechnology and electronics; $200 million acquisition of U.S. software firm
Toray (textiles/fibers)	50 percent of revenues from chemicals, housing, and other nontextiles
Toyota	Recent entry into telecommunications, satellites, and prefabricated houses

Source: J. W. Westphal, Modern change in the Japanese corporation (Master's thesis, University of Virginia, 1991).

covered that diversification itself requires the hiring of new, highly skilled employees, often in midcareer: an apparent solution has turned out to be one of the problems facing permanent employment. Internal competition itself has been the cause for at least some midcareer hiring in Japan. In 1991 (in the midst of a recession), Japan Broadcasting Corporation (NHK) made its first midcareer offers in the network's history. When the company announced that twenty midcareer hires were being sought, they received more than two thousand applications. Most applications came from employees in the industry, but in addition there were doctors, advertising agents, securities dealers, newspaper reporters, and "even a Buddhist priest"—all looking for a career change. The company claims that "the rapidly changing world of multi-channel and multi-media broadcasting" was responsible for the need to hire midcareer (*Understanding Japan,* June 1992, 3).

The competition for workers has also been a reason for at least some midcareer hiring. The famed labor shortage in Japan has caused some companies to diverge from their more traditional hiring patterns. In 1992, for instance, Toyota's business plan called for hiring some nineteen hundred high school graduates but the company could not attract enough applicants, so hired only seventeen hundred graduates. The shortage of such workers was further illustrated by the fact that of the workers hired in 1990, almost one in four quit the job and joined another company within two years. Sixty-five percent of these job-changers claimed that the job with Toyota was just "too hard" (*Understanding Japan,* June 1992, 3).

The labor shortage has been a phenomenon among blue-collar work-ers; it has certainly not been the cause of much midcareer mobility among the corporate elite. In fact, recruiting prospects for 1993 college graduates appears grim. The economic downturn and consequential lack of hiring in the securities industry are part of the reason for less reliance on college graduates in corporations in Japan. But the attitudes of these new graduates toward work is also scaring away companies that would have never thought of midcareer hiring only a few years ago. As one computer software company recruiter put it in an April 24, 1992, article in *Shūkan Asahi,*

> We won't go out of our way to recruit only new graduates. If we hire below-standard students just for the sake of meeting a quota, we will end up paying the price later. Last year's new employees were really troublesome. It's better to hire someone in mid-term because he knows what he wants and he has been trained. (Trans. in *Japan Times Weekly,* April 27–May 3, 1992, 22)

One reason Japanese firms are giving in to the demands to hire midca-reer is that they are undergoing increasing pressure to compete on a worldwide stage. Despite the importance of demographic, internal economic, and technological pressures, internationalization appears to have had the most powerful effect on attitudes and behaviors surrounding the lifetime employment system.

Internationalization

In July 1988 the *Los Angeles Times* described changes in the Japanese employment system as being fundamentally caused by the internationalization of the nation's economy:

Job-jumping [in Japan] is becoming more acceptable, if not commonplace—a by-product of the globalization of Japan's economy and one aspect of the changing face of its labor force . . . Japanese workers are beginning to have, and exercise, more freedom in determining their own career paths. The big corporations are making adjustments in their personnel practices and management techniques. The underpinnings—a hard-working, dedicated work force that applied the elbow grease in Japan's postwar economic "miracle" and became the envy of the world—are being loosened . . . Some of the sociological and economic changes that have been ricocheting through Japan's employment practices in the past decade have been accidental—the result of other cultures rubbing up against and leaving their impressions on the surface of Japan's . . . Some of the changes have been forced: By reaching deeper into Western markets, Japanese industries also have had to come to grips with the ups and downs of the worldwide economy. (*LAT,* July 9, 1988)

The environmental changes discussed above—an aging society, slower economic growth, and diversification—have all combined to create rising levels of job discontent in Japan. It was not until international markets began to impinge on the country, however, that much opportunity existed for job changing. An unhappy salaryman in early postwar Japan was faced with the no-win decision of joining a much smaller and less prestigious firm, starting his own business, or remaining in his present organization forever. Recently, for the first time in Japan's modern era, internationalization opened the labor market and began to allow for some job changing to foreign capitalized firms or to large Japanese firms faced with the need to compete internationally.

Some analysts of modern Japan believe the Nixon shock (the floating of the dollar against the yen in 1971) and the oil shocks marked the beginning of Japan's internationalization in the postwar era. Before that time, Japan had been allowed to function as an isolated entity in the world market. The Japanese themselves seemed devoted to the belief that they were, indeed, a self-sufficient island nation. The shocks of the 1970s shocked much of the populace into realizing that they were part of the world economy.

It was not until the late 1970s that most people in developed countries began to recognize that Japan was an economic force with which to be reckoned. During most of the postwar era developed countries were eager to have the Japanese establish a strong domestic market as a sign of total recovery from defeat in the war. Japanese forays into the export market were tolerated almost in the spirit of benevolence to a poor, ailing younger sister. Only as it became apparent that Japan had captured the worldwide steel and shipbuilding markets and was quickly moving into a dominant position in automobiles and electronics did Western countries begin to demand that Japan play the international business game on a "level playing field." This phrase came to be the war cry of Western nations desiring to gain a foothold in the Japanese domestic market. Japanese domestic deregulation was put in place only when Western nations imposed quotas and heavy duties on Japanese goods.

During this economic dosàdos, Japan was internationalizing on another front as well. Japanese people were becoming more and more exposed to Western cultural phenomena. An entire generation of Japanese young people grew up watching "Sesame Street" on television, more and more English books were being translated into Japanese, and Western movies subtitled in Japanese were always the biggest draws at the box office. As Japanese companies expanded the export business into distant reaches of the earth, they sent employees (and often their families) to oversee the foreign operations. In 1962 there were only about twenty-five thousand Japanese living abroad. By 1987 that number had increased to five hundred thousand. It was estimated that in the mid-1980s fifteen thousand of the twenty-five thousand Japanese citizens returning home from periods of living abroad were businesspeople.[7] That these returning expatriates face the stigma of being "tainted with foreignness" may in part be due to their being undeniable evidence of Japan's increasing integration with non-Japanese people, places, and practices.

Considering their willingness to risk being "tainted," it is not surprising that the one group of Japanese salarymen to whom income and career progress seem to matter much more than social approbation appears to be those who have actually spent a fair amount of time abroad. These Japanese "have a different feeling about them," said an official of a top bank in Tokyo. "They don't seem to feel guilty about changing jobs."[8] Analysis of data from our job-changing survey suggests that those corporate elite who have spent more time abroad are more likely to talk to family and friends about the possibility of changing jobs.[9] Whatever the exigencies that are leading more and more Japanese executives to live or work outside Japan, once salarymen have gone through this experience they are likely to contribute to the recent changes in Japanese attitudes and behaviors toward job changing.

FOREIGN FIRMS IN JAPAN

While increasing numbers of Japanese are forced to travel or live abroad as their firms internationalize, foreign firms are trying to establish a foothold in Japan. In the last decade or so Japanese have had more opportunity to become internationalized right in their own back yards without travel to foreign lands, through contact with the large number of foreign firms that have opened offices in Japanese cities since 1975.[10] Many had thought that as the dollar declined relative to the yen, American investment in Japan would slow. In fact, direct foreign investments have been growing in Japan at the rate of about 16 percent per year, from $299 billion in 1980 to $938 billion in 1986. Further, a survey of executives in 398 corporations in Japan in 1987 revealed "a growing conviction that no major corporations can be global competitors unless present in Japan" (*KN*, September 28, 1987).

This increase in foreign investment has not been limited to firms that were already established in Japan before the economic seas began to roughen. Each year during the 1980s hundreds of new foreign firms were set up in Japan. In 1981, some 401 new foreign-capitalized firms registered with MITI. That number climbed to 588 in 1983 and to 679 in 1985 (*AS*, August 8, 1988).[11] By September 1988, there were 2,600 foreign firms in Japan (*AS*, September 12, 1988). American companies alone were opening Japanese subsidiaries at the rate of almost 200 a year through the mid-1980s (*AS*, October 22, 1986).[12] And each of the nearly 700 new foreign subsidiaries opened in Japan every year during this period needed as many new presidents and many more top-level leaders (Takita 1987, 340). The opening of Japan-based foreign subsidiaries has itself brought more Japanese into contact with Western thinking and business practice than ever before.

Recognizing both the Japanese bias against working for non-Japanese enterprises and the increasing frustrations that beset elite workers in Japanese firms, foreign companies try to attract Japanese employees with high salaries and the promise of quick promotion. In 1986, beginning executive employees fresh out of college were paid about ¥144,000 per month by a typical Japanese company. A foreign firm had to start the employee at ¥180,000 to ¥190,000 to be competitive.[13] Zoltan Jaszai, who runs Helpmates International, an executive search firm in Tokyo, explains that Japanese recruits may expect to earn more from a foreign company than the foreign firm expects to pay. By the time he reached the age of thirty, for instance, a Japanese executive in a foreign firm would make somewhere between ¥9 million and ¥12 million annually. Because of various nonincome benefits, however, the cost of this employee to the company is actually double that amount. Nevertheless, the American firm that offers a potential job changer "only" a 20–30 percent premium over his present salary is likely to be rebuffed. "When a person considers an offer from a foreign company, the minimum he will settle for is a 50 percent increase in his actual income, but usually he will ask for double" (Brender 1986, 19).

Harold Hodgson, vice-president of Executive Search International in Tokyo, suggests that some Japanese might join a foreign firm hoping that their talents will be more readily recognized and their promotion track consequently faster than they would be in a Japanese firm. Jaszai cautions, however, that "if you look at 100 businessmen of accomplishment, perhaps one would be attracted to the challenge" (Brender 1986, 20). One problem foreign employers encounter is that most Japanese are under the impression that a Japanese employee will probably never head the Tokyo office of a multinational firm, let alone climb the corporate hierarchy beyond that. These impressions are correct to a certain extent. A survey of the Ministry of Labor in 1988 showed that in 990 foreign-capitalized firms (with more than 50 percent investment from abroad) 4 percent of the total employees were foreigners; in these same firms, 20 percent of the top officials and 33 percent of the presidents are foreigners (AS, June 2, 1988). While the fact that 33 percent of the foreign firms use foreigners for subsidiary presidents lowers the odds that a Japanese will be able to climb on the "fast track" to the top of a multinational organization, these figures are still lower than many Japanese executives might guess.

As this survey shows, foreign firms in Japan do not limit their hiring of Japanese citizens to a few top leadership positions in the organizations. Another Labor Ministry survey of 990 foreign companies showed that 152,378 Japanese citizens were employed by these firms (JEJ, June 25, 1988, 10). In 1987, 77.4 percent of the companies surveyed had hired new employees—16,591 in total. Thus almost 17,000 Japanese a year are experiencing Western organizational policies and practices. This familiarity with Western ways may well have some impact on the Japanese employees' attitudes toward work. More important to the present argument, however, is that 56 percent of the total new employees brought on board by foreign firms in Japan during 1987 were midcareer hires.

In sum, the many foreign firms in Japan today have created a new labor market for those Japanese executives who are disgruntled with their present job or organization and want a change. In the past, the dissatisfied worker had to take a tremendous cut in pay, prestige, and stability if he left the company he joined immediately after school. He was faced with the loss of the safety net provided by the lifetime employment system. The foreign firms in Japan today may offer the employee less prestige than that accorded to a salaryman in a Japanese company, but there are compensations. Salary tends to be higher (¥273,000 for a thirty-year-old male college graduate versus the Labor Ministry's surveyed average of ¥234,000) and working conditions better (77.2 percent of the foreign companies surveyed by the Ministry of Labor required fewer than forty hours a week of their employees) (*JEJ*, June 25, 1988, 10). Furthermore, most foreign firms are acutely aware of the Japanese belief in the instability of non-Japanese companies. Fear of losing reputation in Japan forces them consciously to avoid even the appearance of instability, which means that most employees' jobs (particularly white-collar jobs) are quite secure.[14]

JAPANESE FIRMS AND INTERNATIONALIZATION

Foreign firms are not the only organizations contributing to the internationalization of Japan. Japanese firms, too, recognize that they are members of a global economy. Jorge Ribeiro notes that non-Japanese companies are no longer alone in bringing change to Japan's employment system:

> Foreign firms in Japan trying to recruit trained workers were once the only ones throwing stones at the hallowed walls of lifelong employment. They virtually created the head-hunting business in Japan, giving it legitimacy and driving salaries upward, but these days the rapidly expanding financial services sector and the legions of understaffed small- and medium-sized firms are not only snapping up personnel but are also trying to create incentives for more people to change jobs. In other words, Japanese companies themselves are contributing to the demise of the lifelong employment system (Ribeiro 1988, 27).

Rapid internationalization has made this unprecedented behavior more and more necessary to ensure the survival of Japanese companies in the world market. During the export era of the Japanese economy, it was enough for a Japanese manager or two to be sent to outposts around the world to monitor the sales activities of local staff. Today a lack of international expertise at headquarters could thwart corporate strategy and reduce or remove profits.

In Yoshino and Lifson's study of Japan's large trading firms, the authors describe the concern of managers in the *sōgō shōsha* about how they are to survive in a global economy. One of the biggest problems for these companies is how to obtain Western ideas and personnel. Yoshino and Lifson suggest three methods that might be used to solve this problem. The first, hiring non-Japanese into career positions with these firms, is dismissed as being "difficult at best"; the second possibility, changing the policies and structures of the trading firms to a more "Western approach," would "destroy" the very foundations of the *sōgō shōsha* (Yoshino and Lifson 1986, 264). The only solution then is to create

> a hybrid that can accommodate the need for developing local management capabilities without destroying the system. Toward this end the sogo shosha are taking several steps. First, virtually all sogo shosha have intensified their search for well-educated and highly qualified local nationals . . . Another step has been to train and develop selected members of the Japanese core staff so that they may gain understanding of the Western, particularly American management approach . . . A third step is to use local nationals in key positions in foreign subsidiaries that are not related to trading, which are the functions that require the closest integration and coordination with other parts of the organization. (Yoshino and Lifson 1986, 264)

Not all firms have been as critical of the first solution offered by Yoshino and Lifson—hiring foreigners into lifetime career positions—as were the *sōgō shōsha*. As late as 1986 a large firm that hired a foreigner as a regular employee in Japan could expect its action to make headlines.[15] Today a number of large Japanese firms are busily hiring small but significant numbers of foreign employees into their corporate staffs. These are no longer the translators and culture experts traditionally hired by Japanese firms. Executives from companies like Sumitomo Bank and Trust traveled to Massachusetts during each of the last three years of the 1980s to interview Harvard Business School graduates for positions in their international strategy group. Foreigners are even being invited to participate on the economic councils in Japan, to an extent unmatched in the United States. In 1986 the head officers of subsidiaries of ten large foreign firms in Japan were made members of the Keizai Doyukai (Japan Council of Economic Organizations) (*AS*, July 22, 1986).

Even such conservative firms as the Industrial Bank of Japan, which are not bringing foreigners into the boardroom or the executive offices, proudly boast that more than half the directors have international experience. "Especially in banking," a director of the bank explained, "international experience is even necessary for doing domestic business."[16] Whether the reason for acquiring international expertise is to understand customers, to stay abreast of the latest happenings in the market, or to be able to form useful alliances with foreign partners, all Japanese firms in recent years seem to treat the term "internationalization" with deep respect and interest.[17]

International experience or training seems to head the list of needed skills at most of the large corporations (Katou 1987, 239). Perhaps the best example of the effect of internationalization on midcareer hiring can be seen in Japan's financial industry. The incursion of foreign securities and banking institutions into the Japanese market during the 1980s, coupled with a growing awareness among Japanese investors of the need to search not just the Japanese market but also the other world markets for the best returns on investments, meant that Japanese businesspeople have been looking more and more to foreign banks over the past decade. When the intensive internationalization of the financial industry began, most Japanese assumed that foreign commercial and investment banks would have a firmer grasp of worldwide opportunities for investment than their Japanese counterparts—a perception that was accurate in the early 1980s. To stave off the foreign incursion into their turf and to gain a competitive advantage in regard to domestic competition, Yasuda Bank and Trust announced in late 1984 that some slots in the company would be filled through midcareer recruiting. A year later Sumitomo Trust followed Yasuda's lead, and within two years, twenty-four financial institutions had initiated systems of midcareer recruiting (figure 12). Even banks as prestigious as Mitsubishi and Mitsui Bank joined the midcareer recruiting figure 12 leagues. For many of these banks, international skills are not the only ones midcareer recruits are expected to bring with them to the company. Japanese banks have long been known as the epitome of conservatism in the Japanese business world. There was for many years in Japan an almost ritualized method of carrying out financial transactions through a bank. Risk taking was frowned on, and during the high growth years profits flowed smoothly into the bank's coffers without any apparent need for imagination or innovation. The globalization of markets has changed all that. Today's banks are looking for a way to "slough off the traditional cultural skin of a bank [and] bring in a completely new type of human resource."[18] What many banks are looking for in new employees today, in addition to skills that would make an employee competitive in the global economy, is the ability to breathe new life into stagnant, stultifying corporate cultures. As a director of Industrial Bank of Japan (IBJ) put it:

> In financial markets, companies in the slower growing American economy have employed a "leaping" strategy to gain competitive advantage as opposed to the "creeping" strategy in place in traditional Japanese firms. The liberalization of the Japanese financial

Figure 12

Timing of Financial Institutions' Announcements of Mid-Career Hiring

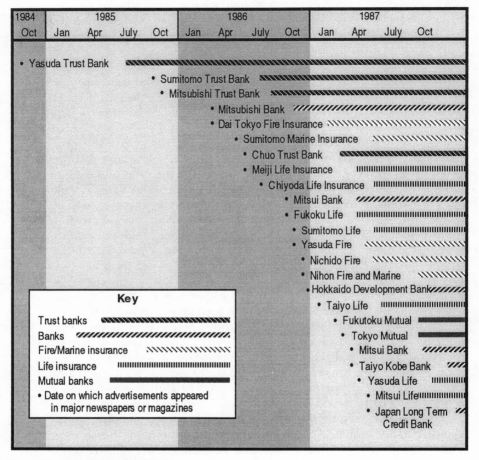

Source: *Nihon Keizai Shinbun* classified ads.

markets may change all that. New structures—mid-career hiring, mergers and acquisitions—and attitudes—risk taking, innovation—that are indicative of a "leaping" strategy may need to be put in place in Japanese financial institutions.[19]

It must be remembered that this statement comes from the director of a bank in which "inbreeding" is the solicited norm: 30 percent of the employees in the Industrial Bank of Japan, including the director quoted above, are graduates of Tokyo University, the uncontested top university in the country. Since its foundation in 1886, Tokyo University has routinely supplied government ministries and commercial enterprises with their top executives. Recent studies have found that there may be some reason, in today's technologically fast-paced world, to reduce reliance on the Tokyo University old boy network.

Nikkei Business Magazine in early 1986 studied traditional educational elitism by looking at the fortunes of the largest employers Tokyo University (Todai) graduates. It found generally an inverse relationship between those Japanese firms with high growth rates in sales and their proportion of Todai graduates. Hitachi Maxell, for example, which has no Todai graduates in its management ranks, has grown 10.3 times in sales over the past ten years. Conversely, companies like Toa Oil, Furukawa Mining, and others who employ a high percentage of Tokyo University graduates (60–80 percent in management) have not been very healthy recently. Apart from simplistic comparison of growth and management, these statistics may also imply the attractiveness of elite graduates to stable, prestigious corporate names.[20]

Some banks, such as the staidly traditional IBJ, have ignored evidence that there may be a need for more heterogeneity in their corporation; there is no talk of midcareer hiring there. But other banks, like Sumitomo Trust, list *konketsu shugi* (literally, "mixed-blood-ism") as one of the major reasons for adopting midcareer recruiting. Top executives appear to be sold on the policy of midcareer hiring as a way to "create a revolution" within the company.[21] In fact, personnel managers at Sumitomo Trust have often favored new employees from foreign firms and from other industries (a department store, for instance) over those with traditional Japanese banking experience.[22] One company official commented: "If you think only of efficiency, it is better to have people who share the same values because they can move under a single flag. But the question is if the company can adjust itself to changes in the future with pure-cultured people" (Kanabayashi 1988).

Banking is not the only industry to see a need for a new type of corporate culture and try to create that culture through hiring decisions. John Ware of Spencer Stuart, a U.S.-based executive search firm, claims that the biggest task facing all Japanese management is "how to breed capable individuals and accommodate new ideas."[23] Sony Corporation's general manager for hiring and training, Nobukazu Ohga, calls the company's most recent emphasis on midcareer recruiting a "stirring-up effect." In 1987 Sony hired seventy midcareer employees, which accounted for almost 13 percent of their total recruiting that year (Kanabayashi 1988). Honda Giken Kogyo and Itoyokado Department Stores have also adopted midcareer hiring to "stir things up" internally (Takita 1987, 221).

When the types of specialists organizations are looking for in midcareer recruiting are broken down by the size of the organization, an interesting mosaic appears (table 5). Larger companies seem to be trying to cope with markets that are globalizing by hiring foreign specialists. The pace of technological change is also a force with which large firms are dealing by hiring planners and researchers. The importance of cultural change and "revolution" is also evident in the largest firms (3,000+) where personnel and general management specialists are the second most important category of midcareer employees being sought.

Smaller Japanese firms have always been more likely to hire personnel in mid-career. Their preferences among midcareer recruits are those that have traditionally been popular. Salesmen are lured away from larger companies in hopes that the personal relationships a salesman has developed in the bigger establishment will be strong enough to bring his clients with him to the new firm. Computer specialists, too, have long been a draw to smaller firms trying to automate many of their internal processes. The importance of finance specialists is perhaps a more recent phenomenon, reflecting the increased sophistication of financial strategies and instruments popular in the Japanese market.

Table 5
Top midcareer personnel needs by size of company

	Number of Employees				
Rankings	3,000+	1,000–2,999	500–999	300–499	Fewer than 300
1st	Foreign specialists	Foreign specialists	Planners/ Researchers	Sales/ Promoters	Sales/ Promoters
2nd	Personnel/ General managers	Planners/ Researchers	Foreign specialists	Computer specialists	Finance specialists
3rd	Planners/ Researchers	Computer specialists	Computer specialists	Finance specialists	Computer specialists
4th	Managerial planners	Personnel/ General managers	Personnel/ General managers	Personnel/ General managers	Personnel/ General managers
5th	Computer specialists	Finance specialists	Finance specialists	Production engineers	Production engineers

Source: Chūto nyūsha būmu! *Next*, July 1987, p. 88.

Headhunting in the Securities and Pharmaceutical Industries

If, as we have argued, the change in Japan's lifetime employment system has been catalyzed by the advent of increased internationalization, then a closer look at internationalization in specific areas of
Japan's economy might provide both an illustration of how this
change operates and a check on the validity of our theoretical stance.
The extent to which internationalization of various industries affects
the attitudes and behaviors of organizations and individuals in those
industries can be seen in the following description of two executive
search assignments undertaken by a large international headhunting
firm in Tokyo in the summer of 1987.

One of these headhunting efforts was an attempt to fill a position in an
investment bank—a highly internationalized industry. The other search
was undertaken to find a manager for a firm in pharmaceuticals, an
industry that has been relatively insulated from the effects of internationalization. Of course, the anecdotal evidence provided by the accounts of
these searches cannot prove unequivocally that internationalization is the
key factor in determining the different responses to the idea of midcareer
job changes within these two industries. However, the variation in the
reactions encountered by headhunters in a very internationalized industry versus an insulated one is interesting and suggestive. It provides an in-
depth qualitative context for the broader but shallower evidence provided by our statistical data.

HEADHUNTING IN INVESTMENT BANKING

In late 1986 an investment bank asked one of the largest headhunters in
Tokyo to find three vice-presidents for the bank's growing corporate
finance group in Japan. The foreign-capitalized investment bank was
looking for thirty-five- to forty-five-year-old bankers in the elite Japanese
commercial or investment banks who had strong domestic experience in
corporate finance. The emphasis was less on intricate knowledge of the
financial instruments than on the ability to build and manage long-term
relationships with clients. For the appropriate individuals, the foreign
investment bank was willing to pay a salary of between ¥20,000,000
and ¥30,000,000 with up to 100 percent in bonuses per year.

The executive recruiters were able to identify two successful candidates for the vice-president positions—men with very impressive career
histories in two commercial banks—soon after the case was accepted.
The search was conducted in stages. First, the headhunters made a series
of phone calls to informants in the financial industry in Tokyo. Next,
they developed a list of sixty professionals in corporate finance of the top
six commercial banks and "big four" investment banks in Tokyo. Two

headhunters divided these lists and contacted the sixty executives over a one-month period. The initial phone calls were all made in English, since language was a necessary skill in the job; those who did not understand the English conversation could be immediately eliminated as possible candidates. Only a handful of the candidates were eliminated because they lacked English skills.

Of the sixty professionals on the contact lists, more than twenty expressed some interest in the job. In the end, however, only ten of these candidates agreed to meet the headhunters face-to-face to discuss the job opportunity. Five of these corporate finance executives were finally presented to the client as meeting the job specifications necessary to carry out the position of vice-president of corporate finance.

HEADHUNTING IN THE PHARMACEUTICAL INDUSTRY

In mid-1986 a large international pharmaceutical firm initiated a search for a vice-president of national sales in Japan. This company had relied on local distributors in Japan for most of its sales there in the past but was interested in developing its own sales capability. The company saw the hiring of a sales director as one of the first steps in this process.

The pharmaceutical firm was looking for a forty- to fifty-year-old bilingual Japanese professional with fifteen to twenty years experience in marketing or sales in Japanese pharmaceutical firms. The ethical pharmaceutical market in Japan is controlled by large hospitals and doctors rather than druggists and pharmacists. Because of the semisocialized nature of medicine in Japan, medical services are not profitable, but the sale of drugs through the doctor's hospital is. Thus, the decision-making unit in pharmaceutical sales is the Japanese physician who is informed about "best" brands by the doctor's college professor. Without a broad contact base in hospitals and universities around the country, a vice-president of national sales could not be effective. Thus, the experience of candidates for this position would be crucial. One final requirement that proved to be a major factor in this search was that the foreign pharmaceutical firm wanted to base its operations in the Kansai region.

The pharmaceutical firm planned to send the new vice-president abroad to headquarters for a year of training and familiarization with company procedures and personalities before having him begin day-to-day responsibilities in Japan. The company suggested that the pay range for a well-qualified candidate would be ¥18,000,000–¥25,000,000 annually.

The headhunters began their search in the usual fashion, contacting friends and acquaintances with the intent of focusing on and pursuing one very attractive candidate. However, in the pharmaceuticals case this simple approach did not yield one interested candidate. Next, the headhunters made up a list of sales and marketing managers in the top Japanese pharmaceutical firms. Because of the low priority given to this search in the executive search firm, the phone calls on this list were made over the course of four or five months. Not a single candidate emerged from all of the phone calls.

After the client firm pressured the headhunting firm, this search received higher priority, and one executive recruiter was assigned full-time to the search. Since the majority of corporate sales and marketing executives in Japanese firms had been approached to no avail, this head-hunter decided to focus his search on foreign-capitalized firms and regional sales managers in Japanese firms. In all, 120 executives were contacted in twenty-one Japanese firms and ten foreign firms. Of these, only nine showed any interest in the position. The recruiters met with seven of the potential candidates, all of whom were qualified for the position, but one of these declined participation after further thought. Of the six remaining candidates, all were presented to the client.

During the first six months of this search, the headhunters realized that finding a Japanese executive with English skill, a desire to live in the Kansai region, a deep knowledge of the Japanese pharmaceutical markets, and the ability to manage a large national sales force would be difficult. For this reason, English ability and living in Kansai were not mentioned as requirements for the job when the initial contact was made with the 120 potential candidates. (The executive recruiters thought that for the right individual, the foreign pharmaceutical firm might be willing to work around both of these requirements.) Even without these requirements, only nine individuals—all from foreign-capitalized firms—showed any interest whatsoever in the new job.

WHAT THE SEARCHES SHOW

For the corporate finance job, then, a full 33 percent of those contacted showed some interest in the job; 17 percent were willing to meet face-to-face with the headhunters. In the pharmaceutical search only 8 percent showed interest in the job and fewer than than 6 percent were willing to meet to discuss the job. The lack of interest in the job of vice-president of sales for this well-respected international pharmaceutical firm is somewhat surprising when compared with the interest in the investment bank search. While differences in the salary level and location of the two jobs may have had some effect on the varying interest levels, we would argue the interest variation is indicative of the difference in the internationalization of industries and attitudes of executives in the two industries studied.

Certainly, the salary levels for the corporate finance job were higher than those for the pharmaceutical position, but when the average salary levels of potential candidates is examined, those differences disappear. The six final candidates for the investment bank position had salaries ranging from ¥15,000,000 to ¥18,000,000 and were interested in a job with a salary ranging from ¥20,000,000 to ¥30,000,000. The maximum premium for changing jobs in this case was a 200 percent salary increase. In the pharmaceutical search, salaries of the five final candidates ranged from ¥10,000,000 to ¥12,000,000, and the salary range for the new job was from ¥18,000,000 to ¥25,000,000. If the lowest-paid candidate could have convinced the foreign firm to offer him the highest possible salary, he would have had a 250 percent increase in salary.

The location of the job also appears to be important to the Japanese executive. There is a feeling among some businessmen that jobs in Tokyo are higher status than those in Osaka. Osaka is less cosmopolitan and exciting as a business location. However, the location should have had very little to do with those who showed interest in the pharmaceutical position. For one thing, the location of the job was not mentioned to the potential candidates in the initial conversation. The headhunters were also careful to try to include on their list of 120 executives as many as possible who had been born, educated, or worked in the Kansai region. In the end, more than half the pharmaceutical businessmen contacted had some affiliation with Kansai.

The strongest explanation of the difference in interest between these two jobs seems to be the variation in degrees of internationalization in the industries and the executives who staff those industries. At the industry level, the deregulation of securities allows foreign firms to operate on almost an equal footing with domestic Japanese firms. This level of equality is still not present in the pharmaceutical industry. In a global industry like investment banking, the labor market is also global. In other words, firms from any of the major markets in these industries are trying to attract executives from any of the major markets to run their business. At the personal level, executives in both industries who were interested in changing jobs usually had very international backgrounds.

When foreign firms began taking seats on the Tokyo Stock Exchange, the domestic investment banking industry in Japan changed considerably. In the ten years between 1975 and 1985, twelve foreign securities firms set up offices in Japan. In the year between 1985 and 1986, twelve more offices opened. Suddenly, foreign banks were scrambling for talented Japanese traders, analysts, and relationship managers to help their firms gain a foothold in this new market. Between June of 1986 and December 1987 the total number of Japanese employees working in foreign securities firms in Tokyo rose from 1,996 to 4,943 (table 6). Of those only 200 were new graduates; the rest were all midcareer hires (*Tokyo Financial Letter*, July 27, 1987, 6–7). The foreign firms were

Table 6
Foreign securities firms in Japan

Company	Total Work Force				New Graduates Employed	
	June 1986	Dec. 1986	June 1987	Dec. 1987	April 1987	April 1984
Merrill Lynch Japan, Inc.	290	322	373	410	12	—
Vickers da Costa Ltd.	174	182	245	270	20	30–40
Prudential Bache	50	60	110	170	a few	
Smith Barney	60	75	115	130	8	0–15
Jardine Fleming	105	122	150	180	8	10
Salomon Brothers	112	173	270	350	20	30–40
Kidder Peabody	43	52	65	75	4	5
Goldman Sachs	107	162	259	320	12	20
Morgan Stanley	208	300	404	500	14	30
S. G. Warburg	74	89	133	178	23	14–15
W. I. Carr	50	3	543	58	3	5
First Boston	78	103	164	220	9	25
Drexel Burnham Lambert	32	53	72	90	0	—
Kleinwort Benson	64	71	94	130	0	10–15
E. F. Hutton	50	55	60	70	10	15
Schroder Securities	36	38	46	65	0	0
Paine Webber	19	21	26	30	0	0
Hoare Govett	31	33	45	70	0	0
DB Capital Markets	41	56	74	100	7	7
Shearson Lehman Brothers	70	91	142	180	16	30
Baring Securities	40	54	80	100	0	10
SBCI Securities	17	63	94	145	2	15
County NatWest	25	40	70	100	5	15–20
UBS Phillips & Drew	19	46	101	150	4	10
James Capel	25	50	79	95	5	5
J. P. Morgan Securities	—	—	80	130	4	15
Barclays de Zoete Wedd	14	45	88	100	0	20
19 other firms	162	214	517	730	12	57
Total	1,996	2,623	4,000	4,943	198	410
Increase from previous period		131%	152%	123%		207%

Source: Changes in workforce at foreign securities houses in Japan, *Tokyo Financial Letter.* 1.17 (July 7, 1987): 6–7.

willing to pay extravagant salaries and benefits to attract the best and brightest of the Japanese investment world. The internal labor markets that had governed Japanese employment systems for years were exploited by foreign firms in the exorbitant salaries they were willing to offer to attract executives from lower-paying domestic firms.

The response of Japanese investment houses and trust banks was to begin a system of midcareer hiring themselves. Part of the reason for this hiring was to find qualified Japanese to compete with foreign firms abroad. But at least some of the credit must go to the idea of attracting midlevel specialists who could compete with the foreign firms in the development of new financial instruments for the Japanese market itself. With the offer of high salaries from foreign firms and the knowledge that one could return to a Japanese firm safely in midcareer, Japanese investment bank employees began to seriously consider offers from a variety of foreign and domestic firms.

The history of Japan's pharmaceutical industry is a very different story. There are signs that this industry too may be deregulated in the future; thus, foreign firms like the headhunter's client are making more decisive moves to enter the Japanese market. In the past, however, foreigners have claimed that the government's process for approval of new drugs has taken just long enough for the Japanese pharmaceutical firms to introduce a similar product, thus blocking foreign drugs from the Japanese market. Graduates of top universities recognize that foreign firms have had a distinct competitive disadvantage in pharmaceuticals and consequently prefer to enter Japanese firms. Foreign firms have also been unwilling to pursue top-ranking personnel because of the extra expense in recruiting, which may not be compensated for in the marketplace. They have been content to hire new graduates from the second-tier public and private universities and midcareer employees from a number of different backgrounds. With more and more signs that deregulation may occur, foreign firms may begin to offer higher salaries to elite university graduates and aggressively pursue a policy of hiring their competitors' executive talent.

Finally, the personal characteristics of executives interested in changing jobs in the pharmaceutical industry and investment banking industry were different. The most glaring difference was that all the investment bankers came from domestically capitalized firms while the pharmaceutical sales people who expressed interest were from foreign firms. In fact, of the six pharmaceutical company employees who were presented to the client, two had made midcareer job changes into their present firms. None of the investment bankers had changed companies before in their lives.

The international experience of all of those wanting to change jobs in both industries was also impressive. All the corporate finance executives had been stationed abroad. Three of the final five candidates for the investment bank position had received graduate education abroad. In the pharmaceutical industry, three of the eight businessmen who expressed interest had lived abroad; the other five had traveled extensively. In fact, in both of the searches, the executive recruiters report that the correlation between English ability and interest in talking to the headhunter about new job possibilities was very high.

The influence of varying exposure to internationalization in these two industries, pharmaceuticals and investment banking, appears to have been a very marked if not primary determinant of the ways in which individual salarymen responded to the idea of changing jobs. As Japan continues to become more economically integrated with the rest of the global market, it seems likely that the influence of internationalization will continue to expand. This possibility has not gone unnoticed by the Japanese. On September 18, 1988, the *Asahi Shinbun* carried a full-page article entitled "Business Elites Are Targeted: Companies Fighting a Defensive War on All Fronts." The article began with this paragraph:

> The number of people who think it is good to work for more than one company during their lifetime has been increasing. Elite managers who have been sent overseas as students or in other capacities during the last ten years seem to leave the company as soon as they reach the prime of their life. The business elites have been going to the foreign companies that have made a successful entry into the Japanese market—the banks, securities firms, and pharmaceutical companies. And more recently, they have even been finding jobs in Japanese city banks, trust banks, securities firms, and other related companies. Personnel departments of large companies that until quite recently thought that they did not need to worry because quitting meant the end of an employee's career are now confused by this new era in which the best employees are starting to resign. These companies are responding in ways that reveal that, in trying to defend against this kind of labor mobility, the lifeblood is being squeezed from them.

While this journalistic treatment of the effects of internationalization on the lifetime employment system might be justly accused of verbal histrionics, our research shows its claims to be at least partially supported by a wide variety of evidence. Both the broad-scale and in-depth investigations of internationalization and its effect on job changing presented in this section suggest that the integration of Japan with the rest of the global market is contributing to the softening of the strictures that have maintained the lifetime employment system.

Summary

This chapter has adumbrated some of the more obvious macrosocial reasons for the increase in job mobility described in chapter 4. Included in these are the aging of Japan's population, which places pressures on individuals to seek out better promotion opportunities; the slowing of economic growth, which has exacerbated such pressures; the related diversification of Japanese corporations, which often requires the hiring of new personnel; and finally the heavy impact of internationalization on the structures and attitudes that support lifetime employment. All these factors are relatively recent and unprecedented, and all serve to undermine the employment system that has been a hallmark of Japanese management throughout the postwar period. In following chapters we describe the increasing propensity of organizations to hire executives in midcareer and the consequential motivations for Japanese "lifetime" employees to change jobs. We argue that while the influence of economic and demographic factors on organizational and individual actions is primary, there is a cyclical nature to this influence. Some of the macrosocial data reported in this chapter are actually influenced by organizational and individual decisions discussed in chapters 6 and 7. For example, the internationalization of Japan's domestic finance market has altered the way that organizations and executives think about job changing. However, if the individuals and organizations had not been able or willing to alter their structures and attitudes, the internationalization of these markets would not have occurred as rapidly as it did. In the next two chapters we try to point out this sort of interaction between levels of analysis.

CHAPTER SIX

Opportunity for Change

NO MATTER HOW strong the incentives might be for a Japanese executive to change jobs, job hopping would not be occurring in Japan today if no alternative jobs were open to dissatisfied employees. Much of the increase in turnover rates in Japan has been achieved because of increased opportunity for midcareer hiring. March and Simon's classic model of organizations, published in 1963, proposed a two-step break-down of job changing. The first step was an individual's dissatisfaction with his or her present job and desire to find new employment. The second factor was the opportunity for the dissatisfied employee to change jobs (March and Simon 1958). This chapter focuses on the second condition required by March and Simon's model. This condition—opportunity—was not present in Japanese postwar society to the extent found in the late 1980s. Our data suggest a considerable increase in midcareer hiring opportunities for Japanese salarymen; these increased opportunities may help to explain the recent increase in job changing.

The fame of Japan's lifetime employment system has contributed to the impression, both in Japan and abroad, that opportunity for job changing in that country is almost nonexistent. This has never been strictly true, although by comparison to Western nations Japan's business environment has indeed done very little to encourage job changing in the past. The most obvious evidence of this is the relative historical absence in Japan of deliberate recruiting of midcareer workers. Individual salary-men may have long been fulfilling March and Simon's first requirement for job changing by dreaming of greener pastures (we discuss this further in chapter 7), but for much of the postwar period those "pastures"—in other words, most large, reputable Japanese firms—have taken pains to fence out stray employees from other firms. Very few would even have considered inviting midcareer employees into the fold by actively recruiting them.

In this chapter we consider recent changes in the historically negative Japanese stance on midcareer recruiting. First, we explain the ways in which Japanese firms have adapted structurally to the changes in the business environment described in chapter 5. Next we focus on midcareer recruiting specifically. We discuss the methods Japanese firms are using to accomplish midcareer recruiting, as well as some of the ways in which companies themselves are being restructured in order to accommodate the growing presence of midcareer hiring as a fact of Japanese corporate life. Finally we show that there are certain types of firms in Japan that are most likely to involve themselves in midcareer recruiting and show evidence of the success these firms have had in enticing the corporate elite to join their companies. We argue that the growing presence of companies that are not only willing but determined to hire elite salary-men away from other firms represents a dramatic rise in opportunity for lifetime employees to act on whatever motivations they may have to change jobs.

Structural Changes

The rise in the number of midcareer hires among elite employees in Japan is partly a manifestation of a number of structural and systems changes taking place in Japanese firms. Japanese companies have used a variety of different methods in addition to midcareer hiring and firing to rationalize their executive resource systems and meet the demands of a changing environment. Some of these programs, such as the *shukkō* system, have been in place for many years and are simply finding wider usage today. Others, like outplacement, are completely new methods of coping with changes taking place in the wider society. The following section discusses the organizational and structural changes that have served to encourage midcareer job changing among elite employees in Japan.

Intercompany Transfers

In the mid- to late-1970s, the system of *shukkō* was seen as a threat to the survivability of the lifetime employment system. In the *shukkō* system an employee could be either temporarily or permanently transferred from one company to another. The transfers usually took place between companies in the same industrial group, and the direction of the transfer was usually from big company to small company. As a temporary assignment, it was usually designed to give an employee experience in a new industry related to the main business of the company. In its permanent form, it was a replacement for retirement. Yoshino and Lifson note in their book on *sōgō shōsha* that the percentage of employees on *shukkō* climbs as the average age of those holding the position increases.[1] *Amakudari* was one method of opening more leadership positions in the lead group of a firm by sending a number of the leadership-age employees to manage groups in related firms.

Japan's Koyo Sokushin Jigyodan (Employment Development Group) recently surveyed 148 companies on the first section of the Tokyo Stock Exchange and 3,318 of their related companies. The results of the survey show some of the practices and trends associated with *shukkō* in these firms (Yoshino 1986, 6–7). In the five years before the administration of the survey in 1986, 66 percent of the responding companies had experienced an increase in the number of employees transfered from parent firms. Only 12 percent responded that the number had decreased. Fifty-nine percent of the firms expected increases above the 1986 level in the future, and only 4 percent thought the number of transfer employees would decrease.

Parent companies in the survey had an average of 562 employees on the *shukkō* system at the time of this survey. That number represented 7 percent of all their employees. A subsidiary firm can expect to receive an average of twenty employees (or 11 percent of total subsidiary employees) from the parent company each year. Of those only nine (or 5 percent of total employees) will remain permanently with the firm. Generally speaking, if the age of the transferee is low, the chances of returning to the parent company increase.

In most cases the transferee's salary was in line with practices at the parent company, but in only 1 percent of the cases did the parent company pay the salary. In 35 percent of the cases the subsidiary paid the entire salary; another 33 percent of the respondents said the parent and subsidiary firm split the costs of the employee.[2]

Many personnel managers were explicitly using the *shukkō* system to reduce their number of older employees before retirement age, and the practice was expected to increase. In a survey by the Koyo Mondai Kenkyukai in 1986, 34.6 percent admitted to using transfers to reduce the number of management personnel in their firms. More striking was that 56.3 percent of the respondents were planning to use transfers for this purpose in the future (Tanaka and Ito, 1989, 4–17).[3]

OUTPLACEMENT

At the beginning of 1982 no major companies in Japan were actively placing their senior people in unrelated companies. In that year C. Itoh, the large trading firm, started an internal division to place executives to smaller companies in Tokyo. Within the following three years, 80 outplacement firms were registered with the Ministry of Labor in Japan

(Yoshii 1987). Most of these firms were divisions or subsidiaries of large companies eager to shed some of their redundant executive talent. In many cases these outplacement firms themselves were a diversification for firms into which employees in the top of the diamond could be put out to pasture. Nippon Steel, not surprisingly, was one of the companies that set up an outplacement firm. That the idea was that this venture—optimistically named "Bright Career"—could be used as a sieve into which to drain excess Nippon Steel managers, who would in turn try to find jobs for other superfluous Nippon Steel personnel, is attested by the fact that all the leaders at Bright Career were formerly managers at Nippon Steel (Tsuchida 1987, 248).

The forming of outplacement firms seemed like a wonderful idea to executives in large firms across Japan. The reasons are obvious, according to Mr. Itakura, president of Talent Refreshment System (TRS), a private outplacement firm. Itakura notes that

> the salary of most of the people being outplaced is ¥10 million. When you add in bonuses and benefits, it comes out to about ¥20 million a year. Thus if a company is willing to pay ¥2 million to an outplacement firm to get that employee another job, it is a good investment. (Tsuchida 1987, 248)

The problem with the outplacement business in Japan, in general, is that while the fifty-year-old executive does have many skills that a smaller company might want to use in its operations, most of these people come from the oil, steel, shipbuilding, and textile industries. Therefore they may not have exact skills or mind set that a small firm would need in the 1980s. These people are also usually in their late forties or early fifties, graduates of the best universities, and have been making ¥10 million a year in salary. "So," concludes Atsuhiko Tateuchi, president of Drake, Bean, Morin–Japan, "it is hard to find jobs for them" (Tsuchida 1987, 245).

When a large company like C. Itoh sends an employee with twenty-five years of in-house experience to its internal outplacement firm, Career Planning Center, it is unlikely that the employee will find a job easily. The employee, naturally, feels that he can expect C. Itoh to take care of him in the manner to which he has grown accustomed. However, if he expects to continue at his present salary and with the same benefits, he is being offered by the outplacement firm to an external labor market at a very high premium. The Career Planning Center's experience in its first years of existence was often to relent and find the employee a shukkō position within the C. Itoh group (Ribeiro 1988, 27).[4]

In the early 1980s, all the petrochemical competitors in Japan met and agreed to reduce capacity from 6.2 to 4.0 million tons per year. Because of this reduction in industry capacity, Mitsubishi Petrochemical determined that it would have to cut more than five hundred college graduate employees. In 1985 Mitsubishi Corporation and Mitsubishi Petrochemical formed an outplacement firm called Able Bodies. Their research indicated that companies like NEC, NTT, Hitachi, Fujitsu, Toyota, and Kyocera were all interested in finding mature employees with technical or trading experience. They had assumed, when this venture was formed, that older Mitsubishi employees would easily find new jobs in these prestigious, growing companies. The experience of the last few years has proven their expectations wrong. While most of the job seekers handled by Able Bodies are finding jobs, they are often having to go with second- or third-tier companies. The employees are willing to do so, however, because the options at Mitsubishi Petrochemical or Mitsubishi Corporation could be much worse. Had these employees not been willing to accept jobs found for them by Able Bodies, the alternative would have been three or four years' equivalent salary and very little possibility of finding any kind of new job.

EARLY RETIREMENT

All of the organizational initiatives described in the preceding paragraphs have one major purpose in mind—to reduce the average age of employees in the organization. Accomplishing this goal would reduce personnel costs (since most Japanese employers still base their pay scales on seniority) and increase management opportunities for younger workers. There has long been a core of reality beneath the surface behavior of Japanese who question the validity of the seniority system. Saburo Shiroyama's novel, *Kanryōtachi no Natsu* (The Summer of Bureaucrats), depicts the activities and worries of bureaucrats as they await promotion decisions (Shiroyama 1975). The concerns of these officials as they contemplate the levels to which they might be elevated center on the personalities and the politics of their organizations, not their performance on the job. The depiction of aging personnel as nonproductive social manipulators is one of the most striking elements of Shiroyama's novel, one that many claim to be an accurate representation of elites who hold top positions in Japanese government and large enterprises. The prevalence of this image of aging workers is borne out by interviews with today's business leaders. One official at the Industrial Bank of Japan is of the opinion that consensus decision making is a function of the growth economy. Once the economic engines slow, the individual sources of power in the organizations become more visible.

What really is at work in Japan is a "juniority" not a "seniority" system. Middle managers, those in their late thirties to early forties, are much more important than top leaders as far as real power goes. They are the ones who make decisions; they have the new ideas; they make the older executives look good.[5]

A recent survey by the National Personnel Authority asked more than three hundred personnel directors in large firms in Japan about their perceptions of pay-to-work ratios among different age groups in the firms. Some 38.6 percent of the respondents thought that office workers in their thirties are underpaid, and 44 percent held the same opinion about thirty- to thirty-nine-year-old technical workers. Conversely, more than 40 percent of the personnel administrators thought that technical and office workers in their fifties are overpaid (JEN, May 3, 1988). It is little wonder, then, that companies like Nomura Securities—those actively entangled with Western markets—have recently announced that the average age of directors in the firm will be reduced by replacing "outgoing executives aged between 50 and 56 years old" with "directors from 43 to 50 years" of age (Reuters 1987).

This emphasis on reducing the age of employees in Japanese firms comes just as the government is pushing companies to extend their mandatory retirement age beyond age fifty-five to ages sixty or sixty-five (see chapter 5.) Asahi Kasei has a mandatory retirement policy at age sixty but manages to convince 30 percent of its workers to leave the company at age fifty-five with a retirement bonus. Over the last few years a number of companies have developed programs to encourage employees to voluntarily take an early retirement bonus and leave the firm once they are in their mid-fifties. At IBM Japan, workers and their wives who are fifty years old and over can participate in a Nice Life Plan. This program offers husband and wife ¥600,000 apiece to develop a hobby that will last them into their sunset years (AS, July 30, 1985).

Companies like C. Itoh and Toyo Engineering take their employees and their wives on a weekend excursion to a resort town if they are willing to participate in a series of lectures about ways to make their mature years productive apart from the company. C. Itoh calls its version the Life Plan Seminar (AS, July 30, 1985). Kawasaki Steel has a program called Tenshoku Junbi Kyuka Seido (Job-Change Preparation Vacation System). Under this system, anyone over fifty years of age in the company who has the title of kachō or buchō (about 450 people) can take one year of paid vacation to get the training necessary for finding a new job thereafter (AS, May 22, 1987). Other companies offer similar programs in which older workers take every other day off from work to receive training and to have time to interview with potential employers (AS, March 20, 1985).

Some of the programs for bringing an employee's career with his lifetime employer to an end are even less subtle than those described above. At Daiseru, a tobacco filter company, any son of a present employee who joins the firm gets a very large bonus added to his monthly salary. The hitch is that his father must retire (*MS*, August 18, 1988). At Matsushita workers over fifty years old are forced to choose one of three paths.[6] One allows the employees to stay in their present job but take a cut in pay. The second involves a transfer to a related company in the Matsushita Group. The final path is a job change to a different company (*AS*, July 30, 1985).

Midcareer Hiring (*Chūtosaiyō*)

The methods used by Japanese companies to accomplish the rather daring and direct practice of midcareer recruiting are becoming more familiar to the Japanese business community as companies begin to use them more frequently. In the direct method the company itself contacts potential new employees or uses want ads for the same purpose. In the indirect method the company uses a middleman or a recruiting company. The former method has been used for a number of years in Japan; the latter is a more recent phenomenon linked to Japan's increased need for midcareer recruiting techniques and perhaps to the Japanese system's greater exposure to Western practices.

One way of recruiting directly is the familiar method of placing an ad in the newspaper. As is the case in any Western country, newspapers in Japan have always devoted a section to want ads. In Japan, as in most other countries, these ads are usually directed at hourly workers or other employees near the bottom of a corporation's organizational hierarchy. It has only been recently, with the advent of midcareer recruiting in the financial markets, that newspaper ads have begun to be used for elite corporate employees. When Sumitomo Trust announced its midcareer hiring in November 1985, it placed a seven-by-eight-inch advertisement in the *Nihon Keizai Shinbun* (Japan's equivalent of the *Wall Street Journal*). The headline of the ad read "People who can tell about themselves based on their careers." When Mitsubishi Bank followed Sumitomo's lead and placed an advertisement in the same paper some months later, their headline was even more direct. "Intellectually savaged? Come to Mitsubishi Bank."[7]

In addition to the want ads, there are also magazines filled with advertisements for midcareer job changers. Recruit Company is perhaps the most famous publisher of these magazines.[8] In 1979 Recruit began publishing *Shūkan Shūshoku Jōhō* (Weekly Employment News), which usually listed jobs available in small to middle-sized companies. Because of the success of *Shūkan Shūshoku Jōhō*, Recruit spun off two other magazines in the early 1980s: *Beruf*, for engineers and technical specialists, and *Torabaayu* (Travail) for women.[9] The popularity of these magazines is reflected in the number of companies advertising in them over the past few years. In August 1987 *Shūshoku Jōhō* contained ads from 600 companies. *Beruf* represented 150 companies. In February 1988 the two magazines combined under the title of *B-ing* when the editors at Recruit decided that the market for literature/arts graduates *(bunkakei)* and technical graduates *(rikakei)* was no longer separate in Japan. Some 1,190 companies advertised in the first issue of *B-ing*. By the summer of 1988, *B-ing* had a weekly circulation of 180,000.

As might be expected, the direct method of recruiting midcareer employees has been aimed for the most part at young people. Recruiting magazines, in particular, appear to be read almost exclusively by people in their twenties. With the new breed of young people in Japan today, it is not uncommon for a college graduate to go through the long and drawn out hiring process for a company, attend the initial orientation meetings with his new company, and then upon receiving an initial job assignment that he or she does not like, to decide to leave the firm within a month or two of joining it. Since college recruits start work in April and receive their first assignments in late April or early May, the phenomenon of leaving a company at that time has come to be known (by employers, at any rate) as *gogatsu-byō* (May disease). Many Japanese firms—often the second-tier firms unable to get as many prestigious college graduates as they would like in the initial recruiting—have caught on to this pattern. Starting in May of each year, these companies flood the newspapers and particularly the employment magazines with advertisements for "experienced" employees (*AS*, February 3, 1987).

A 1988 survey of companies involved in midcareer hiring showed that those using direct methods of recruiting had more complaints from their employees than those using indirect methods—specifically, using a scout or headhunter. However, most of the differences in outcomes between direct and indirect methods listed in figure 13 are indicative of the fact that direct methods are more often aimed at younger employees. The employees hired by direct means—and thus almost by definition younger —can be expected to have more dissatisfaction about pay and more worries about the security of their positions. Indirect hiring yields more complaints only when a new employee claims that not to fit in well with the company culture. This complaint is predictably associated with hiring older employees and is evidence of the fact that the company itself is often not much involved in the recruiting process, leaving most of that work to the scout or headhunter.

While most direct recruiting is aimed at younger employees, indirect recruiting covers a range of ages. Different age groups, however, are recruited most effectively by different types of personnel companies. For

Figure 13

Complaints of Dissatisfied Job-changers by Hiring Method

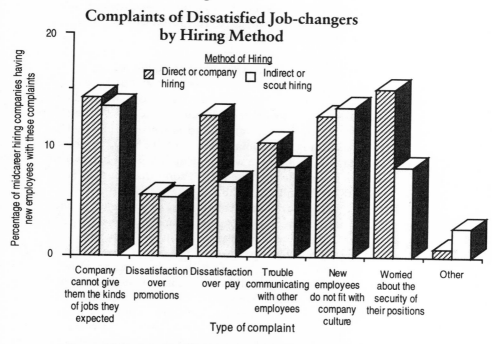

Source: "Dokushin no Kyuyo Taikei ga Shorai Kadai ni" *Sogo Shiryo M&L.*
Jan 1-15 1988, p. 34.

young people aged twenty to thirty-five there are the *tōroku,* for middle managers there are domestic scouting firms, and for top executives there are the headhunting companies. In 1981 there were fewer than twenty personnel companies in Japan. In 1986 there were well over a hundred (*NKS,* June 8, 1987). The placement business had revenues of ¥226.1 billion in 1987 (*KN,* July 5, 1988). Still, direct methods of recruiting are much more popular than indirect methods involving personnel companies. In 1986 some 1,270,000 people changed jobs in Japan; 10 percent of these were white-collar workers. According to Labor Ministry statistics, personnel companies placed 5,402 white-collar workers in 1985 (*NSS,* August 12, 1986). Thus only 5,402 of 127,000 or 4 percent of white-collar job-changers made their moves through personnel companies. Nevertheless the 5,402 white-collar placements through personnel companies reflects a doubling in less than five years.

Over half of the personnel companies in Japan are *tōroku* firms or *jinzai* banks, which cater to younger people (*NKS,* June 8, 1987). These companies record job seekers' names, career interests, and past experiences and make that information available to corporate recruiters who come to examine the records. Both the company and the individual pay a fee. The largest *tōroku* company is Recruit Jinzai Center (another subsidiary of the ubiquitous Recruit Company.) In 1986 more than 12,000 people were on record with the company, and 2,306 were placed through their services (*NSS*, August 12, 1986).[10] The quality of registrants at the *tōroku* firms is evident in data from Imuka, which has 50,000 individuals recorded in its system. Eighty percent are university graduates, and nine percent have graduate degrees. The top three alma maters in terms of numbers are Keio, Waseda, and Chuo universities (*Next,* December 1986, 75). According to Ejima Yutaka of TESCO, a Tokyo-based *tōroku* company, in 1988 there were almost 150 *jinzai* banks (or *tōroku* companies) in Japan. He predicted that "soon that number [would] be more than 200" (*NSS,* July 21, 1988).

Scout firms, which have been around for a long time in Japan, are the most popular personnel companies if an organization is looking for middle managers. Usually these companies are quite small, often with only one or two employees. They go into and out of business with equal ease (*NKK,* June 8, 1987). Technology firms have been particularly prone to using scouts in the past, especially since during the postwar period, only technology firms did much "specialist" midcareer recruiting. A survey conducted by the Japan Productivity Division of the Koyo Taigu Center of 186 large Japanese companies with strong research divisions showed that 28.5 percent of these firms used scouts to help them with midcareer recruiting. Larger companies—135 of the 186 companies surveyed had more than a thousand employees—were more likely to use scouts than were smaller firms. Scouts were ordinarily used to find personnel who would give the company immediate competitive advantage in a current business (51.6 percent) or in a new business (64.9 percent). Other reasons for using scouts included strengthening research management capabilities (9.5 percent) and changing the balance of personalities and skills in a particular division (8.1 percent) (Dokushin no Kyuyo 1988).

To recruit top executives, organizations in Japan use headhunting or executive search firms. The first headhunting firms in Japan were all started by foreign executive search firms. In 1986 there were still only about ten companies in Japan that qualified as executive search firms; five of those were subsidiaries of foreign firms. All but three of the ten had been established after 1983. By 1988 there were sixty domestic executive search firms in Japan, and by 1992 the number had reached more than five hundred. Not only have the number of firms grown, but so has the number of searches completed. Between 1985 and 1987 the combined number of completed searches grew at a rate of 30 percent a year (figure 14) in two of the top foreign headhunting firms.[11] By 1991 Rus-

Figure 14

Searches Completed in Two Tokyo Executive Search Firms 1985–1987

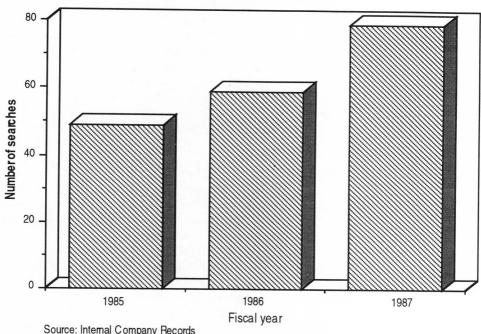

Source: Internal Company Records

sell Reynold itself completed ninety-nine searches, and Korn/Ferry had more than a hundred complete assignments. The Egon Zehnder Company employed only two headhunters from its establishment in 1972 until late in 1984. Since then, the company has been forced to hire four more search consultants to cope with growth rates.[12] Korn/Ferry, which claims to be the oldest foreign executive search firm in the country, also had only two headhunters until the mid-1980s. Now the company boasts ten consultants in the Tokyo office, seven of whom are Japanese.

Much of the increase in the use of headhunters in the period following 1983 has been a result of foreign financial firms' moves into Tokyo. Indirect evidence of this is that of the roughly eight hundred people placed into jobs by the city's ten headhunting firms in 1986, almost 60 percent were investment banking assignments (Takita 1987, 339). One particular executive search firm handled only two searches in the financial area during 1984. By 1987 more than twenty searches in that firm were in banking or securities. Not surprisingly, the clients for almost all these searches were foreign firms. Only one company, Executive Search, claimed that a majority of its clients were Japanese enterprises (*NSS*, August 12, 1986).[13] But other smaller Japanese firms, like Pioneer Headhunting, are increasingly finding Japanese clients for their services.[14] Headhunters also tend to find their recruits for clients—especially foreign clients—in other foreign firms. Ken Whitney of Egon Zehnder estimated that in 1987 some 65 percent of his company's placements came from other foreign firms in Japan, indicating that much of the elite external market in Japan is made up of a highly mobile group of executives who transfer from foreign firm to foreign firm. That at least 35 percent of the placements come from Japanese firms,[15] however, indicates a much more mobile group of Japanese corporate elites than existed in 1980, when almost all the placements came from other foreign firms.

Organizational Accommodation of Job-changers

One of the problems that many personnel companies confront as they attempt to place employees in new firms is that the new firm does not have a structure or culture conducive to midcareer job changers. Along with the need to create methodologies for recruiting employees in midcareer, Japanese companies that want to recruit employees in midcareer are faced with structural barriers inside their own organizations that may discourage or even preclude the successful hiring of job-hoppers. That some large Japanese corporations are attempting to restructure their organizations to accommodate the recent rise in job mobility attests to the impact of changing attitudes and behaviors toward lifetime employment in present-day Japan.

During most of the postwar period any person who changed jobs into a large Japanese company suffered serious discrimination as a result of the job change. Most of those who changed jobs did so because their former employer was unbearable or because they were so devoted to a particular vocation that they did not mind taking on a "specialist" title, which eliminated any possibility of their being promoted up the corporate ladder. Almost without exception, job-changers received lower pay and fewer benefits in their new organizations than did lifetime employees. Even today, if one asks a midcareer hire about his experience in a Japanese company, it is not unlikely that the response will be, "Chūtosaiyō dakara . . . " This phrase, which literally means "Because I was hired midcareer . . . " brings to mind a collage of images, all negative and discriminatory. It means "Because I was hired midcareer I have no hope of being promoted; I receive low wages; I do not receive benefits that real employees my age receive; my family and I are not included in the social networks in the corporation; I do my work and go straight home at night; I know that if the company comes on hard times I will be one of the first let go."

Companies that have decided to make midcareer recruiting a major part of their personnel strategies have had to fight such images of the fate of job-changers—images that have been sustained and built up during the whole of the postwar period. The first changes an organization must make to attract positive attention from potential midcareer recruits are structural ones. At Mitsui Bank new recruits are promised that "salary, position, and future raises and promotions are exactly the same as the people who join the firm right out of college. It is no handicap to one's career to be hired mid-career any more" (Takita 1987, 222).

Companies doing midcareer recruiting are often trying to recruit an employee who is very different from other personnel in the firm. The new employees they seek are often the *shinjinrui* of Japan, concerned with finding a job that interests them, making a larger sum of money than people their age have traditionally made in Japan, and having many interests in life besides the company. To attract these employees, companies put out publicity that reflects what they believe a potential job-changer would like to hear. An example of a magazine article directed at *shinjinrui* recruits was published in the April 1985 issue of *Beruf*. It is taken from an interview with Nippon Motorola's new president, Takashi Irie, himself a job-changer from NEC after holding a directorship there (see chapter 7). He addressed the engineers:

> For Motorola to gain market share in Japan, the participation of you young engineers is absolutely necessary. There are two things I wish young engineers would always do. First, I wish they would set goals that they personally want to achieve. I am not talking about goals for your company, I am talking about personal goals that you set for yourselves. I think it is very important for you to strive to meet those goals with positive attitude.
>
> Second, I believe it is important to develop the ability to picture for yourself what you can be and what you can do. By exercising this ability to set your own goals daily, I believe that you will all rise to greater heights than you might have otherwise.

To attract and retain the type of employee Irie is describing, however, the company must create different promotion and career paths than have traditionally existed in Japanese firms. The structural norms from which these new paths must diverge are clearly marked in traditional Japanese companies. For example, in the large trading companies there have normally been five career paths, according to Yoshino and Lifson: (1) the generalist stars—"the true 'fair-haired boys' of the organization"; (2) the system specialists—those involved in the production system; (3) the periphery controllers—those who become managers of subsidiaries and affiliates; (4) the staffers—those fixed in support staff functions; and (5) the locals and administrators—those unable to handle coordination functions (Yoshino and Lifson 1986, 170–172). While each of these five career paths is open to all employees, Yoshino and Lifson claim, only one would lead to the upper echelons of the company—the path of the generalist.[16]

The type of new employee modern companies want to recruit deplores the rigidity of this traditional promotional structure. Consequently, some firms are attempting to put into place new paths to corporate success. With the *shinjinrui* and the need for diversity among its employees in mind, Daiei, the large department store, has designed three different employment systems within its firm. An employee joining the company must decide which of these paths to follow. The first is the traditional path: the employee is willing to move all over the country at the company's whim and for this sacrifice has the potential to rise to the highest levels of the corporation. The second path involves a regional career. The employee is promised a job within a specified region. Thus the family can buy a home and expect to live there for an entire lifetime, with the employee spending most nonwork time at home. Employees with ailing parents or who are concerned about their children's educations and the deleterious effects of uprooting them would be the most likely to opt for this career path. The regional career employee could rise to no higher position in the firm than that of regional manager. The third career path is for the employee who does not want to do any more travel than the commute between home and the nearest Daiei department store. This path is the city career. Employees would be assigned to one city (and often only one store) for their entire career. The highest position attainable in such a career would be store manager (*AS*, May 6, 1985).

Besides promotional structures, salary structure is also a valid concern for midcareer job-changers. In the past, a Japanese executive's salary was based only on seniority within the company. Thus the job-changer was at a serious disadvantage. As recently as the summer of 1987, companies like Nippon Steel and Kobe Steel—which are busily diversifying with the help of midcareer recruits—adopted salaries based 100 percent on ability and not seniority (Shibuya, 1987). The ability wage is particularly applicable to managers of these steel firms (*KN*, September 28, 1987). Asahi Glass is another firm well known for its midcareer recruiting. It has adopted executive bonuses based on individual performance rather than seniority or corporate performance. Mr. Tomozawa, the director of personnel for Asahi Glass, calls such bonuses a "controversial idea." "But," he adds, "if we don't have change, we can't internationalize" (*WSJ*, November 14, 1988, R14).

Another characteristic of *shinjinrui* is their interest in benefits—an interest that approaches anxiety in the case of an executive contemplating a job change. Because of the traditional practice of extending extravagant benefits to lifetime employees but not to midcareer hires, many *shinjinrui*

> attach as much importance to company welfare as to job satisfaction and pay . . . although some are uneasy about the company subsidizing everything from leisure to housing for its workers. Large Japanese companies, in return for worker loyalty under the lifetime employment system, have traditionally provided their workers with a total welfare system in such areas as housing, family support, recreation, education and retirement. (JEN, May 27, 1988)

Small firms have generally been unable to offer such benefits to their workers and since, in the past, small firms were the main employers of midcareer job-changers, job change became associated with a significant loss of benefits. Companies that are presently trying to recruit midcareer employees have found that a healthy system of benefits is one major drawing card. Consequently, companies as diverse as securities firms, banks, and heavy industries have decided to help their employees with housing loans. Nomura Securities offers its employees housing loans of up to ¥50 million at 3 percent interest. Mitsubishi Heavy Industries has taken a different tack by paying 9.49 percent interest on employee savings for housing. Other benefits offered by companies in the midcareer market include the free use of company resorts, such as those established in Australia by Daiwa and Nikko Securities for the entertainment of their weary dealers and traders. Finally, midcareer recruiter Asahi Glass made a press event out of the president's and other top executives' nine-day summer vacation in 1987. During the summer of 1988, the company called on all employees to take a sixteen-day paid vacation (JEN, May 27, 1988). In a country where using accumulated vacation time has long been against corporate norms, the ostentatious display of vacation taking may be very appealing to talented workers considering a job change.

The snowball effect of organizational responses to individual job-changers is not limited to a few large corporations, any more than it is to a single market sector. As more and more large companies have started to cater to individual job-changers, small companies have felt the pressure to respond by matching the flexibility of larger firms. Many smaller companies, no longer secure in the belief that employees must stay with them for life, have had to begin offering benefits in line with those of large companies. Housing loans, golf club memberships, and overseas company vacations are "deducted as corporate welfare expenses" so that smaller companies will "not be outdone by larger corporations" (JEN, May 27, 1988).

Organizational Efforts to Minimize Effects of Increased Job-changing Opportunities

Of course, even the companies, large or small, that may benefit from the increased familiarity of midcareer recruiting and job hopping in the Japanese business world must also deal with the threat this change poses to their own employee population. Japanese companies have used a number of different approaches to try to cope with this threat. Organizational responses to midcareer hiring have included explicit rejection of such hiring practices, containment activities (creating special "quarantined" organizational tracks where job changing may be allowed to occur while being prevented from "spreading" to other areas of the organization), and enthusiastic acceptance of external labor market activities.

One *Nihon Keizai Shinbun* article, after describing the rise of job changing in Japan, reported on organizational initiatives to stop the slow leak of foreign-educated employees from major firms. Some of the most prestigious companies in Japan have prided themselves for years on sending their best executives overseas for graduate training. Companies like Industrial Bank of Japan, Nomura, Nippon Steel, DKB, and Mitsubishi each have more than a hundred foreign-trained MBAs in their companies (*NKS*, August 10, 1987). It is little wonder that firms react nervously to news that foreign-trained executives are changing jobs in greater and greater numbers, since these employees comprise the managerial hearts of many companies. Nomura Securities has been said to fine employees $75,000 if they leave the company within five years of graduate education overseas. Many companies have even resorted to contracts that forbid an employee from leaving the firm for a certain period following training abroad (Holden 1989, 58). Mitsubishi Corporation has quietly phased out the policy of paying for students' graduate educations, instead encouraging their executives to take seminars closer to home. Firms without such specific sanctions have learned to be careful in picking those to be sent abroad—they try to instill a high degree of *giri* before allowing employees to leave for their schooling.

Another way in which one large Tokyo firm, the Industrial Bank of Japan, is trying to exorcise the specter of job hopping from its ranks is by requiring that any employee contact with a headhunter must be reported. While top officials will not either confirm or deny the existence of this policy, less senior management staff claimed in interviews that any contact with headhunters was to be reported on a special form, which was distributed to all personnel in the company. The firm kept track of the date on which such calls were made, the company in which a position was being offered, what the position was, how much the new job would pay, and similar data. This list offered the company excellent competitive information about which market areas were being encroached on by other (particularly foreign) firms. It also served as an evaluative indicator, showing which IBJ employees were most highly esteemed by their peers in other companies. Most important, it allowed the firm to intervene whenever an executive might be tempted to change jobs.

Many Japanese companies have given up trying to enforce strict rules against job changing and have turned their attention instead to containing the problem. The containment response of some organizations has been to create a special division or career track in the company for both midcareer hires and employees who are considered likely to change jobs, such as performance-based specialists. These separate divisions are not a new idea; electronics firms have been using them for much of the postwar period. Engineers who were hired away from other companies understood that they were involved in a specialist career track and that they would be able to work on projects they enjoyed but would never rise to top management positions in the firm. A specialist may have become *buchō* over a group of others in his own field of operations, but his usefulness to the company was limited by the fact that he had changed jobs at least once. The directorships and most top general manager positions were reserved for generalists who had submitted themselves to the whims of the personnel department's transfer system.

Engineering companies have thus always contained the contagion of job hopping, keeping it away from managerial employees by using separate career tracks to contain both job-changers and employees who were considered likely to change jobs because of their specialist expertise and/ or their personalities.[17] While manufacturing firms have had technologist tracks for some time, Sumitomo Metals was among the first to develop a career track in which specialists can rise to director levels (Westphal 1991, 73). In banks, such separate specialist tracks are a new phenomenon. Kazuteru Tanaka, the foreign exchange chief at the Bank of Tokyo, had watched a dozen or more specialist employees move from his firm to Citibank, Chemical Bank, and others. Tanaka decided that his division had become nothing more than "a school for traders." He began considering a "special employment track with a separate pay scale pegged to performance" for certain employees (Holden 1989, 58). Sanwa Bank, which has refused to follow the lead of Mitsubishi and Mitsui banks by doing midcareer recruiting, has nonetheless developed a new internal system for internationalists that is supposed to prevent "people with international strengths being drawn away to other companies."[18] These employees are paid the same salary as others their age in the company, but they are allowed to do specialist work throughout their careers rather than be transferred from division to division.

Most banks have taken this kind of cautious containment strategy to cope with a growing number of job-changers in their field. However, contingency plans exist in most companies to launch a full-fledged embrace of the external labor market if push comes to shove. One strategic planner in a well-known Tokyo bank explained his company's contingency plan to us.

> If three or four of our top executive-track employees were to leave the bank to go to a competitor we would be forced to adopt an entirely new structure at the bank. Presently our operations, which can roughly be divided into commercial, merchant, and investment banking, are all housed within the same company. This gives us some competitive advantages over American firms in the U.S. market where investment banking, at least, has to be a separate entity. The top personnel in the bank usually find their way into the investment bank part of our company, the next best do commercial banking, and retail banking is the bottom rung. All of these people, however, are paid the same salary—a salary that is not high by investment banker standards, but is good for commercial banking. If we were to lose people we expect it would be from the investment banking part of our operation. And if we lost enough of these people in one year (three or four) we would be forced to divide our bank into three different banks so that we could pay our investment bankers higher investment banker wages and commercial bankers lower commercial banker wages. The restructuring of the bank to justify differential wages would probably also have significant impact on the way we do business.[19]

In this organization, contingency plans for containing the impact of midcareer job changing would change the bank into a very different entity (figure 15). If many banks in Japan felt that they had to carry out similar restructuring, the effect on the entire Japanese financial market would be dramatic.

In some companies the embrace of midcareer hiring and performance-based pay scales has gone beyond the planning stage. Nikko Securities announced in April 1988 that some employees would be allowed to "avoid the typical routine of a new job every two years" and instead be encouraged to become "higher paid specialists in areas they enjoy." The hitch is that, as in most external labor markets, they "now face dismissal if they don't perform up to expectations." The personnel director at Nikko explained that this system became necessary because "so many headhunters were scouting our employees, we had to come up with a response" (Holden 1989, 58). Mitsui and Company also treats its new financial specialists to compensation "superior to that of general managers" in order to attract and retain the necessary personnel (Westphal 1991, 73).

Figure 15

Bank Restructuring

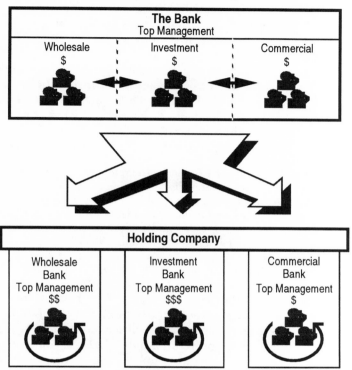

Wherever organizational policies are changing to embrace policies of midcareer hiring or other external labor market practices, the companies explain the changes as a response to individual job changing decisions. *Shūkan Tōyō Keizai,* a weekly economic report, announced that because large Japanese investment banks "do not seem able to stop the foreign banks from hiring" their personnel, their "only method of responding to losing good people so quickly has been for these companies to begin stealing personnel from other smaller firms" (July 25, 1987, 72–73). At the Bank of Tokyo, foreign exchange chief Kazuteru Tanaka believes that since foreign firms have been so effective in demonstrating the utility of midcareer hiring and performance-based pay, "it may also be useful to us" (Holden 1989, 58).

While some Japanese firms have adopted more Western employment practices with a measure of resentment, many other managers believe that these practices are useful in the economic climate of the late 1980s. Ken Moroi, the chief executive of Chichibu Cement, has been leading his company through a diversification effort into high-technology ceramics. He has decided that patterns of lifetime employment are no longer viable for companies—such as his own—with high aspirations for success: "In the past, we sacrificed the small number of talented people for the high morale of the masses. In the future we won't sacrifice. In the 1990s, we have to go more to the Western style of management" (*WSJ*, November 14, 1988, R14).

The problem is that as more and more companies offer midcareer positions to employees, even in a limited area, their actions have the potential to professionalize the labor market in Japan. The cycle created by a growing number of individuals in the external labor market might then feed back up to the organizational level, as new professionals become able to demand more and more freedom from the organization.

> The growing movement of experienced employees and "contract employees" from enterprise to enterprise is creating a horizontal labor market of true "professionals" who can find jobs freely, overriding the corporate framework. This also makes it necessary for enterprises to treat personnel according to their ability and create a corporate environment where such personnel can work well. (Koyama 1988, 8–9)

It is not only the policy of midcareer hiring that leads to a breakdown of corporate loyalty. In a survey of four hundred personnel directors in firms with more than a thousand employees, 75 percent of those asked thought that "a policy of promoting the early retirement of middle-aged employees with long-term firm service will have the effect of lowering loyalty to the firm by all employees" (Tsuda 1982). In some companies this breakdown of loyalty is already a topic of much concern. At Nissan the breakdown of seniority pay systems and midcareer hiring worries managers in charge of personnel. They fear that those who are loyal and stay with the firms will develop "doubts and jealousies" as "companies jack up the pay for employees they fear losing to other firms" (Kanabayashi 1977, 1). Overall, organizational responses to increasing numbers of job changes by individuals seem to be unavoidable in the near future.

Success in Midcareer Recruiting

The first part of this chapter has shown the organizational changes taking place in Japan that allow for mobility among the executive ranks in these firms. The willingness of organizations in Japan to restructure in order to allow for midcareer mobility (both in to and out of the organization) of elite employees is in part driven by the well-known successes of a variety of companies that have tried this in the past or that are restructuring for midcareer mobility now. Some firms in Japan are becoming adept at midcareer recruiting, a phenomenon that greatly increases the availability and visibility of job-changing opportunities for Japanese salarymen.

There are three types of organizations in which mid-career recruiting for elite employees has succeeded in Japan: foreign firms eager to scout Japanese managers and technicians; large Japanese high-tech firms looking for specialists and engineers or nontechnology firms trying to diversify into new technologies; and Japanese service firms, usually in financial markets or information services, looking for specialists and greater international access.

Other firms are involved in midcareer hiring and firing, but their emphasis is not on elite workers. The small firm that is trying to grow quickly has little access to elites unless it has a new technology or market that is particularly intriguing to some elite specialists. An example of this type of firm is Nihon Densan in Kyoto, which started with only four employees in 1973. Now it is a leader in the miniature motor market with eleven hundred employees, 55 percent of whom are midcareer hires. When one looks at the management levels of the organization (*kachō* and above), a whopping 98 percent are job-changers. All of these corporate elite have made good on their decision to switch companies. Nihon Densan is a good example of a firm that has entered the ranks of respectable firms from very humble beginnings. Such powerhouses as Sony and Kyocera also were unable to attract appropriate new college graduates when they first started operations but were able to interest midcareer changers in their technologies.

Another type of company in which elite midcareer recruiting has long occurred, but which does not fall into our definition of midcareer job changing (and which is not accounted for in government statistics) is the *kogaisha* (subsidiaries; literally, "children companies") of *keiretsu* (company networks) in which fifty-year-old executives "retire" from large parent companies into positions of authority in smaller, related firms through *shukkō* or *amakudari*.

Foreign Firms

Foreign firms have always been at the forefront of midcareer hiring in Japan. They have occupied this position more out of desperation than out of a philosophical commitment to the idea of such hiring. Most foreign firms in Japan complain bitterly about the need to hire their people on the "used" market rather than being able to hire college "fresh-outs" as their Japanese competitors are able. (A few foreign firms do appear on the Japanese college seniors' lists of most popular firms. IBM is almost always on the list, and Arthur Andersen has recently gained considerable popularity, as has Motorola.) Nevertheless, all of the complaining about the inability to attract college seniors does not change the fact that many foreign firms in Japan are ill-equipped to handle the training necessary for turning college graduates into business people. The story of a young man named Hiroshi is a good example of the problem.

Hiroshi, a Waseda University senior, was very interested in joining a foreign company. Not only was he intrigued with the salaries offered by foreign firms, but he had attended high school in the United States when his father had been on assignment there for a large Japanese trading firm. Hiroshi had entered the commerce faculty at Waseda intent on joining an American or British firm after graduation. However, the summer of 1988 found him debating his own decision. As Hiroshi consulted with people in U.S. and British subsidiaries in Tokyo, he found himself questioning the advisability of pursuing his long-held goal.

As long as he was talking to the executives who worked in the foreign firms, Hiroshi heard glowing accounts of what he would be able to do in a foreign firm, the career path that would open before him, and his ability to lead a much larger Japan-based operation in the very near future. The foreigners never let him forget the increased salary he would receive by joining a foreign firm rather than a Japanese firm. But the Japanese employees in these same foreign subsidiaries painted a different picture. Often midcareer recruits themselves, they tended to extol the virtues of working in a Japanese firm for the first few years of one's career—"to learn the proper way" to do business in Japan. They noted that U.S. and British subsidiaries, unlike their Japanese counterparts, generally did not have large training programs for college graduates. The work life at foreign firms was much less structured than at a Japanese firm, and most of them noted that they found working at a foreign company somewhat lonely. Instead of going out for obligatory drinking sessions with office staff at nights, most of the Japanese staffers in these foreign firms returned home well before 8 P.M., soon after the foreign staffers went home to their own wives and families. The Japanese employees in these firms noted that this type of early evening was no life for a young man just entering the work world.

Hiroshi was somewhat disappointed by the Japanese employees' recommendations that he move from college into a Japanese firm, but he believed them. He reluctantly accepted their advice, turning down the opportunity to speak English regularly and to earn twice the salary of his fellow graduates from Waseda. He took a job with a Japanese trading firm the following spring, still intent on joining a foreign firm once he had received proper training in Japanese business practice, earned a few likely contacts, and perhaps married so that he would have a family to go home to after work like his non-Japanese colleagues.

Another young executive, now with a foreign firm, gave a similar explanation for joining Mitsui Company fresh out of college.

It was never my intention to remain with Mitsui past the first few years of training. By accepting a job with Mitsui, I not only was able to learn a great deal about doing business as a *shōsha* man, I also gained a kind of certification for doing business in Japan. I am able to explain to all my business associates that I was a graduate of Keio and my first job was at Mitsui. Even though my present company does not have the history or prestige of Mitsui Company, my associates recognize me as one who voluntarily left Mitsui for my present position. I have the same personal prestige as if I were a lifetime employee of one of the large trading companies.[20]

The lack of success that foreign firms have in hiring new graduates like Hiroshi and our Mitsui Company "graduate" is offset by tremendous success in hiring midcareer employees. As the next chapter will show, the types of Japanese elite employees most likely to want to change jobs are the same types of executives likely to be most attracted to working in a foreign company. These firms, fighting the tradition of Japanese lifetime employment and having no cultural bias against midcareer hiring themselves, often try to entice much-needed Japanese executives with offers of high salaries and generous benefits. A former employee of Mitsubishi Petrochemical, who had moved to a *buchō* position in a new subsidiary at Nippon Steel, discussed the job options he had considered before he moved to Nippon Steel Chemical:

If I moved from my former job to Kyocera, my salary would have gone down by twenty percent. If I went to companies like NEC, Fujitsu, or Hitachi, my salary would have gone up by ten percent. If I decided to join a new venture, I would have made fifty percent less than I did in my previous job. An American firm would have been the best bet for salary. I might have increased my salary by fifty to one hundred percent.[21]

This manager's estimate of the salary he might expect to receive in a foreign firm was well within the bounds of probability. However, the high salaries offered by such companies have become almost legendary among Japanese executives, a phenomenon that has led to exaggerated expectations about the money a Japanese salaryman might earn in a foreign firm. Some of the stories circulated by hopeful executives have the same general tone (and credibility) as the story of Ali Baba and Aladdin's cave: once you gain access to a foreign firm, the rumors intimate, there is nothing to keep you from picking up all the cash you can carry. One twenty-six-year-old man in very well known Osaka-based electronics firm confided to us that he wanted to move to Tokyo because his chances of getting into a foreign firm were better there. "I have a relative about my age who works in a foreign securities firm," he explained conspiratorially. "I heard my aunt say that he makes twenty-five million yen a year. I make 4 million yen. I think I'll change jobs later this year—when the time is right."[22]

Along with the tales of the riches to be found in foreign firms, however, young executives in Japan communicate a certain apprehension. As the *buchō* who changed jobs to Nippon Steel Chemical put it: "Even though the salaries are high at foreign firms, the problem is that the new employee is vulnerable because he could be let go after a couple of years of work."[23] A slightly younger employee at a large bank in Tokyo said: "If some Japanese company would hire me for double the salary, I would move. But I wouldn't consider going to an American firm for less than ten times current salary with a ten-year contract."[24] These attitudes reflect the general belief among Japanese that American firms are prone to using "quick hire, quick fire" practices. Among older employees, with their deeper concern about security, this issue often creates a strong aversion to joining a foreign firm. Younger Japanese elites worry about it to varying degrees but in general seem less concerned than their middle-aged colleagues. A twenty-seven-year-old in a sales position in a high-tech firm asserted firmly that foreign companies in Japan "pay well, have lots of opportunities for promotion, and are more interesting than domestic firms."[25]

But a more usual reality, that faced by our Waseda student, Hiroshi, is evidenced in the comments of a senior at Keio University. "I want to join a Japanese company because I do not want to be considered a local staff member." He claimed that after working in a Japanese firm for a few years he would like to change jobs to a foreign firm and "make more money."[26]

In addition to salary, foreign firms are also able to offer responsibilities, titles, and often travel opportunities unmatched by their local counterparts. The importance of these types of promotion opportunities to the most likely job-changing corporate elites in Japan will be discussed in the next chapter.

SERVICE FIRMS

As we have shown already in the example of internationalization and its effects on job changing at the end of chapter 5, the financial services sector is perhaps the most important industry in Japan for explaining the upsurge in midcareer job changing in the late 1980s. After all, it was the midcareer hiring announcements by Yasuda Trust and Sumitomo Trust Bank that served as the spiritual if not physical starting points of the increase in elite job changing in the 1980s. In 1985, at the time Sumitomo Trust announced midcareer hiring, it was considered a rather daring place to work because of a number of new personnel and strategic policies that had been put into place since the 1970s. In a ranking of the popularity of companies among college seniors in 1979, Sumitomo Trust had been ranked seventy-ninth. By 1985 it had climbed to number forty-one. Partly spurred by the announcement of midcareer hiring and Sumitomo's success with that policy, the ranking in 1988 showed this trust bank to be the fourteenth most popular company in Japan.

Many analysts, while forced to concede the changes in midcareer hiring patterns in the financial industry, believe that the changes will not be felt in Japan's general managerial environment. Abegglen, for example, has predicted that "there will be job mobility in the service businesses of Japan to an increasing extent" but that "mobility will remain limited in the manufacturing sector" (Abegglen 1987). Abegglen's statement reflects the traditional dichotomy of sectors in the Japanese labor market between service industries and manufacturing firms. Historically, Japanese manufacturers have concentrated their college recruiting on candidates who emphasized a science track in college. Service industries drew their employees almost exclusively from college graduates who had specialized in the arts and humanities. There has traditionally been little or no significant overlap—with the exception of manufacturer's sales departments, accountants, and other office support staffs—between the labor pools from which these different sectors hired their elite employees. Thus, many observers argue that even a snowballing increase in midcareer hiring practices within the financial sector would not have significant repercussions in the manufacturing sector.

Despite these expectations, there is evidence that the high salaries and mobile labor patterns that have come to characterize service industries are beginning to spread from this limited sector into a wider sphere. Recently media attention focused on two manufacturers that announced that they would enter the midcareer market "in a serious way." Nissan recounted plans to recruit one hundred midcareer types in fiscal 1988 and 1989, while IBM Japan announced that it was looking for five hundred within the 1988 fiscal year—"a figure to match IBM's recruitment of persons fresh from school or university" (Koyama 1988).

This is not simply the result of manufacturing firms imitating the employment practices of financial organizations. New methodologies and techniques that require scientific training are becoming increasingly important in industries that have traditionally relied on executives without scientific training. The word "*zai*-tech" (rhymes with "high-tech") has been coined recently to refer to these new methodologies: the syllable "*zai*" connotes finance, and the word as a whole compares new financial methods with sophisticated engineering technologies. Because of the need for science-track graduates to deal with *zai*-tech, the understanding that an employee with an engineering background brings to investment decisions on research and development (R&D) decisions, and the expectation that science graduates are brighter because the standards for science faculties are higher, the finance sector has started poaching scientists and engineers right out of college. In 1969 Mitsubishi Bank hired its first science graduate; in 1972 it hired its second. By the spring of 1989 Mitsubishi Bank expected 80 of its 420 new employees would be science and engineering graduates (Aridome 1988, 53). Nomura Securities hired 50 science majors in 1988; Sumitomo Bank hired 77. Both firms almost doubled the number of science and engineering graduates over the number hired the previous year (ST, August 11, 1988).

The increase of science-track graduates going to the financial sector is evident in university data as well as those gathered from the companies themselves. In 1988, some 20.3 percent of the science graduates from Sophia University joined finance firms, compared to 5.8 percent in 1986 (figure 16). College seniors realize that while their starting salaries might not be much different if they went to NEC or to Sumitomo Bank, by their midthirties employees at an electronics firm would be earning ¥7 million a year, compared to ¥10 million at a bank or securities firm (ST, August 11, 1988). With this kind of differential in salaries it is not surprising that Fuji Bank, Sumitomo Bank, and Nomura have recently joined the ranks of science students' top fifty choices for jobs. As organizations in the financial sector increase both their appetite for scientists and their susceptibility to midcareer job changing, they are beginning to encroach on a labor pool that has traditionally been buffered from the more avant garde human resource practices of the service industry.

TECHNOLOGY FIRMS

Without a sense of history in the area of midcareer hiring, one might expect the service industry to be on the cutting edge of breaking down the lifetime employment system. In fact, during the postwar era the technological manufacturing sector has never been significantly buffered from midcareer job changing. Technology firms looking for specialists have always been the most likely to poach employees from another company. Certainly this is no different today. And the success stories of technology firms like Asahi Glass and Canon that hire midcareer employees only serve to encourage other firms to follow their examples.

Ten years ago, Asahi Glass was struggling for life in a stagnant market. Over the past decade the company has moved out of the glass industry into other markets, largely by hiring more than two hundred midcareer employees who understand innovative technologies and how these technologies should be marketed. Currently half of Asahi Glass's revenues come from nonglass products, and stock prices, sales, and profits are at their highest levels ever.

Canon Inc. is almost a household word in the United States because of

Figure 16

Sectors in Which Sophia University Science
Graduates Found Jobs

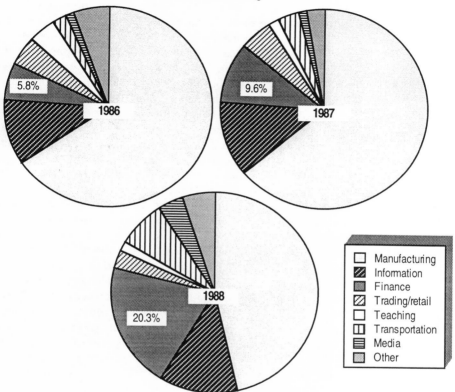

Source: *Business Tokyo*, November 1988, p. 53.

the company's ubiquitous cameras and photocopiers. Much of Canon's success is attributable to its hiring midcareer employees. In fact, in 1985 more than one-third of Canon's college graduate hires were

> not fresh out of college, but technicians and researchers with prior experience in the electronics field. "We believe that Canon's high profitability has resulted, for some part, from our employment policy, which has increased the organization's flexibility," note[d] a personnel department member. (*BT,* May 1987, 41)

Nisshinbo's Midcareer Recruiting

Nisshinbo, a textile firm founded in 1908, began making brake linings before the beginning of World War II. By the early 1980s the company was known as a premier manufacturer of drum and disk brakes. About this time Nisshinbo's planners realized that computer technology was likely to play an important role in brake systems in the near future. Their predictions were well founded: by 1986 most European cars were outfitted with antiskid braking systems (ABS). Only about 4 to 5 percent of Japanese automobiles were similarly equipped. Nisshinbo officials could all too easily imagine their drum and disk brakes becoming outmoded.

In late 1986, Nisshinbo executives established a new department to begin developing an ABS system. The department head was assigned from one of the firm's traditional business groups and told to ask for any personnel he might need to push the new product through as quickly as possible. He immediately began to complain to his superiors that the specialists and technicians needed to complete the project were simply not available in the company. While Nisshinbo had hired some midcareer specialists in the past, there had never been more than one or two college graduate midcareer hires in any given year—and Nisshinbo had not actively recruited those who did join. Under the pressure of the ABS project, however, a decision was finally made to begin midcareer recruiting.

But no one knew how to do it. The company's contacts for normal recruiting had no relationships with the kinds of electronics specialists needed in the new department. Furthermore, Nisshinbo was known as a textile firm and a brake manufacturer, a reputation that did not help in trying to recruit electrical engineers and specialist chemists. Since the search for new personnel could not be handled internally, Nisshinbo decided to turn to electronic specialist scouts and *tōroku* companies. While some Nisshinbo executives worried what the use of such specialists would do to the reputation of their "well-established" firm, others in the company persuaded them that the only way to stay in the brake business was to hire new specialists. The manager of the new department reasoned that those engineers who registered with *tōroku* companies and those acquainted with scouts were probably exactly the kind of specialists Nisshinbo was looking for: men with rare skills, high self-esteem, and pride in their work. After all, if an engineer was not good at what he did or did not want to find challenging work, he would not bother to associate with placement firms. Eventually, Nisshinbo's top executives agreed to allow the use of midcareer placement companies on the condition that only the firms with the highest reputation in the industry be employed. Since 1986, the ABS department has hired twelve to thirteen new midcareer employees annually. The most expeditious of these hiring decisions was made in only one week.

The benefits the ABS department enjoyed after this midcareer hiring began became evident to the rest of the company immediately. Other departments who lacked manufacturing, design, marketing, or managerial talent within their own ranks were suddenly appealing to top executives for the chance to hire midcareer specialists. Permission was given in several of these cases, and the company now hires twenty to thirty midcareer specialists every year to fulfill many different functions in a variety of departments. The decision to use midcareer placement firms and scouts has also stood the test of time. The company tried newspaper and magazine want ads to attract new personnel but found that these methods resulted in a flood of four hundred to five hundred applications for every few jobs to be filled. To avoid spending too much administrative time and effort processing applications, Nisshinbo decided to stick to the original strategy of the ABS department. The unorthodox methods of the ABS project have become not only accepted but positively encouraged in the company. Nisshinbo's personnel chief has been quoted as saying that "the company itself is much more satisfied when the number of midcareer recruits is high" (*Gekkan Sōmu*, February 1989, 39).

Increasing Sphere of Influence of Successful Firms

As stories about these and other companies' successes with "experienced" employees have become more popular in Japan, more and more enterprises have joined them on the midcareer hiring bandwagon. A team leader in the personnel division at Mitsubishi Corporation recently announced that his company had decided to take "mid-career hiring as seriously as hiring college graduates"; at Chuo Trust Bank, which had originally announced a limited form of midcareer recruiting, the popularity of this form of employment brought a more recent statement from the personnel director that there would no longer be any limit on hiring midcareer specialists at the bank. "As long as people are good, they will be hired" (Takita 1987, 221). And Tokyo Denryoku (Tokyo Electric) has established itself as one of the most brash of all Japanese companies by admitting publicly that its personnel managers are thinking about not recruiting college seniors because of the high cost of training young employees. Instead, the firm would rely completely on midcareer hiring (*AS,* January 6, 1988). Table 7 shows the emphasis placed on midcareer recruiting during the 1988 hiring season in a number of large Japanese firms.

According to Mr. Mizobuchi of Recruit Jinzai Center, in 1967 there were no large enterprises doing midcareer hiring in Japan. Ten years later 5 percent of these firms had adopted a limited form of midcareer hiring.[27] But even this ten-year perspective is not indicative of the alteration in employment trends. The change in attitudes toward job changing in Japan has been most pronounced in the very recent past. A 1984 study by the National Personnel Authority, which surveyed 336 companies on the first section of the Tokyo Stock Exchange, revealed that in that year

Table 7
A sampling of midcareer hiring versus new hiring, summer 1988

Company	Midcareer Recruits	First-time Job Seekers
Seibu Department Store	235	426
Nikko Securities	159	508
Mitsubishi Bank	40	405
TDK	27	100
Toyota Motor	21	582
Suntory	9	178
Mitsui & Company	0	334

Source: *Nikkei Sangyō Shinbun,* compiled from various issues, Summer 1988.

only 36 percent of companies were hiring employees with prior employment experience. In 1986 that number had climbed to 79 percent (*AS,* May 4, 1988; JEN, May 3, 1988). A survey of 4,100 manufacturing companies by the Ministry of Labor shows a similar trend occurring between 1987 and 1988, a trend that shows no signs of slowing in the future. As figure 17 shows, 46 percent more of the companies surveyed recruited personnel from other companies in January–March 1988 than had done so during a comparable period in 1987 (Koyama 1988, 8).

The apparent success of midcareer hiring does not seem to stem only from the efforts of Japanese organizations to create an environment conducive to job changing. Companies that have adopted policies of recruiting experienced workers have tapped into a segment of the Japanese work force that seems to have long been frustrated by the uniformity of the lifetime employment system in the country's larger enterprises. Without the enthusiasm of individual workers toward policies of midcareer employment it is unlikely that the companies would have made such strong inroads into that system. Table 8 shows the number of executives who applied for jobs with financial institutions following the companies' announcements of midcareer recruiting (*YS,* October 28, 1986). On average, the number of applicants outstripped advertised positions by a ratio of 20 to 1. At Sumitomo Trust alone, fifteen hundred people applied for approximately thirty jobs; at Sumitomo Fire and Marine five hundred applicants applied for ten positions; and Mitsubishi Bank was swamped with more than two hundred phone calls a day for six months following the placement of an ad requesting applications from experienced workers. This kind of enthusiasm is not reserved for direct recruiting. In one month during the summer of 1986, fifteen hundred people registered with one *tōroku* company in Japan for the chance to find a new job. Only 730 jobs were available.

Figure 17
Increases in Percentage of Firms in Three Industries Involved in Mid-Career Recruiting

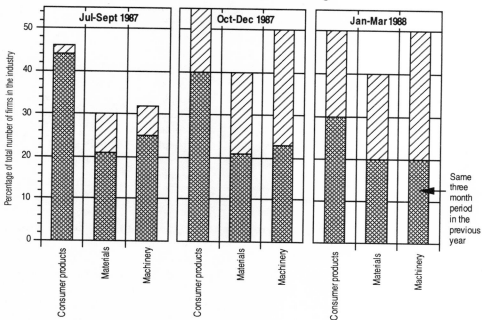

Source: *Nikkei Shinbun*, Summer 1988

That the experienced executive labor supply vastly outstrips demand should not surprise anyone who has observed the viselike grip lifetime employment has had on personnel practices in postwar Japan. What is interesting, however, is that companies seem more than able to satisfy their need for highly qualified new personnel. In a recent survey of high-tech firms, respondents replied that on average they expected to hire 3.2 midcareer employees during the year. In fact they ended up hiring 3.3 (Dokushin no Kyūyo 1988, 33). This kind of data corroborates one personnel manager's lament that after interviews with a number of the mid-career job applicants he would "hire ten times as many people" as top management would allow.[28] The abundance of qualified workers willing to be considered for a position with a new firm has made midcareer hiring easier for organizations.

As companies that hire job-changers continue to show successful results to their employees and their stockholders, news of that success feeds back into a large social consciousness. Stories about companies like Asahi Glass, Canon, Sumitomo Trust, and others appear in the newspa-

Table 8
Applicants for bank midcareer hiring slots

Bank	Ad Date	No. of Applicants	Number of People Hired or Still Interviewing	
Mitsubishi Bank	8/86	580	Fewer than 100 people	Still interviewing
Mitsui Bank	9/86	300	20–30 people	Still interviewing
Yasuda Trust	12/84	60	3 people	Hired
Yasuda Trust	12/85	100	7 people	Hired
Yasuda Trust	10/86	?	No limit	Accepting applications
Sumitomo Trust	11/85	400	4 people	Hired
Sumitomo Trust	11/86	600	10 people	Hired
Sumitomo Trust	11/87	500+	No limit	Accepting applications
Mitsubishi Trust	11/85	60	3 people	Hired

Source: *Yomiuri Shinbun*, October 28, 1986.

pers today without any derogatory tone attached to their hiring "experienced" workers. In the past such accounts often painted job-changers as traitors and their new employers as accomplices in a crime against society. But more than tone has changed in media reports of job changing. The frequency of articles about *tenshoku* and *chūtosaiyō* has increased significantly over the last few years. In 1982, the word *chūtosaiyō* appeared only fifteen times and *tenshoku* only twenty-two times in the *Nihon Keizai Shinbun*. In 1987 those numbers had increased to 183 and 143 respectively (table 9).

The relationship between organizations and the overall business environment is similar to that between the individual employee and the organization. Changes in the broader system are unlikely to occur in response to changes by isolated organizations. Rather, environmental responses occur when aggregations of companies or a few very prestigious organizations decide to change their employment practices. This seems to be occurring to some extent in Japan. After Yasuda Trust took the lead in midcareer hiring, it was nearly a year before other companies in the financial industry began to respond. When they did, however, the pace of change increased very rapidly (see figure 12, chapter 5).

Conclusion

It may well be that the history of Japanese lifetime employment is full of the stories of individuals who wanted to change jobs, but lacked the freedom to do so. It has only been in the past few years that environmental

Table 9
Number of occurrences of terms in the *Nikkei Shinbun*, 1982–1987*

Year	*Chūtosaiyō*	*Tenshoku*
1982	15	22
1983	24	40
1984	37	49
1985	75	63
1986	162	82
1987	183	143

*Word counts come from computerized Nikkei database. The number indicated represents the number of articles including these terms in these years.

and organizational changes have created an expanding external labor market in Japan such that elite corporation employees can move to companies of size and stature comparable to their original firms. This chapter discussed the growing body of evidence that such companies may be increasingly willing not only to entertain the notion of midcareer hiring but to actively encourage it through recruiting employees away from other firms. While Japanese midcareer recruiting is still nowhere near the levels found in the Western business world, the increase in the practice provides an unprecedented level of opportunity for a dissatisfied Japanese executive to desert his "lifetime" employer for some other firm, where he may perhaps have a more interesting life and a better time.

CHAPTER SEVEN

Motivations for Change

CONSIDERING that the Japanese have long thought of job hopping as a breach of values so severe as to be almost criminal, it seems fitting to approach the increases in midcareer job changing among Japan's elite salaryman from the perspective of March and Simon's theoretical position, which seeks to establish motive and opportunity as prerequisites for a job change much the way detectives search for the same elements in the commission of a felony. The previous chapter considered one of the conditions that presage job changing according to March and Simon (opportunity); this chapter discusses the motives Japanese businessmen may have to leave "permanent" employment positions. In it we discuss evidence that attitudes toward job changing are undergoing a pronounced change in Japan, away from traditional values of absolute loyalty to the corporation and toward a more individualistic and merit-based perspective on employment. We then propose a taxonomy of Japanese elite job-changers and consider the various pressures that these groups face in considering a midcareer move. Finally we discuss the ways in which changes in motivation for job changing "feed back" to enhance the organizational and environmental strucutres that encouraged job changing in the first place.

Changes in Attitudes toward Job Changing

The attitude of Japanese workers toward their companies and their jobs has long been the subject of envy among Western managers. As we discussed in chapters 2 and 3, the primacy of the company in a worker's life is one of the longstanding traits of Japanese society. This attitude dates back to the Tokugawa period, when the Japanese proverb *"Nikun ni mamiezu"* (A samurai cannot obey two masters) was introduced. Today this proverb is still used to justify the refusal of some Japanese to consider a strong commitment to any activity outside the work world. It is also grounds for some employers to refuse to hire a midcareer employee. In the Japan of the mid-1980s, male employees still seemed to get more psychic satisfaction from work than did their American counterparts. A survey of 240 top managers in six American and six Japanese firms showed that Japanese were more prone to overwork, found more satisfaction in their work lives, had been with their present firm longer, and were more inclined to expect that they would stay with their present firm until retirement (*NKS*, Jan. 18, 1986).

Most observers who put themselves in the place of an individual Japanese salaryman would agree that the social pressures not to change jobs have been pervasive and compelling for the country's corporate elite. But these pressures are not the only contingencies that affect the lives of almost every Japanese executive. The very strength of traditional reactions against job changing attests to the existence of other factors that might encourage lifetime employees to leave their firms: there is little need to guard a person who has no reason to escape. Of course, every salaryman has personal and unique reasons for staying in or leaving his firm. However, some motivations for changing jobs are experienced by virtually every Japanese executive. Others are felt particularly strongly by groups of Japanese businessmen at different stages in their careers. Consideration of these motivating forces is crucial for understanding the turnover decision of the individual salaryman.

Japanese executives face many of the same difficulties and drudgeries that might make a job seem less than enticing to any white-collar worker anywhere in the world. In fact, in many instances the Japanese seem to work under less appealing conditions than their counterparts in the West. The Japanese are certainly not oblivious to the everyday inconveniences and irritations many of them experience in their jobs. They complain about these problems to their co-workers over sake or beer as they wind down after a day's work. They grumble as they board crowded subways during the morning "commuters' hell" and rub bleary eyes during the endless workday common to almost all elite Japanese salarymen. It is not uncommon to hear a Japanese executive musing about the possibility of a job change that might "take me away from all this." The vast majority of such suggestions are not to be taken seriously. They can be placed in the same category as the constant complaints Japanese housewives make to each other about their husbands; rather than presaging the end of a tenuous commitment, they function to build camaraderie and to give the grumbler an outlet that eases the tensions inherent in a permanent relationship.

Nevertheless, the number of Japanese workers who claim to want to change jobs has been growing. For example, in a Ministry of Labor survey conducted in 1974, some 2,200,000 Japanese claimed they wanted to change jobs. In 1984 that number had climbed to 3,580,000. This growth does not appear to be based on some faddish surge of job hopping; rather it reflects attitudes that have been gaining strength throughout the postwar period. For instance, in 1981 Marsh and Mannari found that

> male employees in Japan do not uniformly support lifetime commitment norms and values, even in large, leading firms. Their "commitment" is not an absolute moral value of unconditional loyalty to the firm. Rather, it is more of a contingent, conditional norm: under certain conditions, I shall stay in the firm and give it my loyalty; but under other conditions, I shall quit the firm if given the opportunity . . . The source of lifetime commitment, then, is not some generalized propensity of "Japaneseness," but rather a set of quite specific, yet universal factors that influence inter-firm mobility rates in other societies as well. (Marsh and Mannari 1981, 452)

Cole noted in 1971 that the more educated workers in his study were less likely to conform rigidly to Japanese social norms. He postulated that qualities of independence were likely to become more prevalent as education levels continued to rise in Japan:

> the cynicism and skepticism . . . their willingness to exercise civil rights, their willingness to oppose management . . . their competitiveness, and their use of *giri* (feelings of obligation toward another person or persons) in an instrumental fashion for their own self-interest are all characteristics that can hardly be described as traditionalistic. It is precisely these characteristics which are increasingly common. (Cole 1971, 277)

Cole's prediction and Marsh and Mannari's conclusions are borne out by survey data that indicate Japanese attitudes toward work and toward sacrifice for societal good have changed significantly through the postwar years. The number of workers who feel that they should work more than the average has declined (figure 18), and the importance placed on "societal needs" is now being challenged by the importance placed on individual life (figure 19).[1]

The Managerial Elites Who Change Jobs

While the above figures are aggregated across the society, this book is intended to focus on the managerial elite and their attitudes and behaviors concerning midcareer job changing and corporate loyalty. Even

Figure 18

To What Extent Should We Work?

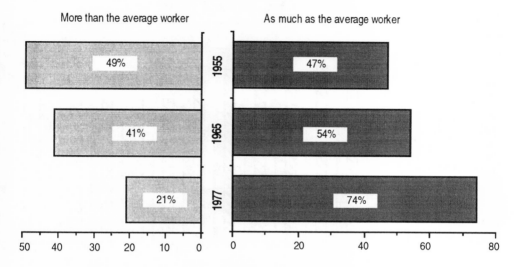

More than the average worker   As much as the average worker

1955   49%   47%
1965   41%   54%
1977   21%   74%

50 40 30 20 10 0   0 20 40 60 80

Source: Prime Minister's Office, Opinion poll, as quoted in *Scenarios 1990, Japan*
(Tokyo: Economic Planning Agency, 1981), p. 83.

within this rather small but important subsection of Japanese population, some elites are more likely to change jobs than others. It would be useful at this point to disaggregate these types and explain their various motivations toward job mobility. The young employee with the freedom to take risks, the older employee who anticipated not being promoted as quickly or as far as he would like within his present organization, and the employee who had already become a part of the mobile elite track in Japan were most likely to change jobs during the late 1980s. In the following sections we discuss each of these types and provide an illustrative case history for each.

THE YOUNG EMPLOYEE

Young people in Japan are more prone than their elders to emphasize their individual needs to the exclusion of societal and national goals and thus are one of the largest groups of job-changers among the corporate elite. Over the past half-century, young Japanese people have come to emphasize the importance of personal pleasure. Their top priorities as listed on attitudinal surveys contrast with responses such as "living a clean, honest life" and "working for the benefit of society," which domi-

Figure 19

Which Needs—Society's or Individual's—Should
Be Emphasized Most?

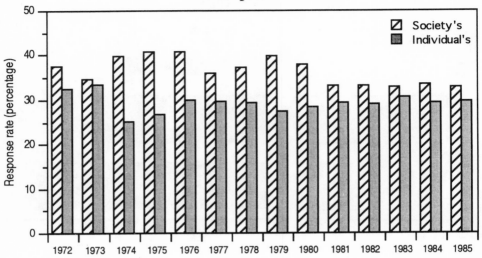

Source: Prime Minister's Office, *Seron Chōsa*, (Tokyo), May 1986, p. 4.

nated responses in the past (figure 20). Twenty- and thirty-year-olds are much less likely than their older counterparts to be willing to sacrifice their personal lives for the sake of the company (figure 21). In 1978 the percentage of Japanese responding that they placed the most emphasis on leisure activities surpassed those emphasizing earning enough money to be able to eat. In 1983, the percentage of leisure seekers surpassed even those who were most intent on finding a way to meet their rent and mortgage payments, making leisure the activity ranked "most important" by young Japanese for the first time in postwar history (figure 22). Because of these attitudes, which are very different from those of their parents, young people today have come to be known as *shinjinrui*.[2]

The members of this "new race" have grown up with a set of societal myths about what leads to success in their world that is quite different from their parents'. One of the popular anecdotes being passed around among college students in the 1980s is the story about a group of graduating seniors vying for entry-level positions at Ajinomoto, the food producer. The story's popularity and the insight it gives into young college graduates' concept of their career development make it worth repeating here.

Ajinomoto's first product, the company's namesake, was monosodium glutamate (MSG), a popular Asian seasoner. Ajinomoto packaged this

Figure 20

Changes in Young People's Values

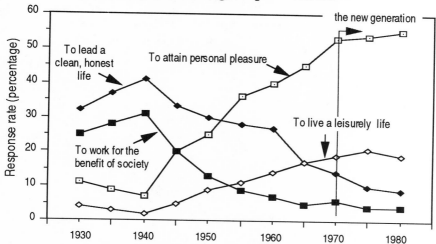

Source: Statistics and Research Center, Ministry of Education, as reported in the
Sanwa Economic Letter, January 1986.
Note: In all cases the respondents were males aged 15-24.

Figure 21

Willingness to Sacrifice Personal Life for the Sake of the Company

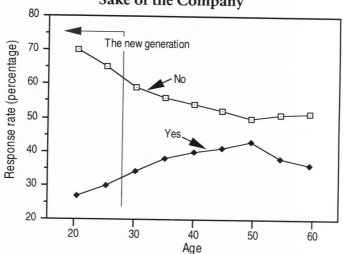

Source: Public Survey Prime Minister's Office, as reported in the
Sanwa Economic Letter, January 1986.

Figure 22

In the Immediate Future, on Which Part of Your Life Do You Expect to Expend the Most Energy?

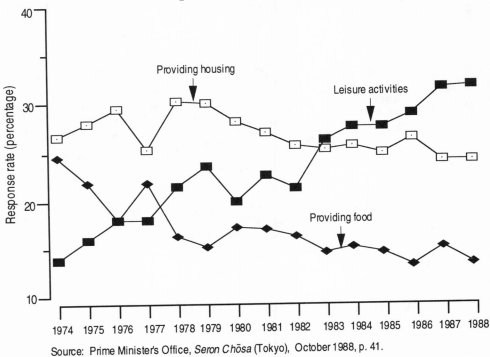

Source: Prime Minister's Office, *Seron Chōsa* (Tokyo), October 1988, p. 41.

powder in brightly colored salt-shaker-like containers and marketed it throughout East Asia. What Kleenex is to facial tissue and McDonald's is to fast food, Ajinomoto is to MSG.

According to the story, three students ended up obtaining an interview with the most important executive at Ajinomoto. Two of the candidates were top students from the top universities in Japan who had done nothing but study during high school so that they were able to pass the necessary entrance exams to join the right kinds of colleges. These two used their alumni connections to enter the formal recruiting process at a number of major Japanese companies. Their decorum throughout the process was excruciatingly proper, and they came to the Ajinomoto interview carefully prepared to answer all possible questions in the expected ways.

The third student, so the story goes, was somewhat out of place. He qualified to enter a good university in Japan, but he was never much interested in studies. He read widely, participated on the American football team at his university, and spent a great deal of time talking with friends about a variety of different topics. In the interview he is said to have behaved almost casually, in sharp contrast to his deferential rivals.

The interviewer reportedly asked these three candidates only one question. "Ajinomoto is the basic product in our company. Recently, however, our sales are down. Top management is worried about this year's sales figure. How would you propose to boost sales as quickly as possible?"

The first student came out immediately with a response carefully crafted to fit in with what he knew of the company's standard procedure. "I would increase the amount and the efficacy of television advertising. Particularly I would use daytime commercials during the most popular soap operas in midafternoon. This is the time that housewives are preparing their shopping lists before they go to the store to buy food for dinner." The interviewer nodded.

The second student was even better versed in Ajinomoto's traditional sales techniques than the first. He responded: "I would use advertising on television and in homemakers' magazines to offer low-price cookbooks to housewives. In these books the company could place recipes that rely on Ajinomoto as a key ingredient. In this way housewives would buy more Ajinomoto." Again the interviewer nodded.

The third student had listened carefully to the first two. When the interviewer finally called on him, he leaned back in his chair, thought for a moment, and said simply, "Widen the holes in the shaker."

The third student was immediately hired.

The young Japanese who tell and listen to this anecdote are always amazed by the innovativeness and boldness and nonstereotypical nature of the third student. They walk away from the story with a new resolve to try to be innovative and an impression that today's Japanese companies are looking for a very different kind of employee than they selected in the past.

Naturally, employers hear these stories, too, and try to adapt their hiring practices to appeal to the new employees who are now graduating from Japanese colleges. Once the *shinjinrui* join the big companies in Japan, however, they often pose significant problems to senior managers who expect them to behave like previously hired employees. One example of this type of problem occurred in Fuji Bank in 1986. Fuji had made more effort than most banks to recruit *shinjinrui* that year. Top management felt that the corporate culture had become too stagnant and *wan patan* (one pattern). They thought that some new and different blood in entry-level positions might solve the problem. Of the 269 people hired by the bank that year, 10 percent quit within the first twelve months of employment. The reason employees cited as most important in their decisions to leave Fuji was that during the recruiting process, the bank represented itself as a company that would allow its employees much more freedom than they were actually given after joining the firm. One new hire reportedly quit after his forty-year-old boss, during an after-work drinking spree, proudly boasted that he had never been home when his children were awake. Faced with the prospect of this much unexpected overtime, the young employee left the firm the next day (*AS*, July 10, 1988).

Japanese executives fresh out of college, besides perhaps possessing the universal confidence of youth, have grown up surrounded by more physical comfort and social freedom than their elders. The reasons young executives give for considering a job change reflect this difference in experience. In 1988 Recruit Research conducted a survey of 2,027 working men between the ages of twenty and thirty-nine in the Tokyo area (Recruit 1988). Of these, 869 were college graduates, of whom 25.4 percent had changed jobs. When these respondents were asked their reasons for changing jobs, thirteen of the seventeen most common responses centered on personal ambitions and dissatisfactions (figure 23). Questions of personal security, which comprised the majority of reasons given by older workers for considering a job change, were given far less prominence by their younger colleagues.

The definition of a "young" employee in job-changing terms is now a person in his twenties or thirties. College graduates during the 1960s and 1970s considered twenty-five to be the cutoff age for any "midcareer" changes in organizational affiliation. At that time, a twenty-five-year-old could reasonably expect a job change to entail only a small move down in the corporate hierarchy. During the late 1970s and early 1980s, the "age limit" for job changing gradually increased, until even employees in their late twenties could potentially change jobs without suffering such downward mobility. Thus, an "elite" employee could consider beginning a career at age twenty-nine with a top-tier firm after having gained experience in another firm until that time. Science-track students were the most likely to be able to effect smooth changes in their later twenties. Nevertheless, the employee who joined a new firm after some experience in another organization was never considered in a viable position for a top position in the firm later in life.

Today want ads generally allow for employees to change jobs up to the age of thirty-five. In fact, Recruit Company's publication *B-ing* includes a special section in the index entitled "Opportunities for those over 35." Of the 1,190 companies offering jobs in the February 25, 1988, edition of *B-ing*, only thirty-four advertisements made special reference to a willingness to hire those over thirty-five (113). Because of the rising age limit for midcareer changes, the young elites seem to consider employment much more fluid than the salarymen of twenty or thirty years ago.

Figure 23

Why Younger Employees Change Jobs

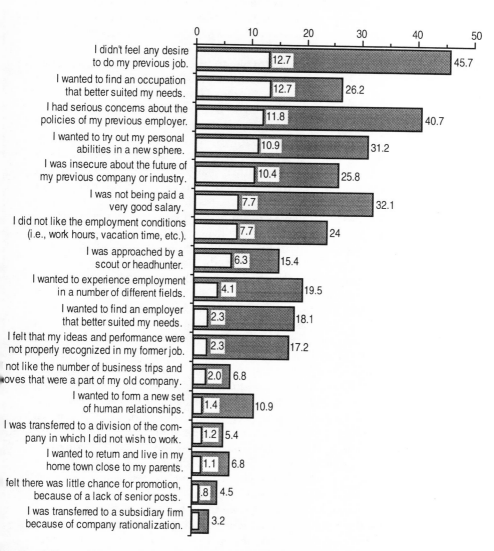

▨ Percentage of respondents listing this as one of their reasons

☐ Percentage of respondents listing this as their *first* reason

Reason	First reason	One of their reasons
I didn't feel any desire to do my previous job.	12.7	45.7
I wanted to find an occupation that better suited my needs.	12.7	26.2
I had serious concerns about the policies of my previous employer.	11.8	40.7
I wanted to try out my personal abilities in a new sphere.	10.9	31.2
I was insecure about the future of my previous company or industry.	10.4	25.8
I was not being paid a very good salary.	7.7	32.1
I did not like the employment conditions (i.e., work hours, vacation time, etc.).	7.7	24
I was approached by a scout or headhunter.	6.3	15.4
I wanted to experience employment in a number of different fields.	4.1	19.5
I wanted to find an employer that better suited my needs.	2.3	18.1
I felt that my ideas and performance were not properly recognized in my former job.	2.3	17.2
not like the number of business trips and moves that were a part of my old company.	2.0	6.8
I wanted to form a new set of human relationships.	1.4	10.9
I was transferred to a division of the company in which I did not wish to work.	1.2	5.4
I wanted to return and live in my home town close to my parents.	1.1	6.8
felt there was little chance for promotion, because of a lack of senior posts.	8	4.5
I was transferred to a subsidiary firm because of company rationalization.		3.2

ce: Recruit Research Company, *Tenshoku Jittai Chōsa 1988* (Tokyo, 1988).

Case Study: Shinji Kato

There are several things that Shinji Kato considers worth doing once in his lifetime. Some of these things—like skydiving, rafting down the Amazon, and gambling the night away in a Riviera casino—Kato has yet to accomplish. Others he has already done—once—and although he has no particular intention of repeating these experiences, he is glad to have had them. So far, the list of Kato's once-in-a-lifetime achievements includes nude sunbathing on the roof of his college dormitory, racing through Tokyo at night in a friend's trimmed-down, souped-up sportscar, attending a Michael Jackson concert, and changing jobs.

When Kato decided to leave Itoyokado, the department store where he had gone to work after his graduation from Tokyo University, some of his friends thought him rather daring. Those who had changed jobs themselves or who were planning to do so in the future seemed to admire him for the move, and the misgivings of those who were still too timid to leave their own firms had been laced with envy. Kato wasn't reckless. He simply knew what he wanted—and what he deserved. After an entire childhood spent studying in the leather chair at the desk his parents had bought him when his legs were still too short to touch the floor; after endless evenings cramming facts into his brain at after-school *juku* classes; after surviving Japan's "exam hell" to go on to the most prestigious university in the nation—after all this, Kato felt he should have a little freedom. Why endure so much drudgery during one's youth just to continue it as an adult? He and his friends should be expected to have a chance to switch jobs once they had been in the work force long enough to decide what they really enjoyed.

What Kato really enjoys is finance. How could he have known that before he tried it? He was a sociology major at Tokyo University, and although his skills had served him well in the "people" side of business they hadn't introduced him to the excitement of dealing with real money in the real world. A department store had seemed like just the organization for Kato, the New College Graduate. The work was hardly thrilling, but all young salarymen had boring jobs during their first few years. For Kato the initial assignment had been conducting floor sales in one of Itoyokado's outlets. The excruciating dullness of his daily duties had not mattered as much to Kato as the fact that his immediate superior had been a man of youthful character. He acted almost as young as Kato himself. Having such a boss had been important to Kato. He wanted to work with someone who understood him. The gray-haired men with their old-fashioned attitudes who had interviewed him for most of his prospective jobs were not the kind of people who would understand that a rafting trip down the Amazon, just for the hell of it, might be a trip worth taking.

Itoyokado had been good to Kato. He appreciated the company personnel for their generosity and even more for having moved him out of sales and into finance during his third year with the firm. That was when Kato's brain, lulled by the restful atmosphere of the forgiving Japanese college system and the menswear department of the department store, had found itself being suddenly and pleasantly awakened by his job. Kato liked manipulating Itoyokado's finances. Even more than that, he liked matching wits with the sharp-witted representatives of the banks with whom he regularly dealt. It was not long before Kato found himself resenting the parochial, unambitious atmosphere of the department store. Retailing bored and irritated him. He knew he would be happier doing real finance, in a real bank with real bankers. He was unmarried, independent, and not attached by any particular title to Itoyokado. In fact, after seven years with the store he had not yet been made *kachō*. With the number of employees waiting in line for titles, there was little chance Kato would be more than an anonymous drudge at Itoyokado for another three or four years. Yes, he decided, it was a good thing to change jobs one time, and for Kato that time had come.

Kato put out some feelers with friends he knew in banking. He didn't tell them outright that he was considering going into finance, but he let them know that he was open to the idea. Either these efforts paid off, or it was serendipity that led a scout to call Kato not long after his decision to change jobs. The scout was working for Mitsubishi Bank, whose directors were looking to hire a few bright young salarymen from the more aggressive corporate culture of retailing to add zest to their own rather stodgy tradition. Mitsubishi Bank also wanted men who could not only learn banking quickly but bring with them the perspectives of client firms to help with strategic planning. If the bank hired Kato, his salary would rise by 50 percent; he might even be given a title. Kato thought about it. Once in his lifetime, he planned to open the hatch of an airplane and jump out with nothing more than a packed-up piece of cloth on his back. This wasn't much different—a bit scary, but exhilarating. Kato agreed to an interview with Mitsubishi.

Contrary to Kato's expectations, his parents were thrilled by the prospect of having a banker for a son. Their prestige went up in their own eyes before Kato even met with the bank's representatives. His boss at Itoyokado was surprised, and rather hurt. He asked Kato to "think it over one more time," but wistfully admitted that he had no authority to stop his employees from leaving. Kato felt a tug of obligation when he thought that his boss might be discredited by having lost an employee, but his guilt retreated into the furthest corner of his mind when he met with his prospective colleagues at Mitsubishi Bank. The respect they paid him, far from being minimized by his status as a midcareer hire, was greater than he had ever experienced at Itoyokado. Mitsubishi had hired several "experienced" men, and Kato heard from them that the company treated them as well as, if not better than, the "lifers."

Thus, when Mitsubishi offered Kato a job, the incentives to take it far outweighed the reasons for turning it down. True, changing jobs was a newfangled thing to do. True, his boss at Itoyokado might take a little flak. True, some of his friends and co-workers would think he was riding on the wild side. That was all right with Kato. If he ever got an opportunity to spend one divinely decadent night gambling on the Riviera, he planned to jump at the chance. Why not take this one now? When they lowered him into his grave, did he want his survivors to remember a man who had lived a life confined to the obedient drudgery of an older generation? There was no sense in it, no purpose. What good would his life be if he was too busy satisfying public opinion to enjoy it? Kato decided to satisfy himself. In his mind's eye he fastened his parachute, picked up his machete, and shook the dice in his sweating, excited palm. And then he changed jobs—once in a lifetime.

Older Employees

For the elite employees in their late thirties through late forties, little has changed in employment patterns from the time they entered the work force. Very few Japanese firms are recruiting executives who have only ten years of productivity left to join their companies as new employees. Western firms also tend to avoid this age group. Many Western firms either look for the young, still malleable "expert" or seek an "elder statesman" who can carry out the duties of a country representative. This is the age group that is represented in figure 4 (chapter 4) with less than 10 percent having ever changed jobs in their lives.

For the employees in their late forties and early fifties the question whether to change jobs has become more and more pressing in recent years. In Japan's era of high growth and increase in working-age population, elderly workers were assured of employment through their sunset years. Supply did not meet the demands of a thriving economy, and there were many new employees to be trained and managed through the early 1970s. Even if retirement were forced at age fifty-five, and consequently an employee's salary was reduced, he often could continue in the same job he had before retirement—the only difference being the lower level of pay. If the same job were not available, the employee was at least assured of employment somewhere in the corporate family.

When what are now older workers took their jobs, "lifetime employment" meant that the company would take care of them throughout their careers and into their retirement. One middle-aged banker we interviewed voiced a complaint common to his age group, that these days "taking care" often means some "low paying job at a no-name company."[3] A similar lament appeared in a recent volume of the *Japan Quarterly* under the title "Lost: Illusions about Japanese Management":

> When I bump into old schoolmates who were top students in our university days, I am always surprised to find that none of them are very well off. Upon graduation, many of the best students from the most prestigious universities secured positions with first-class companies in the industries that were booming at the time—motion pictures, textiles, steel shipbuilding, and petrochemicals. The recent recession set off a bad slump in all of these once-thriving industries, and employees in their 40s and 50s—in the prime of their career—live in constant fear of being sacked, sent to a subsidiary company, or transferred to an outlying branch office. Those who did not study hard at school and had no choice but to enter a distribution or service industry are now working happily under much more favorable conditions. (Esaka 1987, 423)

The concern of older workers about the company's promise to "take care" of them, a personal history that includes the memory of war, economic upheaval, and nationwide poverty, and the concerns surrounding imminent retirement give the individual turnover choice of the older Japanese salaryman a somewhat different flavor from the same choice being considered by a younger man. Figure 24 shows the responses of a hundred *kachō*-level employees to the question "When would you consider a job change?" For this sample of mature employees, six out of the nine defined responses to this question—("I would consider a change if: (1) I received a better offer; (2) my present company looked unstable; (3) personal relationships in my firm were poor; (4) my promotions were slow; (5) my pay were cut; and (6) I were transferred")—have a direct relationship to the employee's assurance that he is progressing along a stable career track in a secure company. These six reasons seem to stem from the individual's desire for personal well-being, a feature of job stability emphasized particularly by older employees in Japan.

With age pyramids turning into diamonds, slower growth, and restructuring, many Japanese firms are now eager to release their aging employees. These employees in their late forties and early fifties are the most expensive personnel in the company, and in some cases the least productive. While it is difficult to fire employees outright before retirement age, companies have started offering incentives for early retirement. Those who do not take the early retirement incentives cannot be sure that there will be a job for them after they reach the company retirement age. Thus, the organizational responses to aging employees are far different from the responses today's older workers observed in the firm when they first joined.

These organizational initiatives to trim the top-heavy organization

Figure 24

Reasons to Consider a Job Change

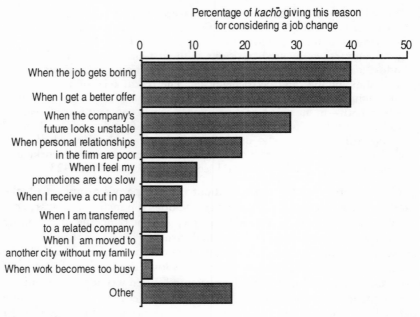

Source: *Nikkei Sangyō Shinbun*, October 9, 1987.

lead individuals nearing retirement to carefully consider opportunities apart from their "lifetime" employers—a point of view that, no matter how unwillingly adopted, represents a dramatic shift in older workers' attitudes toward job changing. As a headhunter, one of the authors noted that the responses of many of this age group seemed to border on desperation. They were not accustomed to talking about or even considering job changes, but when the opportunity arose, a change had to be carefully considered. Foreign firms are eager to hire employees in this age range, as are many smaller and midsized Japanese companies. Both of these potential employers look for the aging employee to bring them contacts in the "elite" Japanese firms and in the employee's industry in general. With retirement age approaching, many older corporate elites consider the offers of Western firms and small Japanese firms preferable to the job opportunities awaiting them after "retirement" in the companies they have been with most of their lives.

An illustration of the extent to which attitudes among younger people differ from those among employees above age thirty-five can be seen in a survey of more than a thousand college graduates working in private enterprises in late 1986 (Recruit 1986). Table 10 shows the differences in personal behavior and beliefs toward job changing among the respondents younger than and older than thirty-five. Those past thirty-five participate much less in job-changing activities than their younger counterparts.[4] These data compare favorably with our Job Changing Survey in which a sharp decline in job-changing behavior can be seen after age thirty-seven. (Those who were thirty-five during the 1986 survey were thirty-seven at the time of our 1988 survey.) Some 30 percent of those thirty-seven or younger had changed jobs compared with 15 percent of those thirty-eight or above. If these young job-changers carry their attitudes and behaviors with them as they grow older and in turn transmit those attitudes to younger employees, general beliefs about lifetime employment are likely to continue to change. Moreover, the period of mobility early in one's career is likely to merge with the period of older job change.

For young and old job-changers alike, the change in attitudes toward lifetime employment and loyalty to one's employer have been exacerbated by slowed economic growth and an aging work force in Japan. These factors have begun to necessitate layoffs in what were previously high-growth, glamorous industries, layoffs that lead many younger employees to wonder how long today's successful industries will remain vital. For example, ten years ago steel and automobiles were the best industries for an engineer to join. Today they are not growing, and the potential for promotion is small. Mr. Mizobuchi of Recruit Jinzai Center believes that many of the younger people he deals with are disillusioned with the sys-

Table 10

Differences between older and younger employees' attitudes and behaviors
(Question: Have you ever thought about changing jobs since you joined your present employer? Answers in percentages.)

	22–34 Years Old	35–44 Years Old
I have been actively involved in job-changing activities.	6.16	3.31
I have not been actively involved, but I do read and collect want ads.	8.22	3.31
I have not been actively involved, but I do think about changing jobs.	38.36	41.72
I have never thought about leaving this company.	47.26	51.66

Source: Recruit Research Company, *Bijinesuman ni kansuru chōsa* (Tokyo, 1986).

tem. "College graduates are best advised to join the best companies in the growth industries today," he says, "and then consider a midcareer move when there is a better industry or company that is doing midcareer hiring." Mizobuchi is convinced that the growing companies and industries are those doing midcareer hiring.[5]

Case Study: Masahiro Suginami

The American employees at the leasing firm where Masahiro Suginami works see him as a pleasant, soft-spoken gentleman. That is how they think of all their Japanese employees: unpredictable, perhaps, but mild-mannered to a fault. The Americans pat Suginami on the back when he enters the office in the morning and trade jocular amenities with him, their voices raised in an illogical but not unusual reaction to his accented English. A few of them wonder from time to time what he really thinks of them, but they know that whatever his opinions, he is far too bland to express any hostility.

The other Japanese executives at the company's Tokyo subsidiary know that the Americans are wrong. Being Japanese, they are alert to the nuances of Suginami's behavior. They know that beneath his social protocol, their co-worker is storing a backlog of anger as volcanic as Mount Fuji itself. They have heard what he sometimes says in the evening, after a few whiskeys, and what he leaves unsaid during the days in the office. They would be alarmed if Suginami's resentment were directed at them. Happily, it is not. In fact, whatever frustration Suginami encounters at his present firm seems to roll off him as though he were waxed and drop into the pool of anger he harbors toward the past, toward *that other leasing firm,* the one the company can no longer do business with, the one whose name Suginami refuses to speak. Sometimes Suginami's Japanese co-workers wonder if *that other firm* was really as bad as Suginami seems to feel. However, none of them has ever wondered why he changed jobs. He makes that clear whenever the percentage of alcohol in his bloodstream rises above zero.

All of Suginami's co-workers, American and Japanese alike, have been told the gist of the story. How Suginami, a blushingly innocent college graduate, had cast his lot with one of the top three leasing firms in Japan. How he trudged through the ranks, year by faithful year, doing his job with devotion Suginami compared to that of Hachiko, the dog who waited for its master at a train station every afternoon for years after the man had died. The admiring citizens of Tokyo had erected a statue in Hachiko's honor in Shibuya Station. Suginami's loyalty had received no such recognition. As he told his colleagues, he had molded his life around his firm, given it his time, his attention, his very soul, well into his middle-aged years. And then, just when he should have been enjoying the promotions and salaries that were supposed to come as his reward for all this devotion, *that other company* had reneged on its half of the unspoken executive deal.

New York. They had sent Suginami to New York. A forty-year-old man, a man deserving of respect and position in his own country, not to mention his own company, was sent to the New York office to deal with the Americans. Of course he went. *He* was not a traitor. *He* was not disloyal. *He* kept his word. Suginami had tolerated the transfer to New York without a murmur. He had set up the office there and even come to appreciate the freedom and novelty of the American post. Moreover, he had done very well for his company in the New York office. Suginami was proud of his work. During the height of the office's success, the director of the company had called from Tokyo to ask Suginami how he felt about his current position, and Suginami had honestly been able to report that he was enjoying his work so much he would like to stay in the United States for at least another year. The director had told him that he was free to choose his own course. Just before they had hung up, the boss had mentioned casually that a few rumors were floating around about Suginami's being given a new assignment but that they were insubstantial and should be ignored.

That was all the warning Suginami had received before two younger employees from *that other leasing firm* had shown up in the New York office and informed him that he was being transferred back to Tokyo. He had two weeks to train these men to perform jobs that he and his subordinates had taken months to master. It was during those two weeks that Suginami reached the limits of his endurance. The injustice of it all, combined with the frenzied pace of the work and the maddeningly subtle insolence of the two new workers (Suginami hadn't realized how accustomed he had become to the relaxed bluntness of American businessmen), made Suginami feel as though he was about to explode. His wife, apparently no less tainted by American attitudes than Suginami himself, had suggested that they spend an extra day or two in Hawaii on their way back to Japan. When he arrived at the Tokyo office, Suginami found that because of his unexplained two-day absence, which accounted for only a fraction of his unused vacation time, *that other leasing firm* had cut his salary by a small but noticeable amount. Suginami, nearly blinded by the headache that arose from his anger, had kept enough of his presence of mind to do a bit of detective work that day. His research confirmed his suspicions: the company was in financial trouble. The disorganization and mismanagement were no accident. It was symptomatic of what looked to Suginami like the company's impending decline.

That had been on November 3. On November 12, Suginami's eye had caught a headline in an industry journal about an American leasing firm that was accepting applications from experienced Japanese workers. He read the article carefully, then read it again. He had heard of the American company: one of his acquaintances in New York had frequently worked with it. It was a good firm, with a solid and growing reputation in the industry. On November 20, Suginami told his wife that he intended to apply for a job with the U.S. company. She shrugged and heaved a sigh, still feeling the sting of the salary cuts her husband had taken after her ill-fated suggestion that they vacation in Hawaii. On November 29, Suginami's forty-third birthday, he was hired as a vice-president in the Tokyo subsidiary.

At the end of January, Suginami informed his superior at his first company—*that other leasing firm*—that he was changing jobs. His boss had grunted and walked directly to the desk of the personnel director. The personnel director, in turn, had headed directly into the office of the company president. Suginami, having watched the proceedings, was not surprised when shortly thereafter he himself had been summoned to the president's office. The president did not mince words.

"I hear you're quitting," he had said to Suginami. "Moving to another firm."

"Yes, sir," Suginami replied.

There followed a full three minutes of complete silence, while the president sat glaring behind his desk. Just when Suginami had decided the man had gone mute with rage, the president spoke again.

"I would imagine this new company of yours would benefit from doing business with us."

"Yes," said Suginami.

"If you leave now," the president told him, "we will have no relationship with your company. Not now, not ever. We have spent a lot of money on you, and a lot of time. We have invested in you, and you would betray us by leaving."

Suginami stood silently, thinking of his lowered salary, of the surety that he would never be promoted as high as the men who had not been shipped off to New York and lost their place in the Japanese corporate hierarchy. The president glared at him again.

"Get out," he had said.

And so Suginami left *that other leasing firm*. The Americans had reacted good-naturedly to his former president's threats. In a year or so, they assured him, the old man will be gone, and the tension will fade. If Suginami worked hard and helped their operation succeed, soon his old company would have to accept them for simple economic reasons. This archaic Japanese code of chivalry could be taken only so far. When it started to interfere with economics, even Suginami's old firm would change its ways. His new bosses consoled Suginami with a 15 percent increase over the very reasonable salary he had been making at *that other firm* and took pains to treat him with respect. Even now, three years later, the Americans at the firm are still willing to listen with bland and uncomprehending faces as the story of Suginami's betrayal spurts out in intermittent eruptions, which they do not recognize as anger.

The Japanese he works with listen, too, and feel simultaneously sorry and glad for Suginami. It is sad that he was given less than he wanted at *that other firm,* but after all, didn't most older workers reach their promotion limit one day? Suginami was lucky to have had the chance to join another company. Such a thing would have been unheard of just a few years ago. So his Japanese co-workers listen, but they do not trouble themselves much over Suginami's story.

Suginami knows this. He does not mind. When he gets off the train in Shibuya Station after an evening of bitter reminiscing, the statue of Hachiko no longer fuels his fury. He wonders if Hachiko would think that the statue is worth a lifetime of waiting for a master who had never shown up. He hardly thinks so. There will never be a monument of loyalty erected to honor Masahiro Suginami, but at least he had the courage to abandon the empty station where *that other leasing firm* had abandoned him. It seems that he was born to lead the life of a Japanese salaryman, and in some ways it will always be a dog's life. But at least these days in Japan, Suginami thinks with a mixture of anger, pride, and gratitude, even a dog has choices.

THE MOBILE SECTOR

There is a good deal of evidence that a growing number of elite employees are devoted to careers with higher levels of labor mobility. One sign of this is that Japanese executives who change jobs once are very likely to do it again. Interviews with executive search consultants—and our own experience in that same capacity—revealed that most job searches end up finding midcareer hires among the ranks of executives who had already changed jobs. The proportion of searches we observed in which the position was filled by someone who had never changed jobs before was well under half.

This was especially true in industries like the financial sector. Michael Freedman, a mergers and acquisitions specialist at First Boston Corporation in Tokyo, said that his company was losing midcareer job-changers faster than it could hire them: "The velocity is amazing. Once the first corporate ties are broken, then people feel free to change jobs at any time. Since there are a lot of foreign firms in the market place now, there is a lot more moving than there was a few years ago."[6]

Statistics from our Job Changing Survey indicate that those who have changed jobs are likely to have lower levels of organizational commitment and are more likely to be thinking about changing jobs again.[7] It is unclear whether they are unhappy about the job changes they have made and want to get into a better company or want to change jobs again because they had such a good experience the first time.[8] The answers given to the questions addressed to the people with social ties to the job-changer shed some light on the issue of motivation for individuals changing jobs repeatedly. A few questions from our survey were directed to the wife of the executive being polled. A full 70 percent of those responding positively to the question "Should your husband think about changing jobs?" were wives of husbands who had changed jobs before. It is also interesting to note that wives whose husbands have changed jobs give very different reasons for advising a friend to change jobs from those given by the wives of more traditional lifetime employees (figure 25).

A job change by an individual Japanese salaryman thus appears to effect a marked change in the attitudes of his wife, and perhaps of other relatives and friends. Even more important in creating widespread attitudinal change is the effect the job-hopper might have on his co-workers. In our survey, men who had changed jobs were acquainted with significantly more job-changers (an average of 17.72 people) than those who had not changed jobs (12.28).[9] These statistics indicate that either these men had observed others who had changed jobs and then decided to change themselves or that other people who got to know these men saw the job change as a positive experience and decided to follow their acquaintances' example. Whatever the direction of the causality, it is significant that those who knew more people who changed jobs, and therefore were likely to have a clearer picture of the implications of job change, were more likely to change jobs themselves. If this trend continues, the more individuals change jobs the more public opinion will change in favor of job changing. Such attitudinal change may eventually have a strong effect on national norms surrounding other work and work-related attitudes.

Other findings support the data from our survey that indicate that, whether new attitudes about work precede or are a result of job-changing behavior, there is a clear correlation between the two. In a 1986 Recruit Research survey, the work-related attitudes and behaviors of respondents who had changed jobs (in almost all cases to Japanese firms) differed significantly from the attitudes of those who had never changed jobs. Job-changers tended to arrive later for work and get home earlier. They took more vacation time than their permanent employment counterparts. They expressed less desire for promotions, and they did not care as much about the prestige of higher positions. They tended to be employed in companies in which the promotion system was based on skill. They felt that their supervisors' evaluations of their performance was more accu-

Figure 25

Differences in Attitudes of College Educated Job-changers, Non-job-changers, and Their Wives

Most important factors in encouraging a friend to change companies:	Employee	Wife
He would be given a more interesting job.	**-** (1)	**-** ** (1)
He would be promoted to the next level.	**+** (5)	**+** * (7)
The new company's product is better.	**+** (3)	**-** * (5)
The new company's reputation is better.	**+** (7)	**+** (6)
His salary would be higher.	**+** * (2)	**+** (2)
He would be able to live in a bigger city.	**-** (8)	**-** (8)
He could spend more time with his family.	**-** (6)	**-** (3)
He would have a better chance of becoming a director.	**-** * (4)	**+** (4)

ANOVA significant at:

☐ p <.15

* .05 < p < .10

** p < .05

+ indicates those who have changed jobs give this factor greater emphasis than those who have no history of job changing

- indicates less emphasis on this factor by those who have changed jobs

( ) = ranking of the importance of factors by each type of respondent
[1 = most important; 8 = least]

Source: *Job Changing Survey*, 1988.

rate than did lifetime employees. They saw their reason for work as being to support their families. And finally, job-changers had less pride than nonchangers in their companies and in their jobs (Recruit 1986).[10]

It appears that a dual employment system like that described by Piore and Derringer in the United States is developing in the elite employment sector in Japan. Once an employee makes changes jobs, the likelihood of subsequent mobility is greatly increased.

Case Study: Ryo Tsuchida

The younger son of the Tsuchida family was expected to follow his father and brother through the ranks of the Japanese school system, into Waseda University, and on to a top position at the nation's largest steel company. Up to a point, he fulfilled these expectations exactly. He was a promising young man, bright but not brilliant, friendly but not ingratiating, attractive but not really handsome. Nothing about Ryo Tsuchida appeared unusual until it was too late for his family to do anything about it.

The explanation for Tsuchida's aberrant behavior could not be blamed on the way he was raised. Even that his parents gave him permission to attend a college for a year in the United States could hardly be considered unorthodox these days. Many parents allowed and even encouraged their children to spend a year abroad. Ryo's father had been almost eager to see his second son become used to American culture, language, and ways of thinking. The older man was well aware how useful such familiarity could be to a Japanese company. Every day, English language skills and knowledge of Western customs were becoming more and more essential to his own business. He half expected Ryo to take his position with the steel firm one day, and the boy's experience in America would be an invaluable asset when that happened.

But the American year—the only "aberration" the Tsuchidas had allowed during Ryo's upbringing—had other results. The boy had returned from the United States looking and acting as docile and as Japanese as he had when he left. He had returned to Waseda, graduated without any untoward incidents, and gone with all the other new degree holders to interview for jobs with the right kinds of companies—including the one that employed his father and brother. Whatever change the young man had undergone during his time abroad waited until the very last minute to show its effects. After days of standing in line with thousands of pressed and brushed young graduates, after hours of being interviewed by company executives, after undergoing background checks and home visits from the recruiters of various prestigious firms, the younger Tsuchida boy suddenly and dramatically veered from his expected course. One day, on his way home from a final interview with an automobile manufacturer, he stopped at the British embassy, applied for a job, obtained an interview, received an offer, and signed on as an embassy translator.

No one could explain it. Ryo's parents were at a loss. His brother was speechless. His neighbors, friends, and schoolmates were flabbergasted. Young Tsuchida's own explanation only puzzled them further. He said that the thought of taking a salaryman's job, one position in one company for the rest of his life, had made him feel claustrophobic. He wanted to keep perfecting the English he had struggled so hard to master during his year in the United States. He liked Westerners and Western culture: they intrigued and amused him. The work at the embassy was interesting. These and other equally bizarre reasons were all Tsuchida could offer to explain his deviation from the usual course of Japanese executive life.

The really strange thing was that even after his abnormal behavior, Tsuchida acted so very normal. He did not appear to be ashamed or stigmatized by his strange job choice. He maintained his easygoing, mannerly behavior at home and with college friends. His parents and brother, once they recovered from the initial shock of seeing Ryo join the British embassy, could not help noticing that he seemed happy in his job. The young man's confidence in his own actions eventually lulled them into acceptance of his decision. Ryo showed them his embassy pass, with its special diplomatic sticker on the back. He took them to eat in the embassy lunchroom, where he could buy exotic foreign foodstuffs (not to mention a few bottles of top-quality Scotch whisky) for a fraction of what they would cost anyone without embassy clearance. It was not too long before the Tsuchida family members found themselves boasting to other relatives and friends about Ryo's unusual but fascinating and prestigious job.

For five years, Tsuchida enjoyed the perquisites of embassy life with the understated enthusiasm that typified his personality. By the time he was twenty-seven, he spoke English as well as any Japanese in the embassy. He was so fluent, in fact, that the personal rewards of learning and the challenge of the language were beginning to wear a bit thin. And while his knowledge of the West was becoming more and more impressive, he was beginning to feel uncertain about his own culture. He began to feel nervous one day when a colleague asked him to translate a technical letter from English into Japanese (instead of Japanese to English, as he was used to doing) and he found himself unsure that he was writing the more difficult characters correctly. He had spent so much time socializing with the English that he was growing apart from his Japanese friends. They seemed more tuned in to what was happening in Tokyo— in fact, in Japan generally—than he was. Tsuchida began to worry. He would never truly be British, and he was afraid that at the rate he was going, he would soon find that he wasn't Japanese.

Tsuchida began to look around for job opportunities with a Japanese firm. That was the obvious answer to the question of how he should reintegrate himself into his own society. The very things that had bothered him about a salaryman's position when he was twenty-three were the things he most wanted now. Tsuchida's philosophy was that he would give more to his employers if he himself was benefiting in every possible way from his work. As his needs changed, he expected his jobs to change as well.

He took his time thinking about where he should go. He was not at all concerned that he would not find a suitable position. He had a degree from a good school, and his experience in the U.S. and the embassy could be worth a great deal to a Japanese company interested in expanding its international range. Tsuchida had known this all along—otherwise he would never have passed up his chances at a corporate job after graduating from college. The year in America had opened Tsuchida's eyes. These were not the old days. He had no reason to fear that a few job changes would hurt his future in the long run.

One day, about a month after he decided to switch jobs, Tsuchida ran across a promising-looking advertisement in a recruiting magazine. Nomura Securities was interested in hiring personnel with good foreign-language skills. He sent in his résumé, received a call from the company a few days later, and showed up the next week for interviews. Everything was eerily familiar as he waited in the office with the twenty or thirty other young men who had applied for Nomura's foreign-language positions. It was as though he were finally finishing the recruiting process he had begun five years before—only this time, all the pieces were in place. This time, the Japanese job market not only wanted Tsuchida, but Tsuchida genuinely wanted a place in the Japanese job market. He smiled as he went in to the interview, feeling confident and relaxed. It went very well, and Tsuchida was pleased but not overly surprised to hear, about a week later, that he was one of the twelve new hires selected from among the applicants.

Tsuchida's family ribbed him gently about starting a "real" career at twenty-eight, after his youthful fling with foreign customs and environs. He shrugged his shoulders and grinned. Since he was once again happy in his job, it didn't matter so much to him what the others thought—and besides, he knew quite well that underneath the joking his family were impressed by the way he was adapting to a changing world. He knew they trusted him, and he trusted himself—his valuable skills, his awareness of the ways in which things were changing, and his ability to make the best of his opportunities. Nomura put him through three months of intensive training to teach him the securities trade. For them, that was the easy part. What wasn't so easy for a Japanese firm was the thing Tsuchida was best at. He could take Nomura's operations and put them almost flawlessly into a Western context and a Western language. He was worth a great deal to Nomura. They knew it, and he knew it, and so everyone was happy with his new position.

It has been four years since Tsuchida switched jobs. He has enjoyed his time with Nomura. He has contributed a great deal to the company. Their international operations run more smoothly now that Tsuchida and the other young men who were hired with him have applied their special understanding to setting up communications between cultures. Tsuchida knows a great deal about securities. If he wished to, he could move comfortably into the Nomura corporate hierarchy, leaving behind his special expertise and conforming to the patterned life of every other Japanese salaryman. He does not wish to. He finds himself growing restless again, eager for a chance to learn something new and contribute something new to his organization. It is time to move on.

Once again, Tsuchida is in no hurry to find another job. Something will turn up. There will always be a need for his skills, and as he moves from one job to another he will gain more skills that will make him more valuable the next time he makes a change. One day Ryo Tsuchida will settle down, but not yet. He is still bright, friendly, and attractive, just enough but not too much. He is still a good catch for a thousand Japanese companies who are looking for new people to deal with new problems. He will wait, and look, and enjoy what he is doing until he finds something he might enjoy doing more. Ryo's family watch him with incredulous satisfaction. No, their youngest member did not go on to the steel firm where the family had established its employment legacy. He did not walk the beaten path. Apparently, he is beating a new one, and against all expectations it seems to be an accepted and even admirable way for him to have gone. Ironically, the Tsuchidas who once decided that they would not bear the blame for Ryo's unorthodoxy are beginning to feel that they would like to take some of the credit.

Common Motivations across Job-hopping Types

No matter when the job changes comes for a Japanese managerial elite—whether when they are old or young or whether their first or fourth job change—some common motivations seem to drive them to change jobs. Some of these motivations were documented in a popular book that appeared on Japanese bookstore shelves in 1988, simply entitled *Tenshoku* (Changing Jobs) (Okamoto 1987). In addition to offering helpful hints about how one might best make a move, the author included on the inside front cover a list of nine questions that were supposed to help employees decide if it truly was time to change jobs. The questions ranged from phenomena as commonplace in Japan as a "seemingly endless commute to work" and "working overtime just because others are working overtime" to concerns the Japanese would consider both unusual and serious, such as "trouble getting along with more than two superiors" (figure 26). If readers responded positively to more than four of the nine questions, the author suggested that they seriously consider changing jobs.

While the nine questions cited in *Tenshoku* may be valuable as diagnostic tools in assessing levels of dissatisfaction with one's job, neither Japanese who actually have changed jobs nor close observers of job changing among Japan's elite employees typically mention "seemingly endless commutes" or similar irritations as pivotal reason for a job change. These experts' answers, although varied, tend to hover around the same essential issues. Mr. Mizobuchi of Recruit Jinzai Center listed three reasons Japanese businessmen change jobs: (1) they cannot do their present job (either because they do not want to or do not have the skill), (2) they have poor relationships with their bosses, or (3) they think they should make more money.[11] Mr. Funatsu, the editor of *B-ing*, was even

Figure 26

Nine Questions for Those Thinking About Changing Jobs

1. Does it seem to take you forever to get to work on more than three days a week?
2. Do you have trouble getting along with more than two superiors directly above you?
3. Do you work overtime simply because others around you are working overtime?
4. Do you think salaries in your company are lower than in other firms?
5. Are a lot of employees leaving your company?
6. Is your company's profitability a secret?
7. Does the president of any company in your family of companies have a relative in a high position in the firm that he doesn't get along with? *
8. Were you transfered to a new job that you don't really want?
9. Is your boss often unfair to those below him?

If you answered "yes" to more than four of these questions, you should think about changing your employment conditions.

Source: Okamoto Yoshiyuki. *Tenshoku* (Tokyo: Diamond-sha, 1987).

* This question apparently refers to what the author of this book believe to be a sign of structural instability in a family of companies — familial strife.

more concise: "Money or *yarigai* [job interest] are the only two reasons people change jobs."[12] Mr. Murakami of TMT consultants claimed that there were five ways a company could lure midcareer recruits: "Give them (1) increased pay, (2) title or status, (3) a type of job they want to do, (4) a good working environment, or (5) the promise of a future with the company."[13]

Whether a job-changer is old or young, experienced as a job-changer or a first-timer, there are three motivations mentioned by most experts on the topic: job interest, money, and career trajectory as defined by promotion. The remainder of this section discusses the powerful influence of these factors on the Japanese salaryman's turnover decision.

YARIGAI

Despite the predominance of issues related to stability in the reasons given by older workers for changing jobs, the one reason they found most compelling had nothing to do with material security. More *kachō*-level employees (42 percent of those surveyed) said they would change jobs "when the job gets boring" than because of any other eventuality. A similar percentage of younger workers (approximately 45 percent) said that they would consider changing jobs if "I didn't feel any desire to do my previous job." Both of these questions address an aspect of the Japanese worker's attitude toward his job that has no direct translation in English. Even rather lengthy English definitions fail to describe this phenomenon accurately: "job satisfaction" is altogether inadequate, and the phrase "feelings of innate interest in and excitement about what one is doing" is lacking in both grace and nuance. The single Japanese word that encompasses the meanings of both these phrases occupies a prominent position in a Japanese salaryman's assessment of his employment situation. No description of the individual salaryman's turnover decision would be complete without a discussion of *yarigai*.

Legends about the power of *yarigai* and its ties to job mobility are legion in Japan. One of the reasons for the traditionally higher turnover rates among engineers, for example, has been the ties these employees feel to a certain technology or product. Engineers are famous for having high *yarigai* needs; they are often willing to switch firms to find the freedom to pursue their passion. If the company is slow to adopt a product or technology toward which such an expert feels a high degree of *yarigai*, he or she may try to pursue the dream in another organization. When we interviewed top personnel at Nikon Camera in 1986, the only employee they could readily remember having changed jobs in the previous two or three years was a thirty-year-old engineer. This young man could not convince the company of the utility of a new photographic contraption he had invented. Such was the *yarigai* the engineer felt for the production of this device that he left Nikon to produce it in a small, family-owned company.

Nikon officials claimed that this man was typical of job-changers in fields like camera manufacturing, where they said "changing jobs for pay was rare."[14] Among such engineers, who made up a large proportion of technology-related firms, they maintained, *yarigai* was the reason behind the vast majority of job changes. The claims of the Nikon personnel are supported by examples of successful attempts to hire engineers away from permanent employment positions. Nippon Motorola, for instance, has recruited many of its top Japanese semiconductor engineers from Japanese electronics firms. These engineers, believing that Motorola had the best microprocessor technology in the world, left their Japanese companies not only for the money but in search of a world-class technology.

Recently, changing jobs because one wants to do a particular job has become even more commonplace, as specialists are increasingly more important even in nontechnical industries. The importance attached to certain specialized skills in investment banking, for example, is evident from the number of banks hiring headhunters to perform searches with very specific criteria.[15] Traditionally, Japanese banks and other nontechnical companies rotated their personnel through a variety of jobs and professions within the company. An employee who served in the accounting department for his first five years in a firm might very well become a securities trader for three years before being put in charge of corporate recruiting in the personnel department. Nowadays, this type of procedure often leads an employee to jump ship.

An employee of Industrial Bank of Japan whom we interviewed knew four IBJ employees who had left the company between 1986 and 1987. One of these was a foreign exchange dealer who loved dealing. He decided that forex (foreign exchange) was to be his calling and profession in life. Unfortunately, the powers-that-be at IBJ did not agree. When the man received the news that he was being transferred, he followed the dictates of *yarigai* and left the firm to join First Chicago. Another man was very interested in American financial techniques and thought that IBJ was too conservative when it came to new financial products. He believed that changing jobs for more money would be immoral, but he found ethical grounds to justify his job change in Japanese history. "I'm like a samurai in the Edo [or Tokugawa] period," he said. "I want to work for the best lord." He decided on the "best lord" by determining which firm was most likely to use financial techniques that interested him. This worker moved from IBJ to Solomon Brothers and then on to Banker's Trust, carrying his strong streak of *yarigai* with him.

For Japanese employees with the *yarigai* that often accompanies technical expertise, job changing to preserve one's relationship with a particular project or technology has always been more acceptable than for many other workers. The explosive growth of technological industries, as well as the increase in specialization that characterizes many aspects of postindustrial societies, means that more and more of Japan's elite workers are fitting into the niche of "expert" where *yarigai* tends to encourage job changing.

MONEY

The *Asahi Shinbun* recently conducted a survey asking Japanese employees why they worked. Of the respondents under thirty years of age, an impressive 70 percent said that they work only to support their nonwork life (*AS*, July 28, 1986). This statistic contrasts strikingly with the attitudes of older Japanese, who received most of their satisfaction from "a job well done" and the interaction with co-workers. Nevertheless, Koji Funatsu of Recruit Company estimated that only 10 percent of job-changers switched firms for money, while 90 percent changed for *yarigai*.[16] Part of the reason for the relatively low level of importance given to money in job changing, despite so much emphasis on money among young people, is the historical relationship between salary and job changing. A survey of those who graduated from college in 1955 concluded that "those who followed a 'lifetime' employment pattern have received higher earnings than job-changers despite the decline in returns for education and tenure during economic growth" (Evans 1984).

Another survey, by Asahi Life Insurance, showed that lifetime earnings decreased for all job-changers in Japan (*AS*, August 26, 1986). Part of the reason for this difference was simply that the *taishokukin* (pension) of an employee who changed jobs was calculated from the time he joined the new company. He was unlikely to receive any pension from his former company (Takita 1987, 226). It is not surprising, then, that the Asahi Life Insurance survey revealed that Japanese who change jobs later in life are likely to have a greater decrease in earnings.[17]

The surveys by the *Asahi Shinbun* and Asahi Life Insurance do not differentiate between the Japanese elite college-graduate work force (the subject of this study) and Japanese workers in general. Our questionnaire survey to college graduates in the Tokyo area tells a story similar to that told by Asahi Life Insurance's survey, but it also indicates a trend away from the traditional norm of an automatic reduction in salary for job-changers. Of thirty college graduates in the survey who had changed jobs, those who changed most recently were more likely to have a salary increase than those who changed in past years.[18] In fact, 12 percent of the variation in salary levels after a job change is explained by how long the employees have been in their present job.

Our survey also indicated that a drop in salary after changing jobs might not be as universal a phenomenon as popular belief would have it. The surveys cited above are based on aggregate data from every sector of the Japanese work force. Our analysis of the survey we conducted shows differences between college graduates and nongraduates that are masked by across-the-board survey techniques. In the survey, there was no statistical difference in salaries between *college graduates* who had changed jobs and those who had not.[19] Among nongraduates, however, the differences between the salaries of job-changers and nonchangers were very significant. The survey also shows that nongraduates who have not changed jobs make on average about ¥1 million less per year than do their college-graduate counterparts (¥3 to ¥4 million/year versus ¥4 to ¥5 million/year). And those nongraduates who have changed jobs make much less than college-educated employees (¥2 to ¥3 million/year).[20] Not only have differences always existed between the college-graduate elite in Japan and their less educated countrymen, but as we will explain in more detail below, the financial condition of college-graduate job-changers appears to be improving. This is not true for job-hoppers who are not part of the elite sector. The disparity between the results of our survey and other surveys may be explained by the large and increasing differential b etween the salaries of college-graduate and nongraduate job-changers.[21]

Financial remuneration for elite job-changers has changed significantly in recent years. Companies that are trying to attract midcareer employees have altered or abandoned many of the policies that have traditionally applied to job-changers. For example, Mitsubishi Corporation is now careful to instruct potential midcareer employees that their "pensions will be equalized to a full-time pension" and that they "would still get all the fringe benefits like a club house, health insurance, pension plan, and athletic club."[22] Part of the reason for this kind of policy change is that executive-track employees who are likely to make a midcareer move tend to be acutely aware of the financial consequences. One thirty-five-year-old described the labor market concisely as soon as we introduced the subject of job changing: "At Toshiba I am making $27,500, at Nomura I would make $55,000, and at Mitsubishi I would make $41,000."[23] This man's familiarity with his own market price tends to be typical of prospective job-changers. According to one foreign headhunter in Tokyo, the salaries this man expected to earn after a job switch are not figures that the average (or even the exceptional) salaryman would have been able to quote five years ago.[24] To attract savvy executives as midcareer hires, Japanese firms know they must provide reasonable or generous remuneration.

Slowly but surely the news about recent job changing and higher salary levels—especially among the executive-track employees—is beginning to reach the broad Japanese public. In 1987, *Next* magazine published a information about nineteen college graduates between ages thirty-three and forty-four who had recently changed jobs (*Next*, July 1987).[25] The list included their ages, occupations, original salaries, and salaries after changing jobs. A quick review of this data set shows that the average job-changer's salary went from ¥7.5 million to ¥9.3 million. When the seniority system is taken into account and salaries are regressed by age, an even more interesting picture begins to form. The salary of the average employee on this list increased by ¥40,000 with each birthday. After changing jobs the slope of incremental change in salary by age increased to ¥53,000. In this sample, then, a forty-four-year-old who changed jobs would increase his annual salary by about ¥150,000 more than a thirty-three-year-old job-changer—information that runs contrary to the traditional belief that older hires are less valuable than employees hired at the beginning of their careers. The popular circulation of this kind of information, the legendary tales of salaries available in foreign firms, and the actual increase in salaries for midcareer hires in Japanese firms are beginning for the first time to present the individual salaryman with a financial reason for changing jobs.

PROMOTION

The preceding chapters have discussed the ways in which trends like technological development and internationalization seem to be increasing the strength and number of reasons a Japanese executive might have for changing jobs. Both *yarigai* and money encourage job hopping by pulling the employee toward greener pastures. A third important influence on the individual in today's Japan operates the opposite way, by pushing employees out of a firm within which they feel their opportunities are limited. A few decades ago young Japanese executives rose rapidly to the top of companies, the relative paucity of older males creating a lack of competition for upper-level slots. Now, young salarymen compete with hordes of others their age for senior positions that are already filled. The key signpost of the salaryman's progress in this struggle for success is promotion.

There are many reasons why an individual in Japan might respond seriously, even by such drastic measures as changing jobs, if he or she did not feel promotion was rapid enough. As Yoshino and Lifson tell us, in Japan, "promotion . . . and its timing is an important signal of the direction a managerial career is taking" (Yoshino and Lifson 1986, 149). The position titles that are often applied outside the workplace as well as inside it indicate that the company values an employee. They show to the world, as well as the company, that the employee is successful. These titles have been one of the main symbols of success in Japan since the beginning of the nation's "economic miracle." An executive is likely to be addressed as *kachō* or *buchō* not only by his co-workers but by colleagues from other companies, the hostesses at his favorite after-work bars, and even his neighbors. The title is part of the salaryman's name—the part that establishes his relative rank in almost every social interaction. Corporate rank and personal identity are intermingled in Japan to a far greater extent than in perhaps any other society.

The importance of position makes it seem all the more serious that the evolution of Japan's age structure from World War II to the present is making it harder and harder to gain high-level positions in Japanese companies. At Hitachi, for example, only 50 percent of this year's entering college graduates can expect to become *kachō*. Just ten years ago this number varied between 70 percent and 80 percent.[26] A 1986 survey showed that at that time, 91.8 percent of Japan's college-graduate employees who were fifty to fifty-four years old had been promoted to managerial-level positions. By the year 2000, only 26.6 percent of the same age group of employees are expected to be managers (Ohta 1986, 12). A Ministry of Labor survey of companies with more than a thousand employees shows the percentage of variously aged employees who have been promoted to *kachō* level between 1973 and 1983 (Table 11). This figure shows that although the percentage of employees attaining *kachō* status in these firms has not decreased as it had at Hitachi, the timing of promotions had slowed considerably.

The lifetime employees presently entering the final stages of their careers are just beginning to feel the downturn in promotion for older workers, a slowdown none of them expected when they entered the work force. Even a slight slowdown in promotion possibilities has great impact on the employees of a Japanese company, including those at very senior levels. The significance of promotions is magnified for mature employees because of the intense struggle for promotion at top positions in the firm. Yoshino and Lifson estimated that in one *sōgō shōsha* "at best only 1 to 2 percent of recruits could hope to become members of the board of direc-

Table 11
Promotion to *kachō*
(in percentage)

Age	1973	1978	1983
Late thirties	40	27	17
Early forties	35	46	43
Late forties	10	17	27

Source: Fukada Yūsuke and Koitabashi Jirō, Warera Sarariiman yonjūdai o ika ni kachinokoru ka? *Gendai,* May 1987, p. 113.

tors. For a group of individuals as talented and ambitious as the *sōgō shōsha*'s core staff, this is a severe competitive struggle" (Yoshino and Lifson 1986, 150).

The reasons older workers compete fiercely for promotions and keenly feel even a slight reduction in their possibilities of moving up are manifold. One of the most obvious is economic. Only those Japanese executives who are promoted to the board of directors are able to stay with the company after the mandatory retirement age of fifty-five or sixty. Japanese companies often give their employees only a three- to five-year lump sum payment as pension, and because the average life expectancy for Japanese men is almost seventy-five years, this leaves them with twenty years unsupported by salary (Jones 1987). With the high cost of living in Japan, there are very few Japanese men who can afford not to seek a second job after having retired from their first "lifetime" company. The man who can be promoted to the board of directors is blessed economically by a hefty salary, a lavish expense account, and a reprieve from mandatory retirement.

A second reason for the intense concern over higher-level promotion is closely related to social status. This is the preservation of "face." Even before demographic pressures began to decrease the likelihood of any one individual's reaching the uppermost rungs of Japan's corporate ladder, the competition for positions at the top of this ladder were more intense and obvious than at the lower levels. Not surprisingly, one of the most frequently cited reasons for a mature salaryman's leaving a Japanese company was that the executive had lost out to a co-worker in the competition for a particular high-status position. When Takeo Shina became the president of IBM Japan, Mr. Naruse, a member of the board who had been in contention for the top spot, left the company to become the president of a small woman's wear company. Naruse said that there are only two ways to get rid of competitive feelings: "to become president or to throw away the pride you have about your own abilities and accept the position you have been given." Naruse could not follow this second route, so he left IBM Japan to become a president elsewhere. Takashi Irie, chairman of Nippon Motorola, tells a similar story. He was at the director-level at NEC when he was approached by Motorola to lead their Japanese operation. Irie realized that he would probably never be president of NEC and that before long he would be "retired" to take the lead of a subsidiary company in the NEC family. This did not appeal to him because "such a position would mean that I would be subordinated to people in the parent company that I had been leading for many years." Irie decided to make the move to Nippon Motorola to preserve his pride and his social status.

Finally, promotion has a particularly strong effect on older Japanese workers because differentiation of career paths tends to begin after employees have been with the firm for a considerable time. The first promotions tend to come only after ten or more years with the company. Until that time, according to a former personnel director of one of the large banks in Japan, personnel managers are careful not to allow any differences in promotions or pay that would indicate preferential treatment.[27] Yoshino and Lifson support this view, noting that in the "first decade and a half of a core staff member's career . . . every effort is made to minimize overt recognition of individual differences in achievement" (Yoshino and Lifson 1986, 146). Once some wage differences are introduced into the system after the first ten years, employees often read great meaning into a ¥500 increase in monthly pay.

Promotion has been even more indicative than salary of a college graduate's chances of success in Japan's managerial hierarchy. A year's tardiness in promotion at any level is rarely made up. A personnel director at one well-respected bank in Tokyo could think of only one "resurrection" during his thirty-odd years with the company.[28] A young employee who disliked his boss was promoted a year later than his cohort in the initial promotion. In his next position, however, he worked very hard and demonstrated to his superiors that his initial poor performance appraisal was due to human relations problems and not his overall inability or attitude problems. He was promoted with the first group at the next promotion level. This system of promotions may be one of the reasons that a study of Japanese and American middle managers showed 50.8 percent of Americans expected to "reach a high level in the firm," while only 32.5 percent of the Japanese had the same expectations.[29] Japanese managers seem to understand the probabilities of being promoted to the top of a company to a much greater extent than do their American counterparts.

It is little wonder, then, that issues of livelihood and status that surround promotion in Japanese companies are such motivators for job changing. Young employees, fresh out of college, change jobs because the relationship they have with their first boss is not good and they fear it will negatively impact their entire career with that company; thirty-year-old employees become nervous about their potential to be numbered among the first promotions and begin looking for an out "just in case"; kachō-level employees miss one of the critical promotion dates and immediately understand the writing on the wall; buchō-level managers fear that they will not be made a director in the firm; and directors explore opportunities at other companies to avoid being subordinated to people they used to lead. Headhunters in Japan claim that job-changers have, as one root of their decision to change jobs, a fear about a future promotion or a gripe about a recent promotion.

Besides the age-old complaints of employees who might find their jobs tedious, unfulfilling, or stressful, Japan's elite work force now faces intensifying pressures that might provide strong motivation for some salarymen to change jobs. Even a cursory glance is enough to reveal that the pull of *yarigai* and high salaries and the push of crowded promotional ranks are growing stronger as a result of demographic change, the involvement of Japan in the international market, and other current environmental conditions.

Attitudinal Effects on Organizations and Culture

Japanese labor markets are clearly being forced by environmental pressures to evolve in a way that accommodates increases in midcareer hiring (see chapters 5 and 6). The increase in individual job changing, in turn, has an effect on organizations and environmental structures supporting job mobility. This cyclical nature of mutually reinforcing links between levels of analysis creates the most powerful argument for a significant structured change taking place in Japan's elite employment system. Whenever the success of individuals or companies becomes linked in the minds of the Japanese people to employment practices that differ from the traditional system, the new systems become easier and easier to accept as part of national norms.

There is a whole body of literature in Japan called *Nihonjinron,* literally, "theories of Japaneseness." This literature usually compares the Japanese to people of other nations to try to differentiate that which is unique to Japanese society. *Nihonjinron* has a tangible impact on the thinking of the Japanese. Chapter 3 dealt briefly with the idea that Japanese do not seem to have an absolute value system: right and wrong are determined internally by the group. *Nihonjinron* is in many ways the manifestation of this group-defined morality at a national level. It seems to have a more profound effect on the value system of the Japanese than any other genre of published works. Because it portrays the values and behaviors that are uniquely Japanese, in explicit contradistinction to the outside world, *Nihonjinron* plays into the Japanese cultural norm of closely aligning one's self with the identification group *(uchi)* and rejecting that which surrounds the group and is foreign to it *(soto).* It is not uncommon to hear a Japanese man or woman, when asked about his or her personal beliefs or attitudes, to begin the sentence with "Ware ware Nihonjin . . . " ("We Japanese . . . "). The expressions that follow this kind of preamble usually reflect attitudes that the speaker has been told are exclusively Japanese.

Lifetime employment has long been one of the best-known topics of *Nihonjinron.* As a headhunter contacting potential candidates for a job change, one of the authors was often the recipient of authoritative lectures pointing out that " 'we Japanese' do not change jobs midcareer. You may as well give up. No one will listen to what you have to say. We are not interested." Typical *Nihonjinron* enthusiasts are much perturbed that a growing number of Japanese companies are beginning to practice nontraditional human resource management techniques and that these techniques often prove effective. Mr. Mizobuchi of Recruit Research comments that the history of companies using these nontraditional employment systems is not long, but many of them have been successful. For example:

> It has been only twenty years since supermarket chains were introduced in Japan. They have been very successful, largely because they recruited lots of people from department stores who had retailing experience . . . The success [of these firms, like the success] of Sony depended upon recruiting experienced workers. (*LAT*, July 9, 1988)

Eventually, evidence of the success of such "non-Japanese" enterprises must be accounted for in the literature of *Nihonjinron*. Because of its lack of absolutes, this body of beliefs is highly susceptible to changes in the actual actions taken by Japanese organizations—which, in turn, are affected by the ideas of *Nihonjinron*.

Even one individual can have significant impact on broad attitudinal changes if that individual's actions become famous enough to alter the shape of *Nihonjinron*. Chapter 4 mentioned the frequency with which the job changes of Eiji Wakabayashi, Youichi Watanabe, Yukio Imada, and Sousuke Yamane have been mentioned in the press. The stories of these men and others like them have begun to change the values that surround job changing in Japan. In fact, when Haruo Shimada, labor economist and Keio University professor, talks about the new values surrounding job change in Japan, he points to one event as a key turning point—the job change of Takeo Morimoto. Morimoto had been a famous newscaster at NHK, Japan's public broadcasting system. His face had come to be a symbol of that network: what Walter Cronkite was to CBS, Morimoto was to NHK. In 1985 Morimoto decided to leave NHK to join rival TBS's news department. For this he received a large lump sum three-year contract. That someone so "Japanese" would decide to change his loyalties and defect to a rival network was a shock to many Japanese and was the topic of vigorous debates on television and in the press.[30] It flew in the face of the current *Nihonjinron*, which strongly emphasized the innate corporate loyalty of all Japanese.

There are not many instances of individual job changes having such a direct influence on the thinking of the entire Japanese nation. Unless an individual is so well known that his or her name is virtually integral to Japanese culture, the influence of the person's behavior on social attitudes is likely to come through aggregation with similar actions on the part of similar individuals. One way in which job-changers seem to be exercising influence on overall attitudes is by creating what amounts to a new type of labor market in Japan. Once an elite worker has left the lifetime employment system by changing jobs, he becomes part of a new pool of employees who seem devoted to obtaining status, good pay, and the other amenities of corporate life along with an unprecedented degree of job mobility.

As more and more people change jobs, there is increased likelihood and opportunity for these "values of job-changers" to affect the mainstream of Japanese culture. Already there are signs that younger people—those with the most propensity to change jobs—have begun to shift their primary values from "groupism to decentralization" and "a sense of belonging" to one of "ownership of one's own life" (*Newsweek,* January 13, 1986, 39). Some analysts have gone so far as to explicitly link these alterations in values to the changes in human resource management policies that were discussed in chapter 6. These claims are generally phrased in terms of sweeping generalities, like the opinion of one *Asahi Shinbun* reporter that "since companies are starting to give more pay to people with greater ability, the loyalty ethic is going away" (*AS,* October 9, 1987). Despite their lack of firm theoretical foundation, the appearance of numerous statements like this in the Japanese media seems to indicate that the broad audience of readers may be willing to entertain the notion they are true.

There is some clear evidence that even if the "traditional" values of groupism, belonging, and loyalty are not disappearing, they are being altered in significant ways. Engineers, the popular press tells us, "are beginning to place much less value on the name of a company and more on salary and ability to do what they want to do" (*AS,* August 25, 1985). An official of a bank in Tokyo said that if the bank hires an elite employee "and he goes two or three years without receiving a phone call from a headhunter, it is a sure sign that he has no ability."[31] The concept of loyalty appears to be changing as well. Today "loyalty means not working in the same industry against a former employer."[32] A 1988 *Asahi Shinbun* article warned potential job-changers that "if someone has changed jobs more than three times, companies will probably not be interested in hiring him" (*AS,* February 19, 1988). Not so long ago, even one job change would make an employee undesirable—now that has been expanded to three changes.

Individuals tend to act in accordance with their expectations, and if Japanese come to expect the possible end of lifetime employment, the probability that their actions will not conform with "traditional" customs will probably increase. In light of the influence of public opinion, it is significant that the decline of permanent employment receives the amount of press coverage and *tsukiai* (get-together) conversation that it does. Predictions run from the cautious words of a government official— "Japan must take it for granted that a certain amount of unemployment will continue and that the lifetime employment (policy) must undergo a significant change" (quoted in *LAT,* July 9, 1988)—to the battle cries of headhunters who claim that the era of lifetime employment was an *ashikase ni natte iru jidai* (era of being in fetters)[33] in which the "system was terribly unfair to individuals."[34] Other analysts have predicted that "in the near future Japanese will be able to move from mid-size companies to large companies in Japan, and from foreign firms to large Japanese firms"[35] as the "one-company-for-life era comes to an end."[36]

Conclusion

This chapter has discussed evidence of motivation for job changing on the part of Japan's elite white-collar employees. The reasons many such workers might have for considering a job change, which are increasingly present under current social conditions, are mirrored in a variety of data showing increased acceptance of job hopping in Japanese attitudes. It seems that, even if not every Japanese businessperson has a reason to desert the traditional devotion to lifetime employment, at least a considerable number of salarymen are encountering forces that may weaken their devotion to the system and provide strong motivation to consider a job change. As March and Simon's model points out, this motivation when combined with the opportunity to move to another job is sufficient to catalyze job-changing behavior in ways that are inconsistent with the traditional view of Japan's loyal managerial elite.

CHAPTER EIGHT

Benefiting from the New Plateau

WHEN THE WESTERN business world first began to notice that Japan was equaling most developed nations in economic prosperity and surpassing many of them in growth, the peculiarities of "Japanese management" became the object of intense scrutiny from envious and even intimidated Westerners. The image of the Japanese salaryman as a human automaton, programmed to work steadily and unremittingly for his company until his useful lifetime had ended, was in part a product of Western investigators' culture-shocked reaction to a system of employment grounded in centuries of Japanese tradition. The stability of this system, the high productivity it produced, and the loyalty ethic that engendered it became the target of both envy and repugnance on the part of developed nations who wished to equal Japan's success. Some analysts recommended a wholesale imitation of the lifetime employment system as the only way any economy might expect to achieve Japan-style economic miracles. Others, noting the entrenchment of permanent employment in the unique history and society of Japan, claimed that any attempts at duplicating the system in other nations would be doomed to failure. Both camps in this argument, however, seemed to agree on one thing: that "permanent employment" is now, always has been, and always will be a truly permanent system. It is hard to blame non-Japanese analysts for the overgenerality of this belief, since the norms of Japanese society encourage its citizens to espouse and express it themselves. However, the available data on lifetime employment do not show a historical pattern of undisturbed devotion to the system, even within the elite college-graduate population where lifetime employment has always been most firmly grounded.

Figure 2 (chapter 4) illustrates some of the variations in the Japanese business community's adherence to the permanent employment system. It compares the percentage of new employees taken from the ranks of new college graduates to the proportion hired in midcareer from the years 1967 to 1989. During this approximately two-decade period, the ratio of new to experienced hires has been far from stagnant. Overall, the statistics show a definite increase in midcareer hiring since the mid-1960s, with the "line of best fit" sloping upward at a ratio of about 10 percent per year. This increase in midcareer hiring (and the decrease in adherence to the lifetime employment system it implies) is not surprising when one considers the pressures Japan's economy has been undergoing throughout the postwar era. This book has been devoted to examining some of the conflicts and changes in the Japanese employment system that seem to be growing more pronounced as the nation's economy responds to environmental pressures such as demographic change, technological modernization, and the internationalization of its markets. In light of these factors, the resiliency of lifetime employment in Japan is perhaps more impressive than its recent weakening. This chapter considers some of the questions that arise as a result of the contrast between the myth of permanent employment as an unalterable monolith of Japanese management and the realities of stress and change within the system. We first consider the possible alternatives that might face the lifetime employment system in the near future and then consider some implications present changes may have for managing economic enterprises in Japan.

If, as our data suggest, Japan is presently experiencing a decrease in attitudinal and behavioral support for the lifetime employment system, there are three possible courses the system might be expected to take in the future. First, the lifetime employment system could continue to deteriorate as Japan struggles with environmental economic and social pressures. Second, the rise in job changing and midcareer hiring may fall back from its present level, returning permanent employment to its place as a venerable pillar of Japanese economic practice. A third alternative is that permanent employment may remain at its present levels through the foreseeable future. All of these arguments have their adherents: we discuss each of them in turn.

The Death of Lifetime Employment?

The development theorists of the immediate postwar period (the vast majority of whom hailed from wealthy Western nations) filled the social science literature of their time with the confident assumption that less-developed countries, in order to progress, must abandon local traditional practices and adapt their economic operations to an essentially Western model. Although Japan's startling postwar development dealt a heavy blow to this theoretical position, many analysts are still eager to seize upon evidence of change as a sure sign that the country is becoming progressively and ineluctably more Western in its business and management practices.[1]

Accordingly, some Western analysts are already beginning to memorialize the Japanese lifetime employment system as an institution that, if not actually deceased, is at least terminally and incurably ill. As one journalist bluntly puts it:

> Japan's vaunted lifetime employment system is coming unraveled at both ends. At one end, companies are being forced to let people go—or are actively seeking to hire experienced midlevel managers from outside. On the employees' end, there is less loyalty to the company today than in the past, not only from leisure-loving young people but also from older workers who have found their careers stalled. The result is a change in the way Japanese have thought of employment since the lifelong system first appeared at the end of the war. (Ribeiro 1988)

Predictions about Japan's future based on this type of argument forecast widespread change in many of the country's institutions and practices. The following assertions, which were presented in a recent article in the American press, reportedly represent commonly held opinions in Japan:

> If it becomes increasingly possible for employees to work their way up corporate ladders by changing companies, then the immense emphasis now placed on getting that first job will be reduced. Few except the top graduates from the best universities are recruited by the leading companies, and the pressures on students to achieve a high standing begins early. This system, many complain, turns Japan's youngsters into rote-learning machines and weakens the national university system.
>
> Changes in the employment structure also may affect the rigid leisure habits of Japanese. The older, and still prevailing attitude that the company comes first is a factor in discouraging workers from taking full advantage of vacations and holidays. Many skip them completely—a habit that, while a boon to productivity, also dulls creativity, observers in and outside the country contend. (*LAT,* July 9, 1988)

Not all the observers who expect the demise of permanent employment are Westerners. Yutaka Kosai, professor at the Tokyo Institute of Technology, criticizes the generic argument that small changes in Japan do not have any long-term consequences. Dr. Kosai believes that "even when small shifts occur they deserve analysis to elucidate their import." He sees the "omens of change" in Japan during the mid-1980s as having "far-reaching implications," especially as affluence serves to increase the "fluid and sometimes speculative flows of people, money and goods" in society (*LAT,* July 9, 1988). Many other Japanese seem to agree with Dr. Yutaka's dire predictions. In a recent survey of 186 large technology firms, 70 percent of the respondents predicted that midcareer hiring would increase in the future (Dokushin no Kyūyo 1988). A 1987 survey conducted by the Keizai Doyukai found that 82 percent of the companies associated with this organization forecast the "collapse of Japan's traditional 'lifetime employment' system" (JEN, July 2, 1987). Less than a year later the same organization's white paper "called on Japanese companies to abandon the lifetime employment system in favor of a 'strategic personnel system' tailored to survival in current economic conditions" (JEN, February 1, 1988).

This kind of expression of belief in the disintegration of the lifetime employment system has always been unpopular in Japanese society. Throughout the postwar period such opinions have been seen as bordering on perverseness, if not blasphemy. Many Western Japanologists learn to share this attitude as they become intimate with Japanese ways of thinking and hence more aware of the naiveté of Westerners who cannot conceive of a system achieving success by following a path that lies outside of their own cultural context. As a result, most predictions that lifetime employment is on its last legs have received little serious attention from scholars of Japan. However, the idea that Japanese employment may be forced to change dramatically in the near future is not based merely on Western bias or an alarmist reaction to insignificant changes. To refuse to entertain it as a possibility is to ignore sweeping, unprecedented, and very real changes in the world economy, as well as in Japan itself.

It is true that Japanese society and business are grounded in a long and pervasive loyalty ethic. It is true that, since World War II, the lifetime employment system has found a tenacious foothold in a population of workers and employers who share this ethical foundation. But it is also true that Japan has never before experienced the pressures that are presently impinging on its population and its economy. The dissatisfactions of individuals caught in a demographic trap stemming from a war of unprecedented scope is a reality Japanese culture has never faced before. Nor can Japan's rapid absorption of technologies that have radically altered the societies of other developed nations be expected to leave Japanese custom altogether unchanged. Moreover, Japan's position in the global market (which itself owes much to information and transportation technologies) puts the country in a position it has never occupied in the past. The Japanese themselves often give casual credit for their unique social consistency to the fact that they are an "island nation," historically able and often eager to vitiate all contact with the rest of the world. Now, however, a return to Japanese isolationism is becoming less and less feasible as the country's economy becomes increasingly—if reluctantly—more interdependent and integrated with external markets.

In the previous chapter we attempted to explain some of the links between these unprecedented broad-scale changes in Japan's business environment and recent changes in the lifetime employment system. While these links may not be immediately apparent to a foreign observer, it takes very little logic and even less research to uncover them once the question is examined closely. A casual bar conversation with a Japanese executive or a glance at the country's daily newspapers may reveal analyses of how the pressures of modernization are undermining permanent employment. In-depth research into job changing and statistical analysis of employment patterns bear out such conclusions. Lifetime employment among elite workers in Japan is decreasing, and it is decreasing as a result of environmental changes that are only likely to intensify in the future. The voices that prophesize doom to the permanent employment system are not necessarily misinformed or simplistic, nor do they lack a significant body of evidence to support their position.

Blip Theory

Conversely, many analysts of Japan believe that reports of the death of lifetime employment have been greatly exaggerated. They, too, cite solid arguments and convincing evidence, but their predictions envision a Japan that will quickly regain its equilibrium, reinstate permanent employment as a fundamental tenet of Japanese management, and leave the current decline of the system as an anomalous blip in the history of a tenaciously stable social phenomenon.

"Blip theory" is perhaps one of the most persuasive arguments about the future of the Japanese employment system. It is supported by analysts who are sensitive to the unusual nature of the most recent changes in Japan's elite career patterns but who are still skeptical of the long-term consequences these changes will have on the overall lifetime employment system. These thinkers realize that the differences between Japanese and Western employment patterns have withstood more than three decades of continual predictions that Japan would soon adopt a more Western style. Having witnessed the nation's increasing reliance on the system of lifetime employment at the very time when so many Westerners were predicting an end to that system, these theorists cast a wary and seasoned eye on the renewed flurry of doom saying.

An example of one well-known Japanologist who both acknowledges current changes in the country's employment system and believes that

they will have little long-term affect is James Abegglen. In an article in
Business Tokyo, Abegglen offers a theory of "contained change" taking
place in Japan. The article focuses particularly on the job changing taking place in the financial sector. Abegglen sees the combination of shortage of skills, higher pay, and "individuals who identify more with their
skills than with one employer" creating increased job mobility (Abegglen,
1987). He assents that the number of job-changers in one industry—
finance—is rising. However, he concludes that no overall rise in mobility
patterns will result from this increase. Abegglen cites a Keizai Doyukai
study that determined that the "career employment system will continue
unchanged" into the 1990s. Abegglen claims that in the future, individuals will still change jobs as they always have "to some degree"; but, he
cautions, "reports of the death of Japan's employment system are now as
before, premature" (Abegglen 1987). Abegglen does not make himself
altogether clear about his expectations concerning the longer-term fate of
the Japanese employment system. However, his general implication is
that the changes in lifetime employment now taking place are real and
significant, but only as an aberration in an otherwise consistent pattern
of employment practices.

The basic arguments of the blip theory are summarized in a report to
the Organization for Economic Cooperation and Development (OECD)
in 1988 (Bounine-Cabale, Dore, and Tapiola). The authors of this report
emphasize the proven efficacy and usefulness of Japan's present employment system, which they see as providing an admirable blend of stability
and flexibility. They point out advantages including differentiated career
tracks, intra- and interfirm redeployment of human resources, training,
quality control, and "member motivation effects." The committee who
wrote this report wondered why the myriad evaluations of "the advantages Japanese firms derive" from the lifetime employment system "have
not much inhibited the steady flow of prophecies to the effect that, whatever merits the system might have, it is being forced to change, and
change in a 'Western' direction" (51).

These scholars are clear about their expectations for the future of the
lifetime employment system in Japan. "Far from disappearing," they
expect that the Japanese system of lifetime employment, seniority wages,
and enterprise unions will "retain their centrality" (51). As evidence to
support their predictions, they point in particular to the fact that these
practices have been "trickling down" from the larger enterprises to
smaller ones through the late 1970s and early 1980s.

The OECD report includes information from the 1987 Ministry of
Labor survey (administered every three to five years), which showed the
largest proportion of job changing to total hires in Japan since 1956. But
it concludes that most of the increase in job changing can be accounted

for by increases in turnover among nonpermanent employees and female job-changers. In fact, for male full-time *(jōyōko)* employees the mobility rate in 1987 was slightly lower than in 1974—the year after the first oil shock (65). The report concludes that the 1987 surge in job changing will probably recede as did the 1974 increase and that the 1987 figures were mostly a reflection of a jump in midcareer moves in the R&D and finance sectors (a Tokyo version of the "yuppie boom") and showed no evidence of expanding beyond these two sectors (66–67). Certainly if mobility is only in these two sectors there is ample reason for belief in a blip. The mobility in the finance sector was due in large part to the deregulation of financial markets in Japan. Once the foreign security firms have filled their more senior positions with qualified Japanese employees, their needs for midcareer hiring will decrease significantly. The same argument can be made for R&D personnel in this period of industrial restructuring. Once NKK and Nippon Steel and other industrial firms have completed their diversification, there will be no need for high levels of midcareer hiring.

Previous Blips

During the postwar period, most blip theorists have stood by as eyewitnesses while the Japanese system has undergone pressures that did in fact temporarily increase the level of job changing. In these instances the Japanese have returned to the lifetime employment system with more devotion than ever after those pressures were relieved. During two historical periods since the emergence of lifetime employment in postwar Japan, the system has appeared to be threatened by higher-level environmental phenomena. The first was of these was the shortage among certain categories of workers that existed in the late 1960s; the second, the oil crisis in 1973–1974.

During the 1960s, the relative lack of qualified employees in Japan compared to the country's potential economic growth drove many companies to begin policies of nonseniority wages and midcareer hiring. Analysts at the time saw this as the beginning of the end to the Japanese employment system. However, after this crisis passed, employment patterns began to appear more stable than ever. Immediately following the oil crisis, job changing again increased significantly as some organizations responded to the crisis by laying off redundant workers and as employees moved to industries less reliant on energy supply. This increase in number of people changing jobs also proved to be temporary, however. Within a couple of years, labor mobility rates were lower than they had ever been.

The quick resurgence of lifetime employment after these two declines was largely a result of the fervent emphasis on economic endeavor during

Japan's rise to economic power. Attitudes toward job hopping did not appear to change much as a result of the labor crisis and the oil crisis, even though pragmatic responses to economic pressures forced some behavioral change. Most job mobility during these two periods was downward mobility and was viewed as a disgrace even if it was a necessity. Many of the reasons given by those who believe that the 1980s represent another blip in job changing reflect this same emphasis on social attitudes. Tadashi Natori, general manager of investment banking at Industrial Bank of Japan, believes that foreign hiring in Japan will not make serious inroads into the permanent employment system because "Japanese companies give their employees something they can't get elsewhere" (Holden 1989, 58). A director of Sumitomo Bank claimed that top talent in his firm would not change jobs because Sumitomo has higher status in Japan than any American bank, a job-changer would have to worry about how long he could stay with a foreign firm, and job changing is still looked down on in Japanese society.[2] These analysts all believe that the persistence of attitudes will once again override changes in various economic aspects of the Japanese employment system.

Both blip theory and the theory of a changing Japan can be argued convincingly from current available data. However, there are also strong arguments against both theories. Some of this contradictory evidence is obvious simply from the descriptions of the two positions. Specifically, some social factors and policies in Japan are working against both continued change in the lifetime employment system and a return to previous norms.

Arguments against Breakdown Theory

One of the strongest arguments against the idea that Japanese lifetime employment will eventually disappear is that many forces in the society are likely to intervene in defense of the system. Despite economic and other stresses on job loyalty in Japan, there are obviously many reasons that organizations, industries, the government, the press, or influential individuals may try to save permanent employment from extinction.

For example, many organizations oppose the adoption of midcareer hiring, or at least try to contain it, because they understand that permanent employment is a self-sustaining mechanism. If lifetime employees see increasing numbers of mavericks making huge sums of money while breaking all the rules of the traditional lifetime employment system, the system itself may be jeopardized. Company strategists feel the same way about enterprises in their industry that have adopted midcareer policies that diminish the effectiveness of their own lifetime employment systems. It would not be surprising to find these organizations banding together to ostracize or snub companies that would not commit themselves to a system of lifetime employment.

One explanation given by Japanologists for the continuity of the lifetime employment system is also a very valid reason that higher-level institutions might intervene to save lifetime employment. These analysts point out that in many ways the Japanese system of internal labor markets is much more rational than the Western model of external markets. Especially for companies adopting a strategy of low-cost production (which Japanese firms have traditionally done), systems of lifetime employment, seniority promotions, and bonus pay appear to be crucial.[3] Lester Thurow and Ronald Dore, among others, have suggested that Western firms would be best served by adopting a more Japanese model.

Higher-level political and economic strategists also have clear reasons for cracking down on individuals and organizations that break the rules of lifetime employment. Permanent employment has been seen as one of Japan's key advantages in dozens of areas. Among these are management systems, about which Westerners have marveled that "superiors show little discomfort when a subordinate proves himself more capable than the superior himself" (Yoshino and Lifson 1986, 192). Similar observations apply to cost control, where "relatively highly skilled people worked for relatively low wages year after year."[4] Flexibility of technology systems, long-term strategic planning, and quality control in Japan also owe much to the lifetime employment system: "Clearly, the heart of the Japanese approach to quality control is the extraordinary stability and loyalty of the Japanese labor force and of Japanese management" (Okimoto, Sugano, and Weinstein 1984, 60). Finally, permanent employment has been cited as a fundamental element in Japan's international competitiveness: "Japan's lifetime employment system [is] at the root of U.S. frustration on gaining access to Japanese science."[5]

Certainly the system of not hiring and firing employees in midcareer is directly related to these advantages in some obvious ways. Costs are kept low by not having to rehire and retrain managerial personnel in midcareer. Innovation is kept high by a basic trust in the employee's loyalty to the firm; new practices and products do not have to be kept under lock and key for fear that an opportunistic employee will defect with the ideas. This allows for greater diffusion of and improvement on innovative behavior within the firm.

THE ELEMENTS OF LIFETIME EMPLOYMENT

The main flaw in the arguments against breakdown theory (because of these manifold advantages of lifetime employment) is that many of these advantages are less a function of the "lifetime" part of the system than they are a result of the more basic elements of the Japanese elite employment practices. If one takes meritocratic recruitment, cross-functional training, lockstep promotion, seniority wages, and early retirement as the five basic elements of the elite employment system, many advantages can be seen resulting from the elements rather than from the lifetime nature of the system. (Granted, these elemental parts of the system work more smoothly if the lifetime employment system is in place, but some of the cost and innovation benefits can also accrue independently.) In many cases these elements have a direct impact on two intervening variables we call "uncertainty reduction" and "informal network enhancement" (figure 27). Table 12 shows how these elements affect the intervening variables and consequently the advantages of cost and innovation.

Reduced Uncertainty
Organizations face two basic types of uncertainty—internal and external. External uncertainty can never be wholly eliminated. It exists naturally in business and industry cycles, macroeconomic trends, buyer, sup-

Figure 27

Relationships Among Employment System Elements and Competitive Advantages

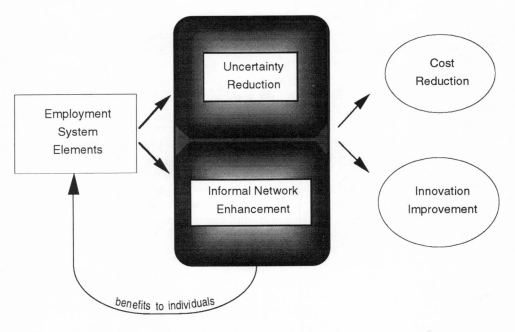

plier, and competitor behavior. Companies learn to cope with this uncertainty by using scenario analysis and contingency planning and by buying insurance. Internal uncertainty is more controllable, and it is in this area that the Japanese gain considerable competitive advantage from the lifetime employment system and its elements. Meritocratic recruitment draws on a limited pool of new recruits, all with very similar backgrounds. This increased uniformity of background (in an already homogeneous Japan) virtually ensures that broad patterns of thought and action will be comparable from manager to manager. Recruiting based on college professors' recommendations also gives the organization some certainty as to the new recruit's ability to think and perform. The training system associated with lifetime employment allows employees in different functional jobs to understand each other. Promotion takes place at predictable times and in an expected fashion. Both individual and organizational uncertainty are diminished; corporate managerial resource planning can occur years in advance, and managers themselves know what is required of them and when they can expect the rewards of even average performance. The seniority system allows organizations to predict payroll expenses, and individuals to forecast earnings, well in advance of the fact. Finally, the early retirement system makes for comparatively simple executive resource planning.

In large companies where corporate elite work, this uncertainty is further reduced by the outplacement of executive talent to smaller, related companies. At an organizational level, this outplacement is perhaps the greatest certainty enhancer of all of the elements of the lifetime employment system. By sending retired employees to subsidiaries, suppliers, and buyer firms, large enterprises in Japan can expect to receive "insider information" about these companies.

Because the lifetime employment system reduces the level of internal uncertainty for Japanese companies, more resources can be devoted to understanding and controlling external uncertainty. In the Japanese system there is little reason for executives to stand around the water cooler speculating about when the next promotions will take place and who will receive the biggest pay increases. Japan's companies lack undercurrents of competition among bosses, co-workers, and subordinates who are not sure "where they come from" and who know they could easily be fired, demoted, or replaced. Instead, the Japanese lifetime employment system has allowed executives to focus their attention outwardly, to their customers and competitors. Executive co-workers in Japan are willing to exchange information about external uncertainties freely because they are not afraid of having that information used against them in ways that may threaten their careers.

Table 12

Elements of the lifetime employment system and types of competitive advantages

Elements of Lifetime Employment System	Competitive Advantages			
	Uncertainty Reduction	Informal Network Enhancement	Cost Reduction	Innovation Improvement
Meritocratic Recruitment	• "Old Boy" network ensures uniformity. • Faculty recommendations and school entrance requirements serve as redundant screen.	• Homogeneity serves as basis of networks. • Alumni recruiters create bonds before employment begins.	• Minimal number of schools are included in recruiting. • Screening is done by faculty and alumni.	• Best and brightest new recruits in the country are hired. • Meritocracy allowed more freedom of thought than others in Japan.
Cross-functional Training (CFT)	• CFT makes it easy to focus resources in crises • CFT builds understanding of other parts of the organization.	• Network extends beyond present position. • No "specialist" cliques develop.	• On-the-Job training saves money. • Transaction costs are reduced in intra-organizational boundary crossing.	• Cross-fertilization of ideas occurs. • Clearer idea of whole organization means greater understanding of real abilities.
Lockstep Promotion	• There is less employee uncertainty because dates of promotion are well established.	• Different-age employees can trust each other. • Same-age employees can expect promotion at similar times.	• Little early career time is spent in speculation about promotion. • Executive resource costs are budgetable.	• Vertical security is built (i.e., new ideas are nonthreatening to superiors).

	• Organizational human resource certainty is also increased			
Seniority Wages	• Individuals can plan future income absolutely. • Organizations correctly forecast human resource costs.	• Seniority perks in form of expense accounts are used to build informal internal and external networks.	• Most productive period is also cheapest. • Few reach highest pay levels. • Slight salary variations can be used to reward most productive.	• Mistakes do not reduce salary significantly. • Creativity and innovation become intrinsic rewards.
Early Retirement	• Least effective employees are weeded out at age of retirement.	• Focus of informal network turns outward to related companies in which retirees are often placed after age of retirement.	• Bulk retirement pay amounts to only a few years' salary. • Only directors who stay after retirement age receive higher pay.	• The way is cleared for younger managers to experiment with new ideas. • Retirees take new ideas to related companies.

Informal Networking

The informal network is also the source of a variety of competitive advantages in a Japanese corporation. In most Western organizations there is a great deal of talk about the difference between company rules and "how it really works." In Japanese firms the lifetime employment system and its elements act to minimize this dichotomy. The familial ideal of the Japanese corporation encourages employees to spend their free time together. Many executives in the United States would find it stifling to spend much of their nonwork time with colleagues from work and would probably expect some form of compensation for the inconvenience. But Japanese elites will spend two or three hours every day (or more usually, every night) with employees of their own firms or members of related firms (customers, suppliers, etc.).

The permanent employment system encourages informal network building simply because employees realize that they will probably spend their entire work lives together. Each element of the lifetime employment system, however, has its own particular influence in building informal networks. The common educational background of executives and cross-functional training means that executive-track employees from all parts of the company have had plentiful opportunities to interact with each other formally and informally. Lockstep promotion negates competition between employees of different age cohorts and minimizes competition between same-age employees because they know that the majority of an age cohort will be promoted simultaneously throughout the early stages of their careers. Seniority wages keep same-company employees of different ages from feeling competitive about compensation—younger employees know that they will be paid similar wages when they reach the requisite age. The large expense accounts that come as perks with the seniority-wage system allow internal and external networks to form through evening activities together. Early retirement is perhaps the most important aspect of interorganizational informal networks, as employees take leaves from their original employer and integrate with the staff at a related firm.

Low-Cost Advantages

Lower uncertainty among executives in Japanese companies naturally results in greater individual productivity, which in turn increases profitability. In addition, costs are reduced by the organizations' certainty about their employees, as well as employee certainty about their organizations. Knowing that almost all employees will be with the company for a lifetime allows Japanese firms to reduce the redundant information systems that exist in most American firms. In Japanese companies, a single employee may serve as the sole repository for enormous amounts of information about the outside world. An individual known as the *mado-guchi* (literally, "window-opening") will oversee all contacts between an external firm (competitor, supplier, customer) and the *madoguchi's* firm. This *madoguchi* will be present at all meetings between the two firms and even at internal planning discussions when the external firm is on the agenda. Because of the lifetime employment system, this *madoguchi* can be expected to serve as a permanently loyal retainer of the firm. Thus, there is no need to put the individual's knowledge into computerized information systems or to have multiple managers as backup in case the *madoguchi* decides to jump ship. This lack of redundant systems in Japan substantially reduces costs to the company.

The informal networks that exist in Japanese firms have been a major factor in Japanese low-cost competitiveness for years. Even since the yen rose sharply against the dollar, Japanese firms have still been able to pursue low-cost strategies because of the minimal transaction costs in their interorganizational and intraorganizational relationships. The "border wars" between functional groups that characterize many internal interactions in American firms simply are not as pervasive in Japanese companies. In most cases, Japanese managers who possess affinities and associative ties that cut across functional groups manage to smooth over the kind of misunderstanding and suspicion that normally exist within Western organizations. Time, effort, and other cost factors associated with implementing change are significantly reduced in Japan because of the lifetime employment system for the corporate elite.

Innovation Advantages

Reduced internal uncertainty and informal networks also allow for greater organizational innovation in Japanese firms. We should distinguish here between individual innovation and organizational innovation. One of the reasons that Japanese firms are increasingly turning to midcareer hiring is that they feel the need for innovative behavior inside their organizations. They need new ideas and new ways of thinking about industries and business areas. Many firms believe that this kind of behavior is initiated by "individualists," and they hope that somehow the "new blood" brought in by midcareer hires will come to permeate their companies with individual innovation. By organizational innovation, however, we are referring to the ability of the organization to adopt new ideas readily. In Japanese firms where backgrounds of managers are homogeneous, turf wars are reduced by functional cross-training, cooperation is highly valued and encouraged by promotion and salary systems, and little is to be gained by personal resistance to new ideas, innovative proposals tend to be implemented more quickly than in most Western firms.

The ability of different functional groups to cooperate because of

cross-functional training and similar educational backgrounds also contributes significantly to corporate Japan's speed-to-market advantages
over the West. Japanese auto makers are able to put out new models
every four years (compared to seven years in the West) largely because
executives overseeing the production, design, marketing, and procure-
ment segments of the process understand at a fundamental level what is
being done in each of the other segments. This allows for simultaneous
development of product strategies in every phase of the manufacturing
and sales process. In addition, many cross-pollination opportunities
come from different units', departments', divisions' and even related
companies' understanding of each other. The fact that a Japanese design
department manager has had experience in marketing and production
functions may allow him to see relationships and glean cost or differentiation advantages in the design stage of a new product. A design manager
in the West who had not had this breadth of experience may be completely oblivious to such useful details.

The stereotypical notion that innovative behavior is beaten out of
youngsters in the educational system in Japan has a degree of truth. Once
graduated from college and into the work force, however, individuals are
rewarded for suggesting innovative ways to improve the company to
which they have devoted a lifetime of loyalty. While young executives in
the West struggle to allay the antagonism of superiors who established
the present systems and who feel threatened by any attempts to improve
on their ideas, young Japanese managerial-track employees enjoy a great
deal of leeway in their early years on the job. Superiors benefit from
smart ideas originating below them, and the new employee has little reason to fear being fired for suggesting a stupid move.

Self-reinforcing Loop

In the end the entire lifetime employment system and its advantages
form a kind of self-reinforcing loop (see figure 30). In many ways this
loop is a byproduct of reduced uncertainty and enhanced informal networks that benefit individuals. We have already noted that individuals
gain a great deal from knowing when promotions will take place and
how much money they will be making throughout their lives. They fit
immediately into the corporate culture of the firm after graduation
because in many ways the company culture is derived from that of their
alma mater. The informal network serves to make individual employees
feel attached to the entire corporate entity through the breadth and depth
of their interaction with other employees. It also supplies these elites with
lifelong friendships, which would probably be severed if they were to
leave their present company for another. Individual employees who have

benefited from the increased certainty and stronger informal networks arising from the lifetime employment system in the past have preached the benefits of this system to the next generation of elites while they devoted themselves to the loyalty ethic.

Arguments against Blip Theory

Blip theorists are the most vocal group to point out the likely reactions against the decline of lifetime employment in Japan. They cite historical precedents and current evidence that greatly weaken the assertion that the system will continue to undergo irreversible change. However, the idea of present circumstances as a simple temporary quirk that will soon be swallowed up in a "return to normalcy" can also be countered with serious questions and opposing evidence.

One of the shortcomings of the blip argument is its failure to consider the social stratum that has been affected by current increases in job changing. It should be noted that many of the data with which blip theorists have dealt are broad-level employment data, and this evidence fails to include (or certainly does not emphasize) elite employees who have always been the mainstay of permanent employment, but who have become much more prone to change jobs in recent years (figure 28). In any society, the attitudes and behaviors of those with status and station in life—such as managerial and professional workers in Japan—are painstakingly copied by those who covet similar positions. Job changing among today's elite Japanese salarymen is much higher than it has been for this group in the past. Furthermore, the recent changes in elite mobility have already lasted three years longer than the oil shock blip of 1973–1974.[6] The unprecedented, sustained pressure and change being experienced within this elite group may have much stronger implications for the lifetime employment system than did job-changing blips among lower-status workers in the past.

Blip theorists tend to presume that current mobility among white-collar workers is simply a result of restructuring. For example, one analyst of Japan pointed out during an interview that once the brewery Suntory has finished its diversification into biotechnology products, it will no longer need midcareer hiring; all of the growth can be internal. This commentator assumed a predictive similarity between diversification within existing production technologies and expansion into new technologies of an altogether different nature. The technological pace of brewing (Suntory's main business) and biotechnology are very different. Developing a work force of generalists in a brewing company is a very competitive strategy, whereas in biotechnology even specialists often can-

Figure 28

Ratio of College Graduate Male Experienced Hires vs New Nonexperienced Graduate Hires, 1967–1989 (with plateaus)

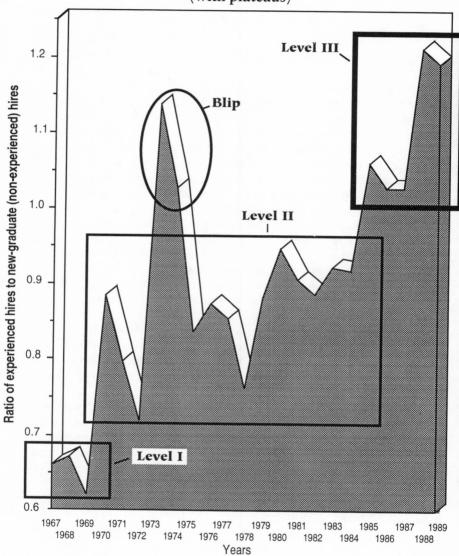

Source: *Rōdō tōkei nenpō*,1967-1989. (Tokyo: Rōdō Homei Kyōkai.)

not stay abreast of all the developments in the field. New products, especially at the levels of technology that will be of increasing importance in the future, often require new personnel (Keizai Doyukai 1987). A blip theory that assumes the technological pace of industry in Japan today can be equated with the pace in the late 1960s or early 1970s is seriously flawed.

The effect of internationalization on the lifetime employment system is also overlooked by most blip theorists. It could be said that both the employment crisis and the oil crisis contained components of internationalization. The employment crisis was the result of the population trough caused by the war and newfound export markets in the 1960s; the oil crisis was a reminder that too much reliance on foreign sources of crucial energy supplies can be dangerous. However, both these previous shocks to lifetime employment exercised their effects indirectly, through economic reactions that affected employment practices as one link in a chain of consequences. Internationalization, in contrast, has itself spurred the recent rise in midcareer hires. Because this internationalization runs in both directions—Western firms having encroached on Japanese territory and the Japanese themselves having eagerly competed as "domestic" companies in foreign countries—it will probably have more long-term effects than did the other crises. Of course, it is also important to remember that the changes taking place in the employment system in the 1980s are not driven by internationalization alone. Had market needs and technology not changed so rapidly and discontinuously in the mid-1980s, the changes in personnel practices might not have been so rapid either.

All of these arguments serve mainly to question the basis of blip theory in the historical record of the lifetime employment system itself. This is not to say that the historical focus of the blip theorists is not a sound analytical stance. In fact, we would argue that a historical basis from which to observe the current events in Japan is absolutely critical. However, we think that the historical examples usually cited by blip theorists are too narrow to provide a predictive comparison for the changes underlying the most recent trends in Japanese employment patterns.

Both breakdown theory and blip theory, then, can be countered by arguments that weaken their persuasiveness as predictors of the future of Japanese lifetime employment. Another position, which we call "plateau theory," argues that current levels of job changing are likely to remain relatively constant throughout the foreseeable future. This position, too, can draw support from the annals of Japanese history both ancient and modern. Because we think this argument is the most powerful predictor of employment practices in Japan in the near future, we discuss its historical and theoretical origins at some length in the following section.

Plateau Theory

Figure 28 illustrates the rise of midcareer hiring in Japan since 1967. It shows at least three types of pattern in the ratio of newly graduated college students hired by elite firms to employees hired in midcareer. The first and most obvious of these patterns is an overall rise in the proportion of midcareer hires. The second is the fluctuation of the system, including the pronounced blip in the early 1970s when the oil shock led to a dramatic but short-lived decline in lifetime employment practices. A third way of interpreting the changes in Japanese employment over the past two decades is to see this graph in terms of a series of plateaus, with job changing responding to various environmental shocks by rising abruptly and then reestablishing its equilibrium, but at a higher level of job mobility than had existed before the system reacted to outside pressures. The plateau of midcareer hiring labeled Level I in figure 31 was first reached during the employment crisis of the 1960s. Job changing rose to Level II in reaction to the oil shocks ten years later. Although job hopping receded from the pronounced surge of 1973, the ratio of midcareer to new-graduate hires never returned to the much lower plateau of the 1960s. The early 1980s show another precipitous climb in Japanese job changing (Level III), and the highest ratio of experienced hires to new graduates was achieved in 1989, the last year for which data are presently available.

The intriguing aspect of Level III is the lack of a clearly evident single reason for decreased loyalty to the traditional procedures of lifetime employment. During the early- to mid-1980s, the Japanese economy did not encounter the kind of obvious internal stresses that had been caused by the management shortage and the oil shocks. It did, however, begin to be more and more seriously affected by the issues we discussed in chapter 4: internationalization, high technology, slowed growth, and an aging worker population. The arguments against breakdown theory are strong enough to convince us that these pressures will not result in the rapid and unrestrained Westernization of the Japanese employment system. However, we also reject the idea that permanent employment is an unchangeable bastion of Japanese tradition that will rebound quickly from any temporary aberrations and return job changing to its lowest historical levels. Instead, we see the recent changes in Japan's employment system as one effect of a struggle to adjust the nation's economy to a new set of political, demographic, and technological conditions. Once those conditions—which include a certain rate of continual change—are being adequately accommodated by the employment system, lifetime employment will remain on a (somewhat uneven) plateau until new kinds of environmental contingencies arise. The historical grounding for this theory is much broader than the blip theorists' consideration of the history of the lifetime employment system itself. Instead of comparing the most recent rise in job changing to previous deviations from the norms of lifetime employment, we will consider the comparison between the present pressures on Japan as a society and similar stresses the nation has faced in the past.

In many ways the internationalization of Japan's economic markets could be compared to two occasions in history when foreign forces have encroached (albeit much more dramatically) on Japanese territory. The first of these occasions was the arrival of the black ships of the U.S. Navy, commanded by Commodore Matthew Perry, demanding that Japan open itself to the West. The second was the penetration of Japanese culture and society by Western influences of all kinds following World War II. Both of these events were seen as incursions from the United States, were military in nature, and profoundly affected virtually all Japanese social institutions. Today's internationalization of Japanese labor markets is not merely an American invasion, is not military in nature, and does not encompass all social institutions. Nevertheless, the similarities are many—especially in light of the fact that after World War II, economics replaced political and military might as the arena in which the Japanese hoped to gain international power.

The real similarities between internationalization and the two historical incursions of foreign powers into Japan can be found in the reactions to these incursions at the various levels of social action. In both the cases of the Meiji Restoration (following the arrival of Admiral Perry) and the reconstruction (following the war), individual Japanese seemed eager to adopt newly imposed behaviors and attitudes. During Meiji, young entrepreneurs without the family ties necessary to have been successful in feudal Japan broke free of the ascriptive society and achieved great wealth, status, and power. Western clothing appeared more and more frequently in Tokyo and even outlying centers. Japanese toured the world trying to adopt as much as possible of Western ways and thinking. Institutions and organizations were not far behind individuals in dropping tradition-bound practices and moving to Westernized practices (including a willingness to consider affiliations with the more mobile members of the society). The effect on the whole social environment of Japan was, needless to say, profound.

Nevertheless, the heady Westernization of the Meiji era soon took on many of the characteristics of a blip in Japanese history. By the turn of the century, Japanese leaders feared that the transformation had been too abrupt. The economy, government, and institutions of social control were staggering under the weight of a nation eager to change too quickly. Strong social actors intervened against Westernization, replacing the spirit of entrepreneurship with fervent nationalism, Saville Row suits with kimonos, and expansive ideals with introspection. Japan once again became a culture far different from the West in its norms, standards, and practices.

After their country's defeat in World War II, most Japanese expected that they would pay dearly for their actions during the war. When the only requirements given to them by the Occupation forces were that they should renounce warfare, become a democratic nation, and rebuild their country, the Japanese were eager to follow the lead of the Western countries. Japan's political system was revamped, its economic institutions were restructured, and its social attitudes were realigned. To the amazement of many Westerners, the Japanese people generally appeared very willing to conform to these new structures and ways of thinking—so willing, in fact, that it seemed Japan would soon become thoroughly Western. It was in this post–World War II period that Western modernization theorists confidently formulated models that assumed that economic development and Westernization in a broad cultural sense were practically identical.

Once again, however, Japanese social forces intervened before a wholesale switch to a Western-style society could occur. Workers who had adopted democratic ideals about labor relations led bloody union conflicts in the late 1940s and early 1950s, and it was not long until some of the democratic concepts that had been adopted wholeheartedly following the war were repealed in favor of more "Japanese" methods of dealing with conflict. The reorganized *zaibatsu* unofficially shaped back into associations and businesses that greatly resembled the outlawed monopolies. The Japanese willingness to try anything indigenous to the victorious West was replaced, as the war receded in time, by attitudes of cultural pride and nationalistic economic competitiveness.

Thus, both the Meiji Restoration and the reconstruction periods could be seen as blips in Japanese history—periods in which foreign impetus caused discontinuous change. The periods that followed these blips could be considered neofeudal (in the case of Meiji) or neonationalist (in the case of the war) periods in Japan. They were periods that took people back to a familiar and comfortable time. These times were in many ways more continuous with the prewar and pre-Perry eras than they were with the blips that immediately followed the advent of these foreign incursions. The Meiji and reconstruction periods were significantly different in kind, as well as in scope, from the oil and employment crises blips discussed above. We think they are more comparable to Japan's present situation than the smaller-scale shocks the lifetime employment system has dealt with during its brief existence.

This present internationalization shock is already being adapted at the organizational and individual levels in ways that never occurred during the previous postwar shocks. Following the oil shock, the individual and organizational systems buffered themselves in such a way that future environmental shocks could not affect them in the same way. In the current shock the reactions have been to embrace internationalization, technological change, demographic shifts, and so forth and to establish new organizational and individual structures that support rather than reject these changes. As we discussed at the end of chapter 7, we are convinced that the current changes in the lifetime employment system for elites are long-lasting because of the cyclical and reinforcing nature of structural effects among levels of analysis (environmental, organizational, and individual).

The lifetime employment system is only one of many indices that show evidence of Japanese society's reaction to a new level of environmental pressures. Like the other aspects of Japan's culture that have absorbed and accommodated such pressures at more dramatic periods in the country's history, permanent employment is likely to change just enough to adapt to current conditions. The increase in job changing among elite Japanese workers is significant in that it represents a new plateau in the nation's managerial philosophy and practice, but it does not mean that Japan is about to discard its uniqueness and revert to Western-style employment. Western businesses that deal with Japan should not expect to see the Japanese becoming ever more similar to themselves, but neither should they refuse to take advantage of the new mobility in the elite work force for fear that lifetime employment will soon snap back to its previous levels. Instead, economic enterprises in Japan should enjoy the unprecedented looseness in the attitudes and behaviors surrounding lifetime employment, while realizing that unforeseen shocks from the environment may result in unpredictable changes in any Japanese institution, including its employment system.

Consequences of Changes in the Lifetime Employment System

Unquestionably, the image of Japanese lifetime employment as eternal and unalterable is not supported by a close look at the system. "Permanent" employment has always been somewhat fluid and has experienced a fair amount of variation since its inception, particularly over the past twenty years. The reasons for the relatively small instabilities in this very resilient system have been related to forces such as internal population change and changes in the external market. The persistence of lifetime employment, on the other hand, is grounded in a far-flung and intricate network of social sanctions, economic strategies, and traditional values.

If our model of change in lifetime employment is correct, however, neither the image of a return to early postwar Japanese practices nor that of a Japan converging rapidly and completely to Western-style employment patterns is likely to prove helpful in dealing with the nation's economic milieu during the coming years. We maintain that lifetime employment will not revert to the level of the 1950s, 1960s, or even 1970s in the near future. Nor will it continue to decline at a rate that will make Japanese employment patterns identical to those found in Western nations. Rather, we think that the present condition of Japan's employment system represents an adaptation to current economic, social, demographic, and political conditions—an adaptation that should prove sufficient for Japan to deal with these issues unless and until the nation encounters another rather dramatic environmental shock.

The most obvious implications of the changes in the lifetime employment system are the increased costs and lowered organizational innovation experienced by Japanese firms. Costs go up when Japanese firms have to retrain executives to replace midcareer job-changers or hire executive search firms and place advertisements to attract experienced employees. The coherence of informal networks and uniformity of thought and action patterns are also disturbed when an outsider is introduced into a social system built around an implicit understanding of common culture and shared experience.

A second implication of changes in the permanent employment system is that innovation in Japanese enterprises is being shifted from the organization to the individual. Firms have opted for some midcareer hiring to bring more diversity to the culture and to strengthen the company's ability to seek out and enter new markets and product areas. In the process, the organization becomes less cohesive. Efforts at corporate change will increasingly have to be explicated and codified, and negative control systems will have to be put into place to keep employees from taking vital information with them if they depart midcareer. Recently designed redundant information systems are coming to litter the corporate terrain in Japan as top executives anticipate the midcareer departure of managerial-track employees, with their vital knowledge of the organization and its environment.

Perhaps the most significant loss that Japanese firms will experience as a result of higher levels of midcareer mobility, however, is the loss of an important nontariff barrier to foreign enterprises entering the Japanese market. In the past, one of the biggest obstacles keeping non-Japanese firms from participating in Japan's market has been the impossibility of hiring talented and well-connected executives (see chapter 6). The recent changes in attitudes and behaviors among Japanese elite have turned that thinking around. Now foreign firms are able to hire some of the very best of the Japanese corporate elite. As a result Japanese firms can expect to lose more and more of their corporate secrets and methodologies to foreign firms who attract Japanese executives. Gradually, the playing field in Japan will be leveled to resemble that used in other foreign corporate contests. While this leveling is taking place, intelligent foreign competitors will move quickly to secure a strong position in the Japanese domestic market and to learn from Japan's past advantages.

Taking Advantage of These Changes

> To meet the enemy's confusion with one's own disciplined array, and to meet the enemy's panic with one's own calmness are the ways to maintain the soldier's morale. One tries to be near the battlefield, while the enemy must come from a long distance; thus one has had a thorough rest and has reorganized, while the enemy is exhausted after a long march.
>
> —*Sunzi,* The Art of War

With the Japanese system of managerial employment changing to look more like the classical system in the West, Western firms now have a distinct advantage in what many businessmen see as the economic battle with the Japanese. For most of the 1980s, Americans were told by the writers of the "Lessons from Japan" school that their management systems should look like those of the Japanese. The paternalistic, close-knit, permanent employment system was given credit for almost all of the Japanese success story in the early 1980s. Indeed, as we have shown in this book, the lifetime employment system and its elements result in powerful competitive advantages. However, one of the reasons we have divided the system into its major elements earlier in this chapter is to show that some of the advantages of the system (while related to and supportive of lifetime employment) can be viewed as separate and independent employment practices. Recent evidence indicates that the battlefield is nearer the Western camp than many analysts once thought, but there may still be a need for Western firms hoping to imitate Japan's success to make a short march, too, and certainly a need to reorganize themselves in preparation for the battle. But Western firms can in fact expect to face a Japanese enemy exhausted from the long march of significant change in its employment system.

REORGANIZING THE ARMY

Although they may modify the lifetime employment system, the Japanese are unlikely to abandon it. They will retain those parts of the system that still give them competitive advantage, while abandoning elements that are at odds with successful international economic competition. Now, while the Japanese are making the "long march" of change, is the time for foreign firms to consider ways to implement in their own organizations some of the elements of the lifetime employment system that might result in major competitive advantages. We turn now to examples of such changes.

Cross-functional Training

Western firms should emphasize cross-functional training and general-ist backgrounds to a greater extent than has been done in the past. Not that everyone in a firm should be a generalist (that has not worked for the Japanese), but neither does every employee need to be a specialist. A corps of generalists who have a variety of functional experiences within the firm become the glue of an organization. They can help their depart-ments better understand the thinking and practices of other parts of the company. They will naturally develop informal ties around the company through job rotation. These understandings and relationships will facili-tate speedier implementation of strategies and enhance innovative think-ing in the firm in general.

Recruiting Networks

Firms should also consider the possibility of establishing relational net-works with potential employees before any formal recruiting takes place. In an increasingly service- and quality-oriented economy, human re-sources become the most important single input to the system—and in many cases the most expensive. The Japanese have provided several examples of ways in which informal networks may be created with potential company members. Among these are hiring college students as part-timers or for summer work, co-opting the relationship between pro-fessors and students so that certain professors in key universities become feeders to the company's hiring process, and relying to a significant degree on recommendations of recently hired employees about potential new hires. For instance, Monitor Company, a strategic consulting firm in Cambridge, Massachusetts, has stopped formal recruiting for second-year MBAs. The company's emphasis has switched to hiring undergradu-ate and first-year MBA students. These undergraduate and first-year stu-dents are usually offered temporary positions of between three months and three years. They are not compensated as highly as MBA-degree holders in the firm, and their temporary position is seen as a testing ground to determine whether or not the firm is satisfied with the employee and vice versa. Turnover has been reduced, and satisfaction levels increased significantly when this policy was put into place.

Interfirm Transfers of Senior Personnel

While we do not advocate early retirement of qualified executives in Western firms as a cost-cutting device, we do think that the informal ties formed by personnel transfers at a senior level are beneficial to the companies involved. Any organizations that regularly cooperate with each other might want to consider a mutual transfer of executive talent. This is not to suggest that the most talented senior executives in a firm should go to work for a supplier, but that other competent managers who may have lost some of their competitive edge can be energized by new surroundings and a new challenge.

TACTICS FOR SUCCEEDING IN JAPAN

This time of significant change in Japanese organizational structure presents an ideal opportunity for subsidiaries of Western firms to gain advantages in the Japanese domestic market. The transition in the thinking of Japan's corporate elites should alter the way that foreign firms conceptualize their own Japanese operations. The most significant change is that subsidiaries in Japan can and should expect to hire better managerial-class employees. Too often executive recruiters in Japan will still tell their clients: "Well, I'm sorry he doesn't meet most of your criteria, but this is Japan, and you must understand that Mr. Tanaka is about the best person you can ever hope to hire." Many midcareer job-changers are leaving their Japanese companies not because "something is wrong with them" but because they are looking for a challenge, enjoyable work, and the pay and prestige levels that foreign firms can offer.

Foreign firms can also expect to hire increasingly talented college graduates from top universities. Our survey of college seniors in one of Japan's best universities indicated that eight out of ten men expected to make at least one midcareer job change during their careers. Five out of ten thought it would be appealing to work for a foreign company at some point during their careers. These unprecedented attitudes among Japan's top graduates support our belief that Western firms can increasingly expect to hire the very best Japanese managerial talent directly out of college.

The implications of both midcareer and "fresh out" recruiting opportunities for Western firms are that foreign subsidiaries can become more successful and autonomous than heretofore in the Japanese marketplace. In the past many Western firms entered into unequal and unfair Japanese joint ventures because of the Westerners' impression that the only way to staff offices in Japan was through a venture with a firm that already possessed a qualified staff. Unfortunately, Japanese partners rarely allowed their best employees to work for the joint venture. Moreover, many of these ventures lasted only as long as the Japanese partner wanted them to. Often the joint-venture employees were reabsorbed into the Japanese firm and the foreign company was left with nothing but a new competitor firm in Japan—one that understood them inside and out.

Motorola is one example of a company that has made some intelligent human resources choices in Japan. The firm initially entered into a joint venture with Toko, a semiconductor firm in northern Japan. Through the joint venture Motorola expected to have a ready location for semiconductor manufacturing and to gain access to a well-functioning work force. Two years later Motorola acquired Toko and began a strategy of internal growth in Japan. A Japanese president for the company was hired away from a large Japanese electronics firm, as were other key engineering and marketing personnel. Motorola also invested huge amounts of time and money in hiring new graduates from the best science universities in Japan. Their first hire of a graduate of Tsukuba Science University in the mid-1980s was cause for much celebration. Today the firm has gained both market share and confidence and expects to continue hiring top graduates and highly qualified midcareer elites.

There may also be a cost advantage that accrues to foreign firms operating in Japan because of increased mobility among the executive class. In the past, Japanese firms have competed with each other on the basis of perquisites such as company housing, vacation resorts, and more recently, retirement communities. Foreign firms offer employees current cash compensation in lieu of these perks. In this way, foreign firms are able to target their incentives at particular employees rather than competing with benefits available to all employees.

Foreign firms are also more agile in the marketplace because of their ability to hire midcareer specialists to deal with changing technology. Japanese companies, when confronted with a significant technological innovation, usually choose to retrain their employees. Such retraining is not cost effective compared to the Western strategy of hiring new and specialized talent. For example, Japan Steel incurred tremendous costs during the 1980s as the company embarked on hundreds of diversification moves—many of which their employees did not have the skills to accommodate. Even if Japanese firms want to hire outside help to cope with changing environments and technologies, their social system usually prevents it. Midcareer hires are still often treated as pariahs or at least second-class citizens in many Japanese corporations. Foreign firms are generally not fettered by these same social strictures. In fact, these transplant companies are generally able to offer higher salaries and higher social status to specialists without fear of losing more employees or causing discontent, as similar measures would in their home country.

Some Japanese companies are losing traditional strength in an attempt to battle the mobility of executive talent. For many years, Japanese firms sent their best employees abroad for management training in graduate programs in North America and Europe. This overseas educational experience usually yielded important international contacts, language skills, and a broader outlook. The export-based economy of the Japanese growth years was directed by many such executives. But just as international management education is becoming more sought-after among globalizing corporations of all nationalities, Japanese corporations are reducing their support of graduate management education. In an effort to deal with a percentage of defections following foreign graduate school, larger Japanese firms either stopped funding graduate education for employees or required executives to establish long-term legal obligations with the firm before embarking on overseas education. Because of this change in policies and attitudes, a large percentage of "free agent" Japanese talent is applying to foreign business schools, but some of Japan's best and brightest are hampered in their quest by unsupportive letters of recommendation from their superiors or outright refusals to write such recommendations.

Finally, foreign companies stand to benefit significantly from the increased knowledge base about their Japanese competitors afforded by a mobile work force. No longer can the Japanese keep their operations, strategies, and corporate philosophies as proprietary as they could when they were assured of the loyalty of all executive-level employees. Foreign firms are now able to hire their rivals' talent, thereby gaining more ability to understand and compete with Japanese companies. Until just a few years ago, this form of competitor analysis was unavailable to foreign firms—whereas Japanese firms were free to hire employees from a foreign firm at any time.

What the new level of job changing in Japan indicates, then, is that enough elite job mobility may now occur to allow Japanese businesses to deal more easily with pressures such as an aging population, technological innovation, slowed economic growth rates, industrial diversification, and internationalization. This adaptation will probably be allowed to the extent that it accommodates the real exigencies of doing business in the Japanese economy—and no further. Even the potential advantages given to foreign firms may give Japanese firms reason to try to reverse the trends to a more mobile executive work force. In the future there are likely to be new environmental stresses—from natural disasters to political upheavals to economic surges—that will push the Japanese employment system to a new level of flexibility. Until such events occur, however, it will be helpful for Japanese and foreign managers alike to recognize that their hiring options are not as limited as the myth of monolithic lifetime employment might lead them to believe.

Conclusions

There is much to learn from both the successes and the shortcomings of Japan's lifetime employment system. The Japanese will probably never adopt a Western model of completely mobile employment, and they will undoubtedly try to retain those aspects of the permanent employment system that prove enduringly beneficial to them. In the current business environment, however, a hybrid of the Japanese and Western employment systems promises to be more robust and more competitive than either model can be alone. The Japanese have already begun to develop such a hybrid from their perspective. We think, however, that the Japanese system is more resistant to change and has further to go than the Western system to achieve a strong integration of Western and Japanese employment practices. We also think, drawing on the imagery of Sunzi in the *Art of War,* that the fact of the Japanese moving in the direction of Western practices does not mean Western companies can expect corporate battles to proceed into their back yards while they simply go about their daily business. We maintain that Western firms could gain a great deal by studying the Japanese employment system. While recognizing the advantages a Western system may have in the international market, they may also benefit by taking a "short march" toward the territory where they can take advantage of the example set by the Japanese, while maximizing their own competitive strengths.

To scholars and Japan-watchers outside the business community, the change in elite job mobility has broader implications. It is yet another illustration of the enigmatic character of a nation in which the more things change, the more they stay the same, and the more things stay the same, the more they seem to change. The lifetime employment system is one of the prime examples of the Japanese love for institutions, relationships, and customs designed to endure forever. It is also an illustration of a culture with a genius for absorbing unheard-of innovations. The alterations in Japan, as reflected in the microcosm of the permanent employment system, do not represent the death of lifetime employment. On the contrary, they are changes in a system that, like all things essential to any life, must remain adaptive to remain vital. Sooner or later, unexpected new forces will again impinge on Japan. Such pressures might necessitate yet more changes in business practices. Until we see them happen, however, we cannot know what those future changes might be. In the meantime, the current state of adaptation in Japan's business world and the accompanying changes in the lifetime employment system testify (as does virtually every other Japanese phenomenon) to the extraordinary sustained fluidity of a unique and remarkable society.

NOTES

Chapter 1

1. To reiterate, *corporate elite* as defined in this work are college graduate males who are likely to be employed in the managerial-track position in elite companies. Traditionally "elite" companies were probably "large" companies (a thousand employees or more). Recently "elite" may apply to smaller firms, especially in the service industry but also in a number of high-tech concerns.

2. That the elite employees were first given lifetime employment and then lower-level employees demanded similar treatment is dealt with in chapter 2.

3. The Japanese government has not been keen on gathering or publishing data that indicate the stratified nature of its people. Most of the data are broken down by prefecture, by age, or by sex, but we argue that these are not valid indicators of the changes taking place among the managerial elite. The only other way that we were able to gather public, broad-level statistics on Japanese workers was to let college education proxy for "eliteness." We approached the Ministry of Labor from a number of different angles to get more exact data. Our inquiries were diverted each time.

4. We have noted with Lincoln and Kelleberg (1990) the propensity for authors on this subject to overqualify their conclusions: "It is almost pro forma to conclude studies of Japanese work organizations and work attitudes with a caveat to the effect that such patterns are undergoing rapid change and [that] forecasts to the future are hazardous" (254). We appreciate the fact that Lincoln and Kalleberg have tried to avoid such tactics in their text. While we disagree with their conclusions, we too have tried to state our hypotheses about the future as clearly as possible.

Chapter 2

1. Since Abegglen first described the system of "lifetime employment" to a Western audience in 1958 *(The Japanese Factory)*, a number of works have called into question the pervasiveness of the lifetime employment system in the working class (e.g., Marsh and Mannari 1971, 1972). Many Japanese blue-collar workers

have been told, and believe, that they will have a full career with the first company they join. Actually, in recent years layoffs of such workers have become more the norm than the exception in Japan. It is the managerial-class Japanese employee who seems most likely to enjoy the benefits of the lifetime employment system.

2. It should be noted here the variety of words that can be translated as "loyalty" in Japan. For the most part, this discussion of loyalty in a corporate context may be translated as *aisha seishin,* but such words as *chūjitsu* (faithfulness) and *chūsei* (loyalty) are also appropriate synonyms.

3. In later Tokugawa a considerable number of samurai appear to have been involved in agriculture. Although it was considered base by most samurai, some were always involved in commerce as well. This relationship was sometimes at arm's length.

4. Hirschmeier and Yui give the example of a sake brewer whose father was a leading samurai leader who kept his status a secret so that his family members would "identify fully with merchant status" (p. 57).

5. Yataro Iwasaki, the founder of Mitsubishi, bought a *goshi* (lowest-class samurai) title at the beginning of the nineteenth century, but by the end of the Tokugawa period, he turned around and sold the title to buy a lumber merchant-ship.

6. Mencius saw these relationships as (1) "affection between father and son," (2) "righteous sense of duty" between master and servant, (3) harmony between husband and wife, (4) "stratification between old and young," and (5) "good faith between friends" (Baker 1979, 10–11).

7. *On* (benevolence to inferiors) and *giri* (obligation to everyone) are two examples of the obligatory actions that all villagers in Tokugawa Japan were supposed to exhibit in their everyday lives (Yoshino 1967, 7).

8. Yataro Iwasaki, the founder of Mitsubishi, was promoted in the shogunate trade office because "his now recognized ability . . . proved sufficient to overcome his humble origins, which, in the last years of feudalism, had become easier to overlook" (Yamamura 1967, 44).

9. This was especially true in the Osaka houses.

10. Larger houses hired several *bantō* with the *shihainin* (chief manager) in charge of the rest.

11. Yamamura contrasts this with the more traditional beliefs about the importance of "samurai spirit" in Hirschmeier (1970) and in Ranis (1955, 81).

12. Ninety-four percent of the total population was commoner. This figure shows that the samurai class did not completely control Meiji business as some have suggested.

13. "In 1867, one French technician at Yokosuka [Naval Shipyard], Francois L. Varney, lamented that workers finally trained with great difficulty in Western skills left for jobs elsewhere, leaving behind only inexperienced workers, thus obstructing operations." Another observer in 1910 suggested that there were no metal workers "of 50 years of age or so" who were not trained in one of the arsenals with foreign technicians (Gordon 1985, 19).

14. "Sotsugyōsei no matsuro," *Nihon no shōnen* 3.3 (February 1, 1891): 2–4.

15. One example of this can be found in "Yuda was hyaku aku no oya," *Eisai Shinshi* (Talent forum), no. 17 (June 30, 1877): 2–3, and referred to in Kinmonth 1981, 77. *Eisai Shinshi* was a type of Meiji weekly reader to which young readers submitted articles for publication. This particular article was about the shame and embarrassment a young student brought to his household by not studying.

16. Yukichi Fukuzawa, *Gakumon no Susume,* trans. and quoted by Kinmonth 1981, 46–47.

17. Translation from *Gakumon no Susume* in Hirschmeier and Yui 1981, 126. "True self-respect should not come from status but from knowledge and business success."

18. "Managers themselves were susceptible to indoctrination at the same time that they were providing an input to the process."

19. *Jitsugyō no Nihon* [Japan's entrepreneurship], 7.6 (1904).

20.

Year	Institutions of higher learning	Students
1885	63	12,382
1905	84	37,180
1915	108	50,470
1925	257	126,842
1935	308	149,030

21. *Nihon rōdō nenkan,* no. 2 (1921), pp. 331–333.

22. The greatest fears: getting fired, 48 percent; illness, 22 percent.

23. "The late 1950s and early 1960s show[ed] the highest persistency recorded in the company's history, with the length of employment lasting 15 to 20 years almost uniformly." The percentage distribution of new employees with prior work experience was as follows: 1918–1930, 15.6 percent; 1932–1948, 31.2 percent; 1949–1976, 53.2 percent.

Tally of entering managerial employees with experience:

Period	Average/year	Rate/100
1918–1930	5.0	.18
1932–1948	8.5	.30
1949–1976	8.6	.22

Chapter 3

1. Vogel cites Baker 1956: "Lower-class Japanese are less likely to have as high aspirations in their society as lower-class Americans do in their society."

2. The results of the survey do not necessarily show that Japanese are virtuous in separating public from private matters. On a question similar to the one above, but with "a relative" replaced with "the son of someone who has been good to" the respondent and to whom the respondent owed a favor, the number answering they would be willing to exert personal influence jumped to 39 percent.

3. On paper, anyway, the process has been outlawed in Japan as well.

4. Interview, summer 1986.

5. Interview with Haruo Shimada, summer 1986.

6. It is only after this first six months that the employee is considered a life-long member of the company.

7. "Because of the long distance from home to work, it is difficult to go home after work and then return to the city for an evening of recreation. Various polls have shown that it takes the husband an average of two to three hours to get home. While commuting may require a long time, the transportation alone could not possibly take that long. It is rather that this is the time for recreation" (Vogel 1963, 103–104).

8. Asked "Would you prefer to work or be idle?"

	Idle (percent)	Work (percent)
Japanese high school	27.3	72.5
College	26.3	72.3
Young workers	19.4	79.9
American high school	8.4	89.6
College	10.8	85.1
Young workers	21.1	75.5

(Source: Prime Minister's Office 1972)

9. *Purejidento* [President magazine], August 1977, p. 40.

10. It was interesting to note the look of frustration on businessmen's faces when a group of my acquaintances from an American consulting firm presented their business cards to a group of Japanese executives. In a very egalitarian manner, the American firm had decided not to print titles on the cards; name, company name, address, and phone number were the only pieces of information listed. Normally visitors will be seated in a room based on their relative status. The first confusion, then, for the Japanese hosts came in not knowing where to seat the American visitors. Once a random seating was decided upon, the conversation took on the characteristics of a subtle interrogation in which the Japanese hosts tried to ascertain the relative seniority of the various members of the American party.

11. Interview with former personnel department employee at Dentsu, September 1986.

12. "When asked about their own personal chances of promotion, only 13% of the Japanese sample, compared with 46% of the British sample said that they had no chance at all. And of those who said that they had little or no chance at all, 28% in Britain, compared with 16% in Hitachi, gave as their reason the injustice of the firm's methods of selection rather than their own lack of qualifications" (Dore 1973, 67).

13. Interview, June 1985.

14. This term has a very derogatory tone. It is still used by some to describe the descent of an "angel" into a management position they were hoping to fill. It is never, however, used to the retiree's face.

15. Dore 1973, 223, mentions that Hitachi's directors are all younger than the president in his study. The process in which directors who are *senpai* and therefore older than a newly installed president has been described in detail to me by a number of directors who have been fearing forced retirement and therefore were contemplating a job change.

16. While this number may appear high to the casual observer, it must be remembered that these individuals' management careers spanned the war years, the economic upheaval at that time, and the consequential higher rates of mobility.

17. Interviews at Nippon Motorola, summer 1985. In the middle of the worldwide semiconductor slump, Japanese management at Motorola urged top management to avoid the urge to lay off workers for fear of never being able to recruit top engineers again. Instead workers and managers were involved in clean-up crews on company time and came to work only three days a week.

18. van Helvoort (1979, 13) estimated that although official unemployment figures stood at 2 percent, they would be 5 or 6 percent or more if "companies would stop honoring the principle of lifetime employment."

Chapter 4

1. It is interesting to note that the slowest growing company had actually "discharged" personnel.

2. The typical layout of a Japanese firm has two rows of desks pushed together and facing each other running down the center of a room. The section chief's desk is situated strategically at the head of these rows so that he can observe constantly the productivity of his charges. Those with desks along sides of a building are not active participants in the core business of a section. These employees, known as the *madogiwazoku* (literally, "window-side tribe"), are usually given menial jobs not requiring much interaction with others in the firm to occupy their time.

3. Interview with K. Funatsu, Recruit Company, June 1987.

4. See, for example, Japan: The end of lifetime jobs, *Business Week,* July 17, 1978, pp. 82–83; "Can lifetime employment in Japan last?" *Economist,* October 1, 1977, pp. 91–92; Kanabayashi 1977, 1; van Helvoort 1982, 26–28.

5. Interview with Mr. Kameyama, National Institute of Employment and Vocational Research, June 1987.

6. Interview, April 1988.

7. Interview, December 1987.

8. Phone conversation, August 10, 1987.

9. Interview, August 1987.

10. Interview with John Ware, Spencer Stuart, Tokyo, December 1987.

11. Interview, July 1987.

12. One account in a recent *Wall Street Journal* article tells of an employee who went "to the local post office, wrote an official letter of voluntary resignation, and signed the document with his 'hanko' or official signature seal" in order to avoid any insinuations by his employer. See Wysocki 1985.

13. Interview, July 1987.

14. Interview, December 1987.

15. Interview with Higashi at Hitachi, September 1986.

16. Interview with John Ware, December 1987.

17. Interviews, Nippon Motorola, Tokyo, June 1985.

18. Interview, August 1987.

19. The obvious gap in the data was in the age thirty-seven to age forty-five category. The company gave the data as an illustration of labor stability. The missing age group would correlate with a group that has been traditionally very stable, but lacks incentives in the recent corporate age structure.

20. Ministry of Labor, *Summary of 1987 Employment Survey* (Tokyo, 1989).

21. Ministry of Labor, *1988 Survey on Employment Trends* (Tokyo, 1990).

22. Management and Coordination Agency, *1990 Employment Survey* (Tokyo, 1991).

23. It should be noted that Recruit Jinzai Center was one of the first executive placement centers in Japan, if not the first; therefore, this increase in numbers is not merely taking market share from other organizations.

24. *East Asian Executive Reports* 8.10 (October 15, 1986): 8.

25. These data come from the Employment Status Survey, which is administered by the Ministry of Labor every three to five years. Data were drawn from the 1987, 1977, and 1968 reports because the survey questions were similar in those years and because those years best represent decade slices of data from the time of the most recent survey, which was in 1987.

26. A recent Recruit Research survey shows that the percentage of twenty- to thirty-nine-year-old college graduates who have changed jobs is the same in 1988 as it was in 1984 (25.4 percent compared with 25.7 percent in 1984). Recruit Research personnel to whom I showed the data in Figure 4 were surprised to see younger respondents changing jobs so much more than their older counterparts. A 1986 survey conducted by this company showed the following data corresponding to Exhibit V.

Age	Years since job change					N
	0–3	4–6	7–9	10–19	20–25	
22–29 (16.7%)	75.6%	24.4%	0%	0%	0%	41
30–39 (30.8%)	25.9%	31.3%	17.0%	25.9%	0%	112
40–45 (35.9%)	10.9%	12.7%	12.7%	56.4%	7.3%	55
All ages	31.7%	25.0%	12.5%	28.9%	1.9%	
	37.46%	22.8%	9.9%	27.4%	2.43%	

27. Interview with Stanley Holt, Boyden Associates, Tokyo, December 22, 1987.

28. Interview with Mr. Murakami, Technology Management Transfer Co. (TMT), December 23, 1987.

29. *East Asian Executive Reports* 8.10 (October 15, 1986): 8.

30. Interview with Ken Whitney, Egon Zehnder—Japan, December 22, 1987.

31. The chi-square probability for this cross-tabulation is p =.0339.

Chapter 5

1. Martin 1982. Peter Drucker made a similar point; quoted in Vogel 1975.

2. Japan's Economic Planning Agency reckons that 21 percent of Japanese will be over sixty-five, compared with 20 percent of (West) Germans, 19 percent of Britons, and 16 percent of Americans.

3. Interview with Ken Whitney, Egon Zehnder, December 22, 1987.

4. "A 1986 survey reported that over 50 percent of corporate employers have adopted a retirement age of 60 years or older. Despite this change, the labor force participation rate for men aged 55–64 years continued to decline from 85.4 percent in 1980 to 83.8 percent in 1984." Jones 1987.

5. From an average of $400 in electronic equipment per car in 1989 to more than $2,000 per car in 1995.

6. Interview, September 1986.

7. Interview, Stanley Holt, Boyden Associates, Tokyo, December 22, 1987.

8. Interview, June 1987.

9. Correlation coefficients show a .221 relationship between talking about quitting one's job and having spent a good deal of time abroad.

10. MITI statistics indicate that the entry of new foreign firms into Japan increased dramatically after 1975. *Asahi Shinbun,* January 10, 1987.

11. *Asahi Shinbun,* August 8, 1988. Forty percent of their offices are in Mina-toku, 30 percent in Chiyodaku, and another 10 percent in other parts of Tokyo.

12.

Year	Number of American companies established in Japan
1982	112
1983	149
1984	182
1985	185
1986	216 (estimated)

13. Thomas Nevins, quoted in Brender 1986. The exception would be foreign firms that are accepted as Japanese (e.g., IBM Japan, DEC, McDonald's).

14. Rather than lay off workers in a recent downturn in the semiconductor market, Motorola employed all of its workers. Many of those who were idle at the factory were encouraged to participate in community clean-up projects on the company's time.

15. Mitsui Bank hires foreigner, *Business Japan,* March 1986.

16. Interview, September 1986.

17. A MITI survey showed that 60 percent of the largest 1,029 Japanese companies wished to have some kind of connection or venture with foreign firms. *Asahi Shinbun,* April 22, 1988.

18. Mr. Takahashi, personnel director at Yasuda Trust Bank, quoted in *Nikkei Sangyō Shinbun,* February 23, 1987, 1.

19. Interview, September 1986.

20. Interview with Ken Whitney, Egon Zehnder, December 22, 1987.

21. Interview with Mr. Nishiura, Boston Consulting Group, July 1987.

22. Interview, April 1988.

23. Interview, December 23, 1987.

Chapter 6

1. Yoshino and Lifson 1986, 159.

Position	Percentage of staff on *shukkō*
Senior manager *(yakuin)*	29.5
Department chief *(buchō)*	22.5
Assistant department chief *(buchō dairi)*	21.6
Section chief *(kachō)*	16.4
Assistant section chief *(kakarichō)*	12.7
Ordinary top grade	7.0

2. The remaining responses indicated a case-by-case treatment of which company paid the transferring employee.

3. The use of transfers to reduce the number of the following types of employees was also expected to increase in the future.

Type of employee	Currently using *shukkō* (percentage)	Plan to use *shukkō* in future (percentage)
Senmonshoku (specialists)	16.8	41.4
Jimu ippanshoku (office workers)	9.6	21.3
Eigyō ippanshoku (sales people)	11.1	21.4

4. At the beginning of the Career Planning Center's existence only about 20 percent of its placements were outside the group; recently that number has climbed to almost 50 percent.

5. Interview, September 1986.

6. This system probably applies only to employees who have no chance of promotion to the Board of Directors.

7. Translation given in interview at Industrial Bank of Japan, September 1986.

8. The company's name has even been bantered about abroad since the Recruit Cosmos stock scandals.

9. *Torabaayu* became such a popular publication for women that it is not uncommon to hear a woman in Japan use the term *torabaayu* as a verb to describe a recent job change. (Example: "Saikin kanojo ga komputaa gaisha ni torabaayu shita wa." "She recently changed jobs to a computer company.")

10. This compares with 104 job-jumpers placed in its first year of operation, 1978, according to the *Los Angeles Times,* July 9, 1988.

11. The other firms in the country experienced similar growth rates over those years according to Takita 1987, 339. Profit levels undoubtedly increased proportionately.

12. Interview with Ken Whitney, Egon Zehnder, December 22, 1987.

13. It is questionable whether or not these searches were on the same level as those done by most of the foreign firms.

14. Kyodo News Service, March 5, 1990. Pioneer claims that 47 percent of its business comes from Japanese clients.

15. Interview, December 22, 1987. This number is low based on my head-hunting experience in another headhunting firm.

16. Interview with Mr. Imagawa at Nikon. "While the specialist is necessary in a firm, only generalists should be at the top of a company. A general management position is one way, however, to groom a specialist into a generalist."

17. An employee who has changed jobs once is always considered likely to try to do it again.

18. Interview with Mr. Sugiyama, Sanwa Bank, June 1987.

19. Interview, July 1987.

20. Interview, May 1989.

21. Interview, June 1987.

22. Interview, December 1987.

23. Interview, August 1986.

24. Interview, July 1987.

25. Interview, January 1988.

26. Interview, June 1987.

27. Interview, June 1987.

28. Interview, February 1988.

Chapter 7

1. That the ratio of the population emphasizing social needs has held steady during the 1980s is very telling in light of the rapidly aging population. Older Japanese have always placed more value on social needs, yet the ratio of social to individual needs has not changed as the population aged.

2. The Foreign Press Center's newsletter, *PressGuide*, defined *shinjinrui* in October 1986.

> The expression *shinjinrui* (new human race or new breed) first appeared in an advertisement for a brand of whiskey targeted at young adults. The whiskey flopped, but the phrase caught on and became a synonym for today's young generation. Though there is no accurate definition of the term, *shinjinrui* generally refers to people born after 1960; sometimes the date is set at 1955. There have been two major influences on this generation: the affluent society, which was the fruit of high economic growth in the 1960s, and television. . . .
>
> The *shinjinrui* generation has several characteristics. First, it is not interested in profundities. Unlike the generation born immediately after the war, which spearheaded the student movement of the 1960s and enjoyed nothing more than revolutionary debate, the new breed is content with, or has come to terms with, the status quo. Second, the *shinjinrui* generation, strongly influenced by video culture, has highly developed audio and visual sensibilities. Third, this is the digital generation. Members of the new breed dislike analogical thinking. They feel no desire to contemplate their existence in the context of history. Fourth, today's young adults feel no solidarity with others. Uninterested in lofty matters, they are a narcissistic breed. They show no interest in what oth-

ers think and live according to their own values. In this way, the *shin-jinrui* generation is representative of the so-called age of the splintered masses. The new breed adapts to society and seeks to live life as fully and comfortably as possible. (Quoted in *Currents* [Tokyo: Japan Echo, 1988], pp. 178–179)

3. Interview, July 1987.

4. An Analysis of Variance (ANOVA) on respondents under age thirty-five and over age thirty-five on these questions showed that the groups differed significantly on their answers (p = .0036). While the analysis of variance probability within groups on the variable increased to p = .102 for respondents in companies with more than a thousand employees, the difference in behavior between those under thirty-five and those over thirty-five was still marked. Some 14 percent of the younger respondents had actively participated in job-changing activities compared with less than 7 percent of those over thirty-five.

5. Mizobuchi interview, Recruit Jinzai Center, Tokyo, June 2, 1987. Naturally, a certain amount of self-interest in evident in Mizobuchi's remarks.

6. Interview, July 1988.

7. The following regression equation explain this relationship.

$$\text{commitment} = 3.19 - .277\,[tenshoku] - .114\,[\text{service industry}] + .12\,[\text{salary}] - .075\,[\text{cosize}]; R2 = .178, p = .034$$

8. There is a third possibility. Once they have been set free from the traditional social sanctions against job changing, they are more able to think about job changing again and again.

9. The ANOVA probability of these numbers being exactly the same is p = .0022.

10. All 1,041 respondents were college graduates; 27.7 percent had changed jobs.

11. Interview, June 1987.

12. Interview, May 1987.

13. Interview, December 1987.

14. Interview at Nikon, September 1986. In young fields like laser technology, however, "changing jobs for more money is becoming more common."

15. One of the authors was involved in a search for a tax specialist for a securities firm; the candidate had to be certified as a Japanese tax specialist, have a working knowledge of American tax laws, and have had experience in the securities industry. An extensive two-month search turned up only one such person in Japan, and he had already been hired by a competitor at an exorbitant salary.

16. Interview, June 4, 1987. Funatsu went on to say that he expected the number changing for money to increase in the future especially among the elite executive-track employees.

17. That those who change jobs later in life receive lower lifetime earnings is not entirely explained by *taishokukin*. Most people who changed jobs in the past, particularly those who changed later in life, changed because their companies were not doing well. Desperate to get another job, they often took lower-paying jobs.

18. The regression equation for this relationship is as follows:

change in salary from previous job = 4.91 − .107 [years in present company]; R^2 = .12, p = .0542

Change in salary from previous job is an ordinal variable that applies only to respondents who had changed jobs.

19. The regression equation for college graduates is as follows:

Salary level = 7.952 − .67 [job-changing experience]; R^2 = .107, p = .1835

Salary level is an ordinal variable. Job-changing experience is a dummy variable. 1 = respondent who has changed jobs; 2 = respondent who has not changed jobs.

20. The corresponding regression equation for noncollege graduates is as follows:

Salary level = 7.00 − 1.46 [job-changing experience] where R^2 = .097, p = .0002

21. Statistically the regression equation linking salary and the number of years one has been with his or her present company has a probability of p = .144 among nongraduates (see n. 18 for comparison to college graduates).

22. Interview, August 1986.

23. Interview, September 1986.

24. Interview, February 1987.

25. It is logical to expect that this article, "Chūto nyūsha būmu!" [Midcareer hiring boom!], did not present a random sample of job-changers in its list. The article had a point to make about the popularity of job changing in Japan, and data were chosen to prove that point. Nevertheless, this article (and the information on salaries included therein) give the Japanese reader one more data point (in what has recently been a long string of positive data about midcareer job changing) on which to hang a newfound belief in the good of job changing.

26. Interview with Mr. Higashi at Hitachi, September 1986.

27. Interview, July 1987.

28. Interview, August 1987.

29. *Nihon Keizai Shinbun,* January 18, 1986. It is interesting to note that 25.8 percent of Americans expected to "reach the top level of the firm in the next five years" while only 0.8 percent of the Japanese answered positively to the same question.

30. Morimoto's popularity did not plummet as many had suspected it might; rather, TBS officials are said to have thought the investment in Morimoto was well worth the increased viewer ratings they received.

31. Interview, spring 1987.

32. Interview with John Ware, December 1987.

33. Mizobuchi interview, Recruit Jinzai Center, June 2, 1987.

34. Interview, John Ware, Spencer Stuart, December 1987. Ware continued:

"Japanese would be better served by taking personal responsibility for their own careers."

35. Interview, Mr. Nishiura, Boston Consulting Group and former personnel planner at Sumitomo Trust, June 1987.

36. Mr. Sato of Mitsubishi Research Institute as quoted in Kanabayashi 1988.

Chapter 8

1. This belief is often expressed best in convergence theories. Thinkers in a variety of fields led by modernizationists assumed that societies would begin to look a great deal more like each other.

2. Interview, August 1986.

3. American companies that have adopted these same policies have been some of the few successful low-cost producers (i.e., Lincoln Electric, People's Express). A different set of human resources management policies may be necessary to successfully implement a differentiated strategy, however.

4. Quote from Tom Murtha, high-tech analyst at Baring Securities, in *Straits Times* (Singapore), August 11, 1988.

5. Quote from Eleanor Westney, associate director of MIT's Japan Science and Technology Program, in *Japan Economic Newswire*, May 10, 1988.

6. In fact, a careful reading of the numbers represented in Figure 28 shows that there was a .05 percent increase in the ratio of experienced to new-graduate hires between 1986 and 1987, from 102.64 percent to 102.69 percent.

SELECT BIBLIOGRAPHY

Abegglen, J. C. 1958. *The Japanese Factory*. Glencoe, IL: Free Press.

———. 1987. Japan's employment system. *Business Tokyo,* May.

The aging of Japanese social security. 1983. *The Economist,* May, p. 95.

Aoki, Masahiko. 1988. *Information, Incentives and Bargaining in the Japanese Economy*. Cambridge: Cambridge University Press.

Aonuma Y. 1965. *Nihon no keisō*. Tokyo: Nihon Keizai Shinbunsha.

Aridome, Osamu. 1988. Scientific yuppies. *Business Tokyo,* November.

Asahi Shinbun. 1985: March 20; May 6; July 30; August 25. 1986: July 22, 28; August 26; October 22. 1987: January 10; February 3; March 11; May 22. 1988: January 6; February 2, 19; April 22, 29; May 4; June 2; July 10; August 8; September 12; October 9.

Baker, Hugh D. R. 1979. *Chinese Family and Kinship*. New York: Columbia University Press.

Baker, Wendell Dean. 1956. A study of selected aspects of Japanese social stratification. Ph.D. diss., Columbia University.

Ballon, R. J., ed. 1969. *The Japanese Employee*. Tokyo: Sophia University.

Ballon, R. J. 1969. Lifelong remuneration system. In *The Japanese Employee,* ed. R. J. Ballon, pp. 123–166. Tokyo: Sophia University Press.

Benedict, Ruth. 1967. *The Chrysanthemum and the Sword*. Cleveland: Meridian Books.

Bennett, J. W., and I. Ishino. 1963. *Paternalism in the Japanese Economy: Anthropological Studies of Oyabun-Kobun Patterns*. Minneapolis: University of Minnesota Press.

Bennett, John W. 1967. Japanese economic growth: Background for social change. In *Aspects of Social Change in Modern Japan,* ed. R. Dore, pp. 411–453. Princeton: Princeton University Press.

Beruf. 1985. April.

Beyond lifetime employment. 1987. *Business Tokyo,* May, pp. 40–42.

Bounine-Cabale, J., R. Dore, and K. Tapiola. 1988. Flexibility in Japanese labour markets. Unpublished report of OECD team. Revised 1989.

Brender, Alan. 1986. Angling for Japanese employees. *Journal of the ACCJ,* July/August, pp. 18–26.

Browning, E. S. 1986. Job hopping in Japan isn't unheard-of, but it is hard to bring off. *Wall Street Journal,* September 9.

Can lifetime employment in Japan last? 1977. *Economist* 265 (October 1): 91–92.

Carlson, R. O. 1962. *Executive Succession and Organizational Change.* Chicago: Midwest Administration Center, University of Chicago.

Changes in workforce at foreign securities houses in Japan. 1987. *Tokyo Financial Letter* 1.17 (July 27): 6–7.

Christopher, Robert C. 1986. *Second to None: American Companies in Japan.* New York: Crown.

Chūto nyūsha būmu! 1987. *Next,* July.

Cole, Robert E. 1971. *Japanese Blue Collar: The Changing Tradition.* Berkeley: University of California Press.

———. 1976. Changing labor force characteristics and their impact on Japanese industrial relations. In *Japan: The Paradox of Progress,* ed. L. Austin. New Haven: Yale University Press.

———. 1978. The late-developer hypothesis: An evaluation of its relevance for Japanese employment practices. *Journal of Japanese Studies* 4.

———. 1979. *Work, Mobility, and Participation.* Berkeley: University of California Press.

Cole, R., and K. Tominaga. 1976. Japan's changing occupational structure. In *Japanese Industrialization and Its Social Consequences,* ed. Hugh Patrick, pp. 52–95. Berkeley: University of California Press.

Cooper, G. 1976. *Would You Care to Comment on That Sir?: A Look at 50 of Japan's Top Businessmen.* Tokyo: Japan Economic Journal.

Cornell, John B. 1963. Local group stability in the Japanese community. *Human Organization* 22:113–125.

Crawcour, Sydney. 1978. The Japanese employment system. *Journal of Japanese Studies* 4.2 (Summer): 225–245.

Daito, Eisuke. 1986. Recruitment and training of middle managers in Japan, 1900–1930. In *The Growth of Managerial Capitalism,* ed. Alfred Chandler. Cambridge: Harvard University Press.

Dokushin no kyūyo taikei ga shōrai kadai ni. 1988. *Sōgō Shiryō M&L,* January 1–15, pp. 25–35.

Dore, R. 1958. *City Life in Japan: A Study of a Tokyo Ward.* Berkeley: University of California Press.

———. 1964. Latin America and Japan compared. In Johnson, J., ed. *Continuity and Change in Latin America,* ed. J. Johnson, p. 238. Stanford, CA: Stanford University Press.

———. 1965. *Education in Tokugawa Japan.* Berkeley: University of California Press.

———, ed. 1967. *Aspects of Social Change in Modern Japan.* Princeton: Princeton University Press.

————. 1973. *British Factory, Japanese Factory.* Berkeley: University of California Press.

East Asian Executive Reports. 1986. 8.10 (October 15).

Edwards, P. K. 1986. *Conflict at Work: A Materialist Analysis of Workplace Relations.* New York: Oxford.

Endo, Calvin M. 1974. Formal management relations practices in Japanese business and industrial organizations. *International Journal of Contemporary Sociology* 11 (January): 23–33.

Esaka, Akira. 1987. Lost: Illusions about Japanese management. *Japan Quarterly,* October–December, pp. 419–423.

————. 1988. Ii kaisha ni chūtonyūsha suru kenkyū. *Next,* January.

Evans, Robert, Jr. 1984. "Lifetime earnings" in Japan for the class of 1955. *Monthly Labor Review,* 107:32–6 April.

Fairbank, John K., Edwin O. Reischauer, and Albert M. Craig. 1978. *East Asia: Tradition and Transformation.* Boston: Houghton Mifflin.

Far Eastern Economic Review (FEER). 1983. April, p. 51, and December, p. 50.

Firms step up raids for mid-career workers. 1988. *Japan Economic Journal,* February 20, p. 19.

Foreign firms see workers slip away: Better salaries, work hours offered but sense of security remains low. 1988. *Japan Economic Journal,* June 25, p. 10.

Foreign Press Center. 1986. *PressGuide,* October.

Fruin, W. Mark. 1978. The Japanese company controversy. *Journal of Japanese Studies* 2.4 (Summer): 267–300.

————. 1983. *Kikkoman: Company, Clan, and Community.* Cambridge: Harvard University Press.

Fukutake, Tadashi. 1974. *Japanese Society Today.* Tokyo: University of Tokyo Press.

Gekkan Sōmu. 1989. February, pp. 38–39.

Gendai Shachō. 1966.

Gerth, H., and C. Mills, eds. 1946. *From Max Weber: Essays in Sociology.* New York: Oxford University Press.

Godet, Michel. 1987. Ten unfashionable and controversial findings on Japan. *Futures* (UK) 19.4 (August): 371–384.

Gordon, Andrew. 1985. *The Evolution of Labor Relations in Japan: Heavy Industry, 1853–1955.* Cambridge, MA: Harvard University, Council on East Asian Studies.

Haitani, Kanji. 1978. Changing characteristics of the Japanese employment system. *Asian Survey* 18.10:1029–1045.

Hamaguchi, Esyun. 1981. The "Japanese disease" or Japanization? *Japan Echo* 2.8:44–55.

Hanke, J., and B. Saxberg. 1985. Isolates and deviants in the United States and Japan: Productive nonconformists or costly troublemakers? *Comparative Social Research* 8:219–243.

Hazama, Hiroshi. 1976. Historical changes in the life style of industrial workers. In *Japanese Industrialization and Its Social Consequences,* ed. Hugh Patrick. Berkeley: University of California Press.

Hearn, Lafcadio. 1923. *Japan: An Attempt at Interpretation.* Boston.

Hirschmeier, Johannes. 1970. The Japanese spirit of enterprise, 1867–1970. *Business History Review 44.*

Hirschmeier, Johannes, and Tsunehiko Yui. 1981. *The Development of Japanese Business, 1600–1980.* 2d ed. London: George Allen and Unwin.

Holden, Ted. 1989. Big bucks vs. a job for life: Why top talent is defecting. *Business Week,* January 9, p. 58.

Horie Yasuzō. 1967. Nihon keieisha ni okeru ie no mondai. *Keieishigaku 2.*

Hoshino Shūichirō. 1937. Hōkyū seikatsu no mitai hōkyū seikatsu. *Shakai Seisaku jihō,* no. 196 (January).

Howard, Ann, Keitaro Shudo, and Miyo Umeshima. 1983. Motivation and values among Japanese and American managers. *Personnel Psychology* 36.4 (Winter): 883–898.

Idemitsu Sazo. 1971. *Nihonjin ni kaere.* Tokyo.

Imazu Kojirō, Hamaguchi Esyun, and Sakuta Keiichi. 1979. Shakai kankyō no henyō to kodomo no hattatsu. *Kodomo no Hattatsu to Kyōiku,* 1:42–94.

Imeeji kawari shūshinkoyō nenkōjoretsu seido o yurugasu. 1987. *Shūkan Tōyō Keizai,* July 25, pp. 72–73.

Japan Economic Newswire, Kyodo News International. 1987: July 2; 1988: February 1; May 3, 10, 27.

Japan: The end of lifetime jobs. 1978. *Business Week,* July 17, pp. 82–83.

Japan Research Center. 1972. *Wakamono ishiki chōsa.* Tokyo: Japan Research Center.

Jitsugyō no Nihon [Japan's entrepreneurship]. 1904. 7.6.

Jones, Randall S. 1987. The economic implications of Japan's aging population. *JEI Report,* no. 12A (March 27).

Kagono Tadao. *Nihon no keiei.* 1984. Tokyo: Nihon Keizai Shinbunsha.

Kanabayashi, Masayoshi. 1977. Fading tradition: economic woes spur firms in Japan to alter lifetime job security; layoffs, early retirements, pay cuts are initiated. *Wall Street Journal,* December 21, p. 1.

———. 1988. In Japan, employees are switching firms for better work, pay. *Wall Street Journal,* October 11, p. 1.

Katou Hitoshi. 1987. Tenshoku: Sukauto sareru kachō, sarenai kachō. *Voice,* pp. 230–243.

Keene, Donald, trans. 1971. *Chūshingura: The Treasury of Loyal Retainers, a Puppet Play.* New York: Columbia University Press.

Keizai Dōyūkai. 1987. *Showa-62-nendo kigyō hakusho.* Tokyo.

Keizai Kikakuchō, Sōgō Keikaku-kyoku. 1986. *Gijutsu kakushin to koyō.* Tokyo.

Kinmonth, Earl H. 1981. *The Self-Made Man in Meiji Japanese Thought: From Samurai to Salary Man.* Berkeley: University of California Press.

Kosai, Y. 1986. *The Era of High-Speed Growth: Notes on the Postwar Japanese Economy,* trans. Jacqueline Kaminski. Tokyo: University of Tokyo Press.

Koyama, Hiroyuki. 1988. Changing corporate behavior hiring practice: Enterprises go hunting for mid-career employees. *Japan Economic Journal,* Summer, pp. 8–9.

Koyama Shoten, ed. 1956. *Watashi wa kōshite shūshoku shita.*

Krackhardt, D., and L. Porter. 1985. When friends leave: A structural analysis of the relationship between turnover and stayers' attitudes. *Administrative Science Quarterly* 30:242–261.

———. 1986. The snowball effect: Turnover embedded in communication networks. *Journal of Applied Psychology* 71:50–55.

Kyodo News. 1987: September 28; 1988: July 5.

Levine, Solomon B., and Hisashi Kawada. 1980. *Human Resources in Japanese Industrial Development*. Princeton: Princeton University Press.

Lincoln, Edward J. 1988. *Japan: Facing Economic Maturity*. Washington, D.C.: Brookings Institution.

Lincoln, James R., and Arne L. Kalleberg. 1990. *Culture, Control, and Commitment*. Cambridge: Cambridge University Press.

Lohdahl, T. 1964. Patterns of job attitudes in two assembly technologies. *Administrative Science Quarterly* 8:482–519.

Los Angeles Times. 1988. July 9.

Maclean's. 1987. Labor section. June 8, p. 42.

Mainichi Shinbun. 1988. August 18.

Mannari Hiroshi. 1965. *Bijinesu eriito, Nihon ni okeru keieisha no jōken*. Tokyo: Kodansha.

———. 1974. *The Japanese Business Leaders*. Tokyo: University of Tokyo Press.

March, J. G., and H. A. Simon. 1958. *Organizations*. New York: John Wiley.

Marsh, R., and H. Mannari. 1971. Lifetime employment in Japan: Roles, norms and values. *American Journal of Sociology* 76:795–812.

———. 1972. A new look at "lifetime commitment" in Japanese industry. *Economic Development and Cultural Change* 20.4 (July): 611–630.

———. 1981. Divergence and convergence in industrial organisations: The Japanese case. In *Management under Differing Value Systems: Political, Social and Economic Perspectives in a Changing World*, ed. G. Dlugos and K. Weiermair, pp. 447–460. Berlin: Walter de Gruyter.

Marshall, Byron K. 1967. *Capitalism and Nationalism in Prewar Japan: The Ideology of the Business Elite, 1868–1941*. Stanford, CA: Stanford University Press.

Martin, Linda G. 1982. Japanese response to an aging labor force. *Population Research and Policy Report* 1 (January): 19–41.

Maverick managers: Breaking tradition, some Japanese firms seek executives who go their own way. 1988. *Wall Street Journal*, November 14, p. R14.

Mitsui Bank hires foreigner. 1986. *Business Japan*, March.

Mitsui Gomei Kaisha. 1933. *The House of Mitsui: A Record of Three Centuries*. Tokyo: Mitsui Gomei Kaisha.

Miyamoto Mataji. 1941. *Kinsei shōnin ishiki no kenkyū*. Tokyo: Yūhikaku.

Mizutani, E. 1972. The changing picture of lifetime employment in Japan. *Japan House Newsletter* 19 (May 1).

Nakamura, Hajime. 1964. *Ways of Thinking of Eastern Peoples: India, China, Tibet, Japan*. Honolulu: East-West Center Press.

———. Conformity in a group situation. 1978. In *Social Psychology in Japan*, ed. J. Misumi, pp. 638–641.

Nakane, Chie. 1970. *Japanese Society*. Berkeley: University of California Press.

Nevins, T. J. 1984. *Labor Pains and the Gaijin Boss: Hiring, Managing, and Firing the Japanese.* Tokyo: Japan Times.
Nihon Keizai Shinbun. 1986: January 18; August 12. 1987: February 23; June 8; August 10; 1988: July 21.
Nihon rōdō nenkan. 1921. No. 2, pp. 331–333.
Nikkei Sangyō Shinbun. 1986: August 12. 1987: October 9. 1988: July 21.
Noda Kazuo. 1960. *Nihon no jūyaku.* Tokyo: Diamond Press.
———. 1975. Big business organizations. In *Modern Japanese Organization and Decision-making,* ed. Ezra Vogel. Berkeley: University of California Press.
Nōshōmushō. 1903. *Shōkō jijō* 3.
OECD. 1977. *The Development of Industrial Relations Systems: Some Implications of the Japanese Experience.* Paris: OECD.
Ohta, Ryuji. 1986. The Japanese employment system in the 1990s. *Journal of the ACCJ,* July/August, pp. 9–13.
Okamoto Yoshiyuki. 1987. *Tenshoku.* Tokyo: Diamond-sha.
Okimoto, Daniel I., Takuo Sugano, and Franklin B. Weinstein. 1984. *Competitive Edge: The Semiconductor Industry in the U.S. and Japan.* Stanford, CA: Stanford University Press.
Ōte jinzai ginkō—Imuka ni tōroku sareteiru gomannin bijinesuman no yarigai, okane, moraru. 1986. *Next,* December, p. 75.
Ouchi, W. 1981. *Theory Z.* Reading, MA: Addison-Wesley.
Patrick, Hugh, ed. 1967. *Japanese Industrialization and Its Social Consequences.* Berkeley: University of California Press.
Plath, David W., ed. 1983. *Work and Lifecourse in Japan.* Albany: State University of New York Press.
Prime Minister's Office. 1972. *First Attitude Survey of the World Youth.* Tokyo: Prime Minister's Office Youth Bureau.
Purejidento [President magazine]. 1977. August, p. 40.
Ranis, Gustav. 1955. The community-centered entrepreneur in Japanese development. *Explorations in Entrepreneurial History* 8.
Recruit Research Company. 1986. *Bijinesuman ni kansuru chōsa* [A survey of businessmen]. Tokyo.
———. 1988. *Tenshoku jittai chōsa 1988.* Tokyo.
Reischauer, Edwin O. 1970. *The United States and Japan.* 3d ed. New York: Viking.
Reuters. 1987. *Financial report,* November 18.
Ribeiro, Jorge. 1988. Sayonara lifetime employment: Is Japan's lifetime employment system crumbling, or are job changers merely the exception? *Business Tokyo,* April, pp. 26–28.
Rōdōshō [Ministry of Labor]. 1988. Shōwa 62-nen kōzō kihon chōsa kekka no yōten.
Rohlen, Thomas P. 1974. *For Harmony and Strength: Japanese White-collar Organization in Anthropological Perspective.* Berkeley: University of California Press.
———. 1975. The company work group. In *Modern Japanese Organization and*

Decision-making, ed. Ezra Vogel, pp. 185–209. Berkeley: University of California Press.

———. 1979. Permanent employment faces recession, slow growth, and an aging work force. *Journal of Japanese Studies* 5.2:235–272.

Rosenstein, Eliezer. 1965. Cooperativeness and advancement of managers. *Human Relations* 38.1:1–22.

Sengoku, Tamotsu. 1985. *Willing Workers: The Work Ethics in Japan, England, and the United States.* Trans. K. Ezaki and Y. Ezaki. Westport, CT: Quorum Books.

Shibuya Kazuhiro. 1987. Sukauto ni nerawareru jyūkō chodai meekaa [Scouts aim at heavy industry firms]. *Nikkei Business* 9.14:244–249.

Shirai, Taishiro, and Haruo Shimada. 1978. Interpreting Japanese industrial relations. In *Labor in the 20th Century,* ed. J. J. Dunlop and Walter Galemon, pp. 242–322. New York: Academic Press.

Shiroyama Saburō. 1975. *Kanryōtachi no natsu.* Tokyo: Shinchōsha.

Smith, Thomas C. 1960. Landlords' sons in the business elite. *Economic Development and Cultural Change* 9.1, part 2 (October).

Sotsugyōsei no matsuro. 1891. *Nihon no shōnen* 3.3 (February 1): 2–4.

Statistics Bureau. 1983. *Japan Statistical Yearbook.* Tokyo: Prime Minister's Office.

———. 1986. *Statistics Yearbook.*

Straits Times (Singapore). 1988. August 11.

Tagawa Yoshio. 1986. Keiretsugaisha ni taisuru shukkō, tenseki no jyokyō. *Denshi,* September, pp. 6–7.

Taichi, Sakaiya. 1981. Debunking the myth of loyalty. *Japan Echo* 8.2:17–29. Trans. Bokutachi no sakkaku. *Bungei Shunjū,* March 1981, pp. 260–279.

Taira, Koji. 1962. Characteristics of Japanese labor markets. *Economic Development and Cultural Change* 10:150–168.

Takagi, Haruo. 1985. *The Flaw in Japanese Management.* Ann Arbor, MI: UMI Research Press.

Takezawa, S., and A. Whitehall. 1981. *Work Ways: Japan and America.* Tokyo: Japan Institute of Labor.

Takita Seiichirō. 1987. 40 dai, 50 dai, jinzai sukauto jijō. *Gendai,* September, pp. 334–346.

Takita Seiichirō and Ōmiya Tomonobu. 1987. Chūtosaiyō daikenkyū. *Next,* January, pp. 220–228.

Tanaka Yoshihiro and Itō Momoko. 1987. Tenshoku jidai—Ima ya "Issha kenmei" (Isshōkenmei) wa owatta. *Shūkan Tōyō Keizai,* June 27, pp. 4–17.

Thayer, Nathaniel. 1969. *How Conservatives Rule Japan.* Princeton: Princeton University Press.

Tsuchida Katsumi. 1987. 45 sai teinen: Autopuresumento no arashi ni anata wa ikinokoreruka?, p. 248.

Tsuda, Masumi. 1982. Perspectives of life-time employment security practice in the Japanese enterprise. In *Employment and Participation: Industrial Democracy in Crisis,* ed. V. Rus, A. Ishikawa, and T. Woodhouse. Tokyo: Chuo University Press.

U.S. Civil Service Commission. 1977. *Planning Your Staffing Needs.* Washington, D.C.: Bureau of Policies and Standards.

van Helvoort, E. J. 1979. *The Japanese Working Man: What Choice? What Reward?* Vancouver: University of British Columbia Press.

———. 1982. The greying of Japan: Japan's rapidly ageing population is demanding increased flexibility in the system of "lifetime employment." *International Management* 37 (June): 26–28.

Vogel, Ezra. 1963. *Japan's New Middle Class: The Salary Man and His Family in a Tokyo Suburb.* 2d ed. Berkeley: University of California Press.

———. 1967. Kinship, structure, migration to the city, and modernization. In *Aspects of Social Change in Modern Japan,* ed. R. P. Dore. Princeton: Princeton University Press.

———. 1979. *Japan as Number One.* Cambridge: Harvard University Press.

Wakamiya Unosuke. 1929. *Morimura o genko roku.* Tokyo: Ōkura Shoten.

Wanous, J. 1980. *Organizational Entry: Recruitment Selection and Socialization of Newcomers.* Reading, MA: Addison-Wesley.

Weber, Max. 1978. *Economy and Society: An Outline of Interpretive Sociology.* Vol. 1. Ed. G. Roth and C. Wittich. Berkeley: University of California Press.

Weick, K. E. 1969. *The Social Psychology of Organizing.* 2d ed. Reading, MA: Addison-Wesley.

Westphal, James Warren. 1991. Modern change in the Japanese corporation. Master's thesis, University of Virginia.

White-collar moonlighters: A new breed of Japanese workers changes the rules. 1986. *Newsweek,* January 13, p. 39.

Whitehill, A. M., and S. Takezawa. 1961. *Cultural Values in Management-Worker Relations.* Chapel Hill: University of North Carolina Press.

Woronoff, Jon. 1983. *Japan: The Coming Social Crisis.* Tokyo: C. E. Tuttle.

Wray, William D. 1984. *Mitsubishi and the N.Y.K. 1870–1914: Business Strategy in the Japanese Shipping Industry.* Cambridge: Harvard University Press, East Asian Monographs.

Wysocki, Bernard, Jr. 1985. Foreign companies are having more success recruiting employees in Japan, although some key obstacles remain. *Wall Street Journal,* January 2.

———. 1986. Hard transition: Japanese are suffering unemployment rise in a shifting economy. *Wall Street Journal* November 6.

Yamamura, Kozo. 1967. The founding of Mitsubishi: A case study in Japanese business history. *Business History Review* 40.2 (Summer).

Yankelovich, D. 1979. Work, values, and the new breed. In *Work in America: The Decade Ahead,* ed. C. Kerr and J. M. Rostow. New York: Van Nostrand.

Yomiuri Shinbun. 1986: August 12, October 28; 1987: October 9; 1988: July 21.

Yonekawa, Shinichi. 1984. University graduates in Japanese enterprises before the Second World War. *Business History* 26.2 (July): 193–218.

Yoshii Shōei. 1987. *Nihon no jinzai gaisha besuto 50.* Tokyo: JCA Shuppan Kyoku.

Yoshimatsu Aonuma. 1965. *Nihon no keieisō*. Tokyo: Nihon Keizai Shin-
   bunsha.
Yoshino, M. 1967. *Japan's Managerial System: Tradition and Innovation*. Cam-
   bridge: MIT Press.
Yoshino, M., and T. Lifson. 1986. *The Invisible Link*. Cambridge: MIT Press.
Yūda wa hyaku aku no oya. 1877. *Eisai Shinshi,* no. 17 (June 30): 2–3.
Yui, Tsunehiko. 1970. The personality and career of Hikojiro Nakamigawa,
   1887–1901. *Business History Review* 44.1 (Spring): 43.

INDEX